D1599257

Adventure Finance

Aunnie Patton Power

Adventure Finance

How to Create a Funding Journey That Blends Profit and Purpose

Aunnie Patton Power
Saïd Business School
University of Oxford
Oxford, UK

ISBN 978-3-030-72427-6   ISBN 978-3-030-72428-3   (eBook)
https://doi.org/10.1007/978-3-030-72428-3

Cover illustration: NeMaria

This Palgrave Macmillan imprint is published by the registered company Springer Nature Switzerland AG
The registered company address is: Gewerbestrasse 11, 6330 Cham, Switzerland

Acknowledgements

Although I had made the decision to write this book in 2019, it wasn't until March 2020 when I hastily flew back from the UK to South Africa that I realized I suddenly had the time. Instead of teaching and conducting workshops in 13 countries throughout the course of 2020, I was restricted to the four walls of our home in Cape Town (and thankfully a tiny garden). Although those first weeks and months of lockdown were stressful and anxiety-ridden, I'll always be grateful for how the mammoth task of creating this book centered me. But it wasn't just Adventure Finance that kept me sane, my husband Sean was an absolute gem through lockdown and the entire book writing process. You've always been unbelievably supportive, but this past year has been something truly unforgettable (in both bad and good ways) and I'm so grateful to have you by my side.

Writing a book is tough work. Writing a book while severely morning sick with your first child is one step beyond difficult. My darling baby girl, we haven't met you yet, but you were definitely part of this book writing journey and I'm excited to share it with you one day (although we'll probably start with Winnie the Pooh before we move onto finance books).

I can't pinpoint when I first fell in love with finance, but it was probably sometime between my father teaching me the Fibonacci sequence at two years old (as a party trick) and my daily reports to him on share prices and company news from the Wall Street Journal in kindergarten. I may be the finance professor, but my Dad will always be my go-to finance teacher. I'm also not the first author in my family. My mother blazed the trail with her books (and now critically acclaimed podcast series) on sexuality and spirituality. In fact, I may be the least interesting writer in our family...

Jessica Pothering, I'll be eternally grateful for your insight and lethal editing skills. You took my mishmash of words and thoughts and sculpted them into something truly remarkable.

Eelco Bennick, Kusi Hornberger and Lisa vanEck, thank you from the bottom of my heart for diving into the original manuscript and helping me to completely restructure and rewrite the entire book. Your stamp on the book is indelible. John Berger, Brian Mikulencak, Chintan Panchal and Juliette Thirsk, you were the core of a true legal dream team. Thank you for your ability to think outside the box and for your willingness to brainstorm and answer all of my inane questions. Karin Iten, Lina Rothman and Maegan Lillis, your work on the early stages of the research and case studies was so foundational to the creation of the book. Thank you so much for all of your efforts. And thank you, Mike Stopworth for pushing me to put everything down on paper in the first place.

Natasha Dinham, Adi Zuk, Lee Zuk, Lianne Du Toit, Kelvin Ivankovic, Marie Ang, Tamara Rose, Bianca Fisher, Sagar Tandon, Cameron St. Ong and Akhil Pawar, your comments on the different drafts and efforts on the glossary were absolutely pivotal. Thank you for your honesty and your insights. Natalie Buckham, your proofreading of the entire book was such a gift. Thank you for your attention to detail.

Alex Kuehl, Alexandra Smith, Alison Linguane, Allie Burns, Aner Ben-Ami, Andrea Coleman, Anita Kover, Antonia Opiah, Antonio Diaz, Bernardo Afonso, Bhavik Basa, Bjoern Strauer, Caroline Bressan, Clemente Villegas, Dami Thompson, Dan Miller, Daniel Goldfarb, Daniel Fireside, Dhun Davar, Ed Diener, Elizabeth Boggs-Davidson, Ella Peinovich-Griffith, Emily Stone, Gene Homicki, Ginny Reyes Llamzon, Jim Villanueva, John Kohler, Jorge de Angulo, Joy Olivier, Karla Gallardo, Kate Cochran, Lars Ortegren, Lilian Mramba, Luke Crowley, Luni Libes, Maggie Cutts, Mariella Belli, Max Slavkin, Michael Bryon, Miguel Garza, Morgan Simon, Nichole Yembra, Rahil Rangwala, Richard Fahy, Rodrigo Villar, Rory Tews, Ross Baird, Ruben Doboin, Sachi Shenoy, Sarah Gelfand, Sietse Wouters, Susan De Witt, Ted Levinson, Tetsuro Narita, Tom Hockaday, Tracy Karty, Tyler Tringas and Wes Selke, thank you for your time and commitment. Each story in the book is based on the work that you've done and were willing to share in interviews. I'm so grateful for your contribution to the space as a pioneer and your generosity in sharing your story and editing the many, many drafts.

Aaron Fu, Adam Boros, Alessia Gianoncelli, Alexandra Chamberlin, Amanda Cotterman, Andrea Armeni, Annie Roberts, Antony Bugg-Levine,

Astrid Scholz, Alex Nicholls, Bill Stodd, Brendan Cosgrove, Brent Kessel, Bruce Campbell, Camille Canon, Candler Young, Cathy Clark, Chris Garner, Christine Looney, Deborah Burand, Debra Schwartz, Dirk Holshausen, Elina Sarkisova, Esme Verity, Fran Seegull, Heather Matranga, Jamie Finney, Janice St Onge, Jed Emerson, Jeff Batton, Jenny Kassan, Jesse Simmons, Joe Silver, John Katovich, Jonathan Bragdon, Jonny Page, Josh Adler, Kirsten Andersen, Laurie Spengler, Lewam Kefela, Liesbet Peeters, Lise Birikundayvi, Lorenzo Bernasconi, Maex Ament, Mark Cheng, Neil Yeoh, Olvia Lloetonma, Priscilla Boiardi, Ravi Chopra, Rob Tashima, Robert Boogaard, Ross Tasker, Scott Taitel, Soushiant Zanganehpour, Stu Fram, Timothy Kyepa, Tom Powell and Wayne Moodaley, this book was built on your wisdom and your experience building innovative funding structures. Thank you for sharing that wisdom with me so generously. Your dedication to innovation and to social and environmental impact is remarkable. I'm so grateful to know you and look forward to so much more collaboration in the future.

Tula Weis, thank you so much for helping shepherd this through the publication process and get it over the finish line.

And finally, Pamela Hartigan, I'm absolutely sure that I wouldn't be where I am today without your guidance. I so wish I could share this book with you. I miss your wisdom and your company.

Introduction

Hi there! Welcome to the world of innovative financing. If you've picked up this book, I'm guessing it's because you are looking to raise capital for your organization, or you are looking to invest capital into organizations, or maybe you're just a curious observer who wants to learn about new ways of investing in **start-ups** and **small businesses**. Well, I'm happy to report that you are in the right place.

This book is meant to take you on a funding journey, where we explore options that suit the needs of all varieties of organizations and businesses. Along the way, we stop to evaluate different types of financial structures that apply creativity and sometimes a bit of technology to allocate capital that makes sense for founders, funders and communities. We'll also delve into the tools that you need to identify and plan for your own funding and investment goals.

My hope is that your experience reading the chapters that follow will feel a little bit like that scene in the Wizard of Oz. Remember the one at the beginning where everything was in black and white, until Dorothy's house lands and she opens the door, and then everything pops out in brilliant technicolor? Right now, you may think that **venture capital** and **bank loans** and **grants** the only funding options out there. But actually, there is a whole rainbow of options that you can explore.

Why Are We Here?
As you've picked up this book, you may already be sold on why we need to take this journey together.

As a **founder**, you might be at your wits end; frustrated that you can't find funding that is appropriate for your business. Maybe you don't want to fit into the traditional venture capital model, but you don't have the right assets and track record to qualify for a bank loan. Perhaps you are building a purpose-driven business that wants to stay true to its mission, a non-profit that is seeking to build sustainable income streams or a community focused organization that doesn't want to take on external shareholders.

As a **funder**, you might also feel as if the current tools at your disposal aren't enough. You see promising founders whose visions don't fit into traditional equity, debt or grant boxes and want to find ways to help them build their businesses.

Perhaps you are a *policy maker, academic, student or advisor* who has seen the issues with early-stage funding and you are determined to find a better way to help support promising young businesses which are engines for job creation and economic growth.

I've spent over a decade helping purpose-driven companies raise capital, and I know exactly how you feel. For this book, I interviewed more than 150 founders and funders, and they expressed similar frustrations in every, single conversation.

Creative Action Network's Funding Struggle

Take, for instance, Aaron Perry Zucker and Max Slavkin of the Creative Action Network (CAN), a for-profit social enterprise built around a global community of artists and designers who make art with and for a purpose. CAN is exactly the kind of company that inspired this book. It's a purpose-driven company that wasn't a good fit for traditional venture capital but nevertheless still needed capital and supportive funders to help the business grow.

Aaron and Max were graphic designers, and also politically passionate, and in 2008 they had a brilliant idea to launch a website where anyone could upload poster art for the U.S. presidential campaign, and anyone could download and print that art for free. It was wildly successful (you know that Obama poster—yes, *that* Obama poster? That was Aaron and Max's website. It was actually originally called Design for Obama.[1]). That website was the seed for CAN.

Like many entrepreneurs, Max and Aaron thought they knew the recipe for start-up success: get into an accelerator program, raise *a lot* of venture capital funding, grow, grow, grow, and then either sell their business to a bigger company or list the company on a public stock exchange. So they

---

[1] Yes THAT famous Obama poster.

tried that route. They got accepted to an accelerator (Matter.Vc, a program for companies "changing media for good"). They made an **investment pitch deck**. They networked their way into the door of venture capital firms in San Francisco. But after fifty meetings and fifty "no thank you's," Max and Aaron realized that CAN wasn't a fit for those investors. **Venture capital firms** they met with were underwhelmed by CAN's potential for scale (and profits) in the **social impact** art marketplace, and they didn't understand Max and Aaron's commitment to the **social mission** of their company, which included long-term ownership of the company by the artists.

The fundraising challenges that CAN encountered are common for **social enterprises**, or even just modest-growth organizations; many mainstream venture investors simply don't understand how social impact and profitability can align.

The Eureka Moment

It wasn't until their third year **bootstrapping** CAN and building up its modest revenues that Aaron and Max discovered the world of **impact investing**, a type of finance that *does* understand that businesses can still make money while doing good—not only that they can, but that they should. CAN's founders were introduced to a venture investing firm called Purpose Ventures, where Max and Aaron first heard about a unique ownership model for companies that needed capital but wanted to stay independent and dedicated to employee ownership. This model, called **Steward Ownership**, was ideal for companies like CAN that exist to do more than maximize shareholder profit, and Purpose was ready to walk Aaron and Max through the process of structuring a deal that would provide CAN with the capital it needed while preserving its mission.

If you're reading this story and thinking, "Yes! I need to find a Purpose Ventures," or "Yes! I want to be a Purpose Ventures," great, that's exactly what most companies need and what most funders aren't. In the mainstream **venture funding** landscape, **venture capital equity funding** is synonymous with **risk capital**, and it's often presumed these days to be the only way for young companies like CAN to raise funding (outside of a traditional bank loan, which also isn't available to most businesses). The problem is traditional **venture capital equity funding** is narrow; it likes **asset-lite, tech-enabled, exponential growth** focused companies. Most companies don't tick those boxes.

That's why this book exists. As a founder or a funder, you should be able to chart your own funding journey—one that works for you and what you are looking to build. That's exactly what this book means to help you do, though a series of in-depth stories similar to Max and Aaron's, and a stockpile of tools, resources, and helpful frameworks. (Deal structuring nerds and textbook appendix lovers, the online companion of this book is for you.)

A Community Focused Funding Solution

Before we get started, do you want to know how Max and Aaron's funding journey with CAN and Purpose Ventures turned out? Meeting Purpose Ventures was obviously the breakthrough CAN's founders had been looking for: Purpose was an investor willing to structure financing that aligned with their vision and mission. Together, they came up with an agreement for an investment model that allowed CAN to access risk capital to grow, while enabling Max and Aaron to maintain ownership of the company in the long term by buying back investors' equityshares with the company's profits.

To be sure, bedding down the details of this model wasn't fast or simple. It took six months to get investors committed, and another six months of legal paperwork. But, in the end, this new structure enabled CAN to raise $380,000, which was $30,000 more than Max and Aaron has targeted to meet CAN's early-stage funding needs.

If spending a year negotiating terms like Max and Aaron did feel overwhelming, you should know that Max and Aaron both feel the time and effort was worth it. Here's why: "By using this model, we've been able to ensure that power stays in the hands of our artists and community, and not the investors, should the founding partners leave Creative Action Network," explains Max.

It's true that these "alternative" funding options can seem overwhelming and confusing. But fear not, we are on this journey together! Some of these instruments are widely available, others will take a bit more initiative on the part of both founders and funders. And as I mentioned, we won't just analyze the instruments in this book, we will also explore the funding process itself, to understand how it can be more inclusive and purpose driven. After all, sometimes the difficulty of venture funding isn't about the structure; it can also be that the process itself excludes promising founders.

Contents

Part I   What If: You Want to Understand Equity and Debt?

1   Helium Health: Our Equity Journey   3

2   SOKO: Our Debt Financing Journey   15

3   Powered by People and Equal Exchange's Trade Finance
    Journey   27

4   Unpacking Our Self-Evaluation   35

5   Reflections on Debt and Equity   51

Part II   What If: You Want to Redesign Risk Capital?

6   Candide Group: Our Structured Exit Journey   63

7   myTurn: Our Redeemable Equity Journey   73

8   Equal Exchange: Our Preferred Stock Journey   83

9   Provive: Our Revenue-Based Mezzanine Debt Journey   91

10 Maya Mountain Cacao: Our Demand Dividend Journey   103

11 GetVantage and VIWALA: Our Revenue-Based Financing
    Journey   113

12 Redesigning Risk Capital   123

Part III   What If: You Want to Be Innovative with Grant Funding?

13   The Studio Museum in Harlem: Our Program Related Investments Journey   135

14   Riders for Health: Our Debt Guarantee Journey   143

15   Upaya Social Ventures: Our Recoverable Grant Journey   151

16   IkamvaYouth: Our Forgivable Loan Journey   159

17   Trackosaurus: Our Convertible Grant Journey   165

18   Innovative Grant Funding   173

Part IV   What If: You Want to Link Financing to Impact?

19   Michael and Susan Dell Foundation: Our Interest Rate Rebate Journey   183

20   Clinicas del Azucar: Our Social Impact Incentives Journey   191

21   My Outcomes-Based Financing Journey   199

22   Linking Financing to Impact   207

Part V   What If: You Want to Redesign the Entire Funding Process?

23   Code for All: Our Crowdfunding Journey   215

24   Village Capital: Our Community Led Capital Journey   223

25   Cal Solar's Journey to Becoming a Worker-Owned Co-Operative   229

26   Redesigning the Entire Funding Process   239

27   Embedding Mission into Contracts   243

Part VI   What If: You Want to Plan Your Journey?

28   Who Are You and What Do You Need?   251

29   What Type of Funder Is Right for You?   267

30   **What Type of Funding Is Right for You?**   277

31   **Glossary**   287

Index   329

How to Use This Book

The material for this book comes from a decade of my own teaching and research. And because I'm not a very patient researcher, it also comes from a lot of doing (I like to call myself a "pracademic" i.e., a practical academic). You can rest assured that this isn't a textbook. Rather, it is a set of stories from founders and funders that have adapted traditional funding methods to make **venture finance** work for the 99% of businesses and non-profits that don't fit with either traditional **venture capital** or a traditional **loan** from a bank. These stories are meant to inspire you as to what is possible. Embedded within them are the tools, and a few frameworks, to help you evaluate your options and shortcut the time it takes you to create your own epic funding journey.

As my students and colleagues know, my classes and workshops generally feature a mix of founders and funders, which seems to make the otherwise somewhat dry topic of finance a little more relatable and tangible, and in turn, stimulates knowledge sharing and integrated learning. In this book, I attempt to speak to both audiences—with the default audience being founders, as your needs should be the foundation of early-stage funding options.

I have also tried to make this material as straightforward and approachable as possible, regardless of your level of financial knowledge and experience. But, if you are brand new to early-stage financing or finance in general, please use the **Glossary** (Chapter 31) as a reference throughout the book. It contains a list of definitions of all of the **bolded words** in the book, as well as additional information that should be helpful.

Founders, unfortunately, there isn't a simple formula to determine the right type of funding for each individual situation, but hopefully the information in these chapters can serve as a guide in helping you make vital decisions about the kind of financing that makes the most sense for your organization. Ideally, one of the biggest takeaways from this book will be a boost in confidence in charting your own funding journey. Having confidence in what you need and what type of funders can best support your growth can help you better identify and engage with funders that mean to be partners in your journey.

Funders, you might find that some of the definitions in the early chapters are too simplified, and so please feel free to skim over them. You might want to come back to them when you are engaging with founders, however, as I have found that there is often significant misunderstanding and miscommunication between founders and funders in negotiating financing agreements. Funders tend to assume that founders understand investment basics and thus, do not explain in simple enough language the implications of the contracts they are considering or negotiating.

Once you have digested the material from this book, you'll likely be keen to really get into the weeds of contracting. In the online companion to this book, I've built out a series of resources to help you structure, navigate and negotiate funding contracts. This material will be continually updated based on changes to accounting, tax and regulations globally.

Right! Let's get started.

Pre-reading: Your Journey Map

Before we dive into others' funding journeys, let's start by taking a moment to think through your own. What do you know (and do you need to learn) about your organization, its funding needs, and the types of funders you want to engage? Funding your business may feel a lot like staring at a completely unknown trail and choosing to… march ahead anyway. Let's make sure you have an idea of where you are starting, where you want to go, and how you want to get there, before you start shopping for gear.

Below is a list of questions that you'll want use as a self-evaluation. You'll want to keep these in mind as you are reading this book. We'll keep circling back to them; first in Chapter 4 where we'll unpack them together (*feel free to skip ahead there now, if you need more information to help you answer these questions*) and finally in Part VI, where we'll revisit these questions based on all of the journeys that we've been on together and all of the funding options that we've explored (Table 1).

Table 1 Founder's self-evaluation checklist

Who are we?	How is our company registered?
	How do we make money? Who are our customers?
	What stage company are we?
	What are our growth projections?

(continued)

Table 1 (continued)

How mission driven are we?	How embedded is our mission in our company?
	Do we have an impact track record?
What are our funding needs?	How much funding do we need?
	What do we need to spend it on?
	How do we want to pay it back?
	What are our ownership expectations in the short/medium term? Long term?
	How involved do we want our funders to be?
What type of funder is right for us?	What types of funders are there?
	What kinds of resources can they provide?
	What level of risk are they comfortable with?
	What kind of return do they require, and when?
	Who are their stakeholders? How does funding get approved?

Now that you have the questions you need to ask yourself while exploring this book, let's chart our adventure through the upcoming chapters. Each of these chapters will introduce you to a new funding option that you can consider (Fig. 1).

Several of the chapters also explore options for making the investment process itself more inclusive and mission focused (Table 2).

Alright, now you have all of the tools you need to start this adventure finance journey. Let's get going!

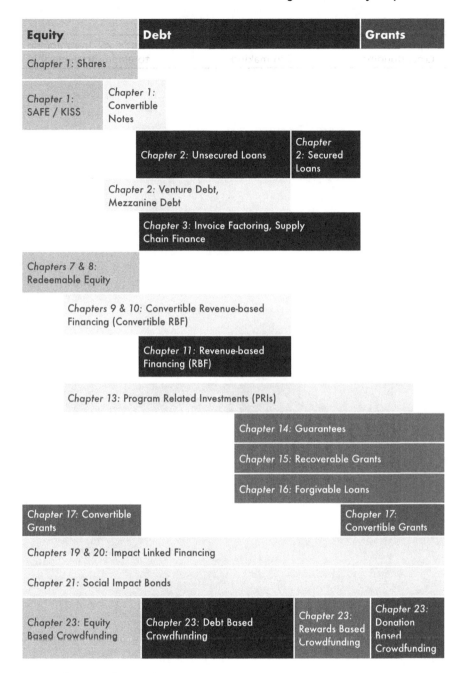

Fig. 1 Adventure finance journey map

Table 2 Investment process chapters

Chapter 23: Crowdfunding	Chapter 24: Peer-based decision making	Chapter 25: Transitioning to employee ownership

List of Figures

Fig. 2.1	Illustration of senior and junior debt in capital structure	23
Fig. 2.2	Illustration of capital structure with cost and risk	24
Fig. 3.1	Cost and risk of factoring options	31
Fig. 4.1	Comparison of Unicorns and Zebras	41
Fig. 18.1	Recoverable grant and forgivable loan decision tree	176
Fig. 20.1	SIINC illustration	193

List of Tables

Table 1.1	Illustrative capitalization table	7
Table 3.1	Types of factoring and their characteristics	30
Table 3.2	Comparison of factoring and supply chain finance	32
Table 4.1	Founder's self-evaluation checklist	35
Table 4.2	Stages of a company's growth	38
Table 4.3	Types of funders	45
Table 4.4	Types of resources	47
Table 5.1	The equity funding lifecycle and players by company stage	53
Table 5.2	Comparison of debt and equity	54
Table 5.3	Summary of options by criteria	55
Table 5.4	Comparison of debt and equity options	56
Table 6.1	Traditional angel/VC portfolio construction, by sport	66
Table 7.1	myTurn illustrative capitalization table	78
Table 7.2	Comparison of types of structured exit repayments	80
Table 9.1	Comparison of types of structured exit repayments	99
Table 12.1	Comparison of structured exits options	128
Table 18.1	Comparison of innovative grant funding options	177
Table 22.1	Impact linked financing options by category	208
Table 22.2	Convertible instruments by type	212
Table 25.1	Sources of capital for employee-owned companies	238
Table 26.1	Chapter overview	240
Table 27.1	Embedding mission options by category	244
Table 28.1	Founder's self-evaluation with relevant terms	251
Table 28.2	Comparison of types of legal structures	253
Table 28.3	Funder approach by type of capital	265

Table 29.1   Fund evaluation   267
Table 29.2   Types of resources with funding options   270
Table 30.1   Summary of options by criteria   278
Table 30.2   Comprehensive summary table of funding options   279
Table 30.3   Linking impact and embedding mission summary   284
Table 31.1   Convertible instruments   291
Table 31.2   Investment process description   305

Part I

What If: You Want to Understand Equity and Debt?

In this first part, we are going to explore the fundamentals of **debt** and **equity** financing with a bit of a twist. In Chapter 1, we will go through an equity fundraising journey alongside the founders of Helium Health. Put simply, **equity** means ownership in a company. When you raise **equity** capital, you are selling ownership in your company.

In Chapters 2 and 3, we will go on **debt** financing journeys with the founders of SOKO, Powered by People and Equal Exchange. **Debt** is when you borrow capital for your business and promise to repay this loan, generally with some amount of interest. Debt providers often require **collateral** in the form of valuable physical assets that they can seize from a company if the company defaults, i.e., stops paying the loan. **Debt** providers also look for a **credit history**, i.e., years of audited financials or a history repaying other loans. As we'll see in these chapters, there are a few innovative ways that you can structure debt without traditional collateral by using **factoring** and **supply chain financing**. We'll also look at **mezzanine** and **venture debt** options that incentivize debt providers to take the additional risk with fast-growing companies through promising them **upside** (additional return).

1

Helium Health: Our Equity Journey

Okay, here we go. Our first journey takes us to Nigeria where Dimeji Sofowora, Tito Ovia and Adegoke Olubusi founded Helium Health in 2016 based on their own experiences and frustrations with the Nigerian healthcare system. We are going to walk with them as they explore their options for raising capital by selling **equity** in their business.

As you'll see below, Helium Health is a rocketship business, i.e., they are projecting **exponential growth** and raising capital from **venture capitalists (VCs)**. Why are we starting out with their story, since I told you in the introduction that this book was for the 99% of companies that aren't projecting rocketship growth? Many of the innovative financing structures that we'll discuss throughout the book use elements of **equity financing**. So, it is important to first understand the basics of how conventional **equity** works before we get creative with it. The Helium Health story is designed to introduce all of the different **equity** options.[1]

Sensing an Opportunity

The starting point for the Helium Health journey is the fact that Nigeria's healthcare sector is in crisis. Nigeria has the seventh-largest population in the world and a healthcare system that is severely underfunded relative to its

---

[1] For more information on equity funding, please see Chapter 4.

© The Author(s), under exclusive license to Springer Nature
Switzerland AG 2021
A. Patton Power, *Adventure Finance*,
https://doi.org/10.1007/978-3-030-72428-3_1

population's needs. Helium's founders Dimeji, Tito and Adegoke experienced this crisis firsthand, and in 2016, began researching the underlying issues to see where they might be able to develop a solution.

What they uncovered was a huge data problem in the Nigerian healthcare sector. Not only was the available data highly fragmented, but it was almost impossible to determine how accurate it was. Dimeji, Tito and Adegoke quickly realized that the only way to solve this problem was to start at the beginning of the data chain and track and record everything that happened from the minute a patient is admitted into the hospital right up until the minute that patient leaves.

The trio founded Helium Health as a Software-as-a-Service (SaaS) platform designed to help hospitals and clinics manage their electronic medical records. Their first step in building the company was designing and piloting an electronic medical records (EMR) system. Early on, the founders realized that digital literacy in Nigeria's healthcare sector was low. However, Nigerians are enthusiastic social media users, so Helium designed the first version of its EMR to mimic a social media experience, with a chat-like feature for notes and a simple user interface (UI). Their interface was so intuitive that when they began demonstrations with nurses, they found they could successfully train staff within a matter of days.

Helium's pilot proved so successful that by the end of its first year, the company had been awarded a prize for promising start-ups by the President of Nigeria and won the country's coveted Etisalat Prize for Innovation. Like many entrepreneurs, Dimeji, Tito and Adegoke had relied on **Friends, Family and 'Fools'** (generally called **the 3Fs**) to get their company off the ground. This very early-stage capital enabled them to build prototypes in the early days of the business.

But Helium needed some serious cash to continue building, so the founders decided it was time for the next step: raising their first round of **equity** funding. Such "pre-seed" or "seed" rounds are generally less than $1 million and are funded by **Angel Investors, Venture Capitalists (VCs) or Incubators**. Angel investors are **high net-worth individuals (HNWI)** or **Networks of HNWIs**, who put capital into fledgling businesses to help them develop intellectual property and attract customers to prove out their business model. **Venture Capitalists (VCs)** are investors who manage other people's capital through pooled funds, which they invest in early-stage businesses with the intent of making a profit. **Incubators** often offer funding alongside programs for cohorts of founders who are keen to build their businesses. **Angel investors** manage their own money, so they can often make investment decisions more quickly than other types of investors.

A Cold Email and a Warm Reception

The Helium founders started by reaching out to anyone whom they thought would be interested in investing in their business. Adegoke had seen a woman named Nichole Yembra in the news for her own fintech start-up and knew that she was interested in investing in emerging fintech companies based on her investments at Greenhouse Capital. The problem was, he didn't know her and couldn't find anyone in his network who did, so he decided he would write a "cold email" to her by trying variations of her name until he found an email address that worked. And it finally did! Nichole replied and they agreed to speak.

For Nichole, it was Helium's healthtech focus that initially attracted her to the company. She saw the value of the healthcare data that Helium was building and knew that they could monetize it down the road, as healthcare data is one of the most expensive data sets to procure.

In the midst of the conversations with Nichole, Helium's founders applied, and were accepted into, Y Combinator (YC), an American start-up accelerator famous for launching and investing in start-ups that have become billion-dollar businesses (so-called **unicorns**) such as Airbnb, Instacart and Dropbox. Nichole was keen to invest in Helium, and the acceptance into Y Combinator made the business even more attractive, so she walked the team through their options from an investment structure perspective.

Helium's first option was to sell shares in the company. These could be **common shares** or **preferred shares. Common shares** are also called ordinary shares and they represent ownership in a company. **Preferred shares** come with certain benefits over **common shares**, including **dividends**, which are payments made to shareholders from the profits of a company, and **liquidation preferences**, which allow **preferred shareholders** to get their money back before **common shareholders** in the event of a **sale** or a **bankruptcy**.[2]

If Helium's founders decided to sell shares in the company, they would need to negotiate with an investor until they agreed how much of the company they would sell and at what price. For instance, they would need to say that they would sell 10% of the company for $50,000. This would then provide a valuation for the company at $450,000 **pre-money** and $500,000 **post-money. The pre-money valuation** is the implied value of the company without the investment capital, and the **post-money valuation** is the value of the company including the investment capital.

---

[2]For more on preference share terms, please see the term sheet guide in the online companions.

For Helium, creating a **valuation** seemed too complex, time-consuming and costly, as they were still a very early-stage business that had not yet launched their healthcare data solution on the market. They were nervous that if they valued the company too low, they would sell too many shares at a low price and potentially lose control of decision-making within the company later on down the line.

Dye in a Bucket

Let's pause from the Helium story for a moment to talk about what selling shares in a company means for the founder. For a founder, having your ownership in a company decrease by selling a portion to investors is called **dilution**. Think of it as a bucket of water with dye in it: if you pour more water, the dye's color becomes less concentrated—it's not as strong. Each time a company raises a new round of equity capital, the founders' ownership stake gets diluted. As a founder, if you have been diluted below 50%, the other shareholders may be able to make strategic decisions on behalf of the company without your approval.

For Helium, which was still so early in getting to market, the founders wanted to raise capital while diluting their ownership as little as possible.

Introducing Convertibility

The second option Nichole presented was a **convertible debt agreement**, which is also called a **convertible note**. In this **convertible debt agreement**, Nichole would provide a loan to Helium, which would be repayable with interest, but that could be converted into shares in Helium when the company successfully raised equity capital in the future. A great advantage of this option would be that Helium's founders would not have to agree to a **valuation** for the company at this point. Nichole walked them through a hypothetical example.

If Nichole agreed to invest $50,000 in Helium in a Seed round using a convertible debt agreement, she would write her convertible debt agreement to say that the $50,000 was a loan and the interest would be 5% per year. Interest rates are common for convertible loans, though interest isn't always repaid in cash. In this structure, the interest would be "rolled up," so instead of being repaid in cash, the interest would be added to the amount of the loan over time.

Her agreement would also include a **discount rate** of 25% that would be applied if the convertible loan converted into equity. This means that Nichole would be able to buy shares at a price that is 25% cheaper than new investors—a provision that is designed to compensate Nichole for the additional risk she is taking on by investing earlier than others. Until an equity round was finalized, Nichole would not own any shares of Helium; rather, her convertible note would sit on the company's balance sheet as **debt**, just like any other type of **loan**.

With these terms, Nichole explained that one year after her initial investment, her total outstanding loan would equal $52,500: $50,000+ the 5% interest of $2,500. When Helium raised its next **equity** round—a Series A round—Nichole could decide to take the $52,500 that would be owed to her and convert the loan into equity.

In a $500,000 Series A round at a **post-money valuation** of $1.5M, this would mean that the new Series A investors would buy 100,000 shares at $5 per share and Nichole would be able to purchase Helium shares at $3.75 per share. Nichole's price would be determined based on a 25% discount to the Series A investors' cost of $5 per share ($5 × 75% = $3.75).

Based on this price, she could purchase 14,000 shares with her $52,500. Nichole would thus own 4.5% of the company, the Series A investors would then own 31.8%, and the founders would retain 63.7%. Below is an illustration of this ownership. This is called a **capitalization table** or **cap table** (Table 1.1).

Table 1.1 Illustrative capitalization table

	Seed round		Series A		
	% Ownership	Shares	% Ownership	Shares	$ invested
Helium	100	200,000	63.7	200,000	
Nichole	0		4.5	14,000	$52,500[a]
Series A			31.8	100,000	$500,000
Total	100	200,000	100	314,000	$552,500

[a]This amount represents the total cash from the Seed round ($50,000) in the form of a convertible note + the interest that is owed ($2,500). It doesn't represent new cash to the company in the Series A.

A Simple Agreement?

Even though a convertible debt agreement can be easy to set up, Nichole presented Helium's founders with a third option that would likely be quicker for them to use. This structure is called a **simple agreement for future equity (SAFE)**. A **SAFE** is an agreement between a founder and a funder that stipulates that the funder will invest in the business but allows the major terms of that investment to be set by the next round of equity funders. The **SAFE** was created by Y Combinator in late 2013. In the years since, it has been used by almost all Y Combinator start-ups and many others for early-stage fundraising.[3]

Let's pause again to quickly discuss how SAFEs work. When negotiating a SAFE, you really only have to negotiate two things: the **valuation cap** and **the discount rate**. The **valuation cap** is the maximum valuation at which the SAFE will convert in the next round. This limits the amount of **dilution** for the SAFE investor as it sets a maximum share price that the SAFE investor will pay for the shares. Unlike a convertible note, this does require the investor and the investee to agree on a valuation of the company.

Let's use the same numbers in the convertible note example above to illustrate a **valuation cap**. If instead of a discount of 25%, Nichole had a **post-money valuation cap** of $1,125,000. She would have also paid $3.75 per share instead of $5 per share.

The **discount rate** is how much less the **SAFE** investors would pay per share than the Series A investors. The same logic as the **convertible note** applies here, in that the **SAFE** investors have invested early into a company and taken more risk by making that early investment, so they should be able to buy the shares at a cheaper price. For **SAFEs, discount rates** can range between 10 and 70%.

Nichole told Helium's founders that from her experience, there were several advantages to a **SAFE**: simplicity, cost and a faster close. As a **SAFE** is a very short document with few terms to negotiate, it would save both Helium and Nichole money in legal fees and reduce the time spent negotiating the terms of the investment. Second, a **SAFE** can be closed as soon as both parties are ready to sign the agreement and the investor is ready to wire the money. For Helium, this would mean that they could get the money they needed right away from Nichole, without waiting for other investors to join a complete round.

---

[3]The SAFE itself has evolved over time and the updated documentation is available on the Y Combinator website, including their SAFE user guide, which explains the details of the instrument from an investor and an entrepreneurs' perspective in great detail.

Based on these arguments, the Helium founders were convinced that a **SAFE** was the right instrument for them for their pre-seed round.

Signing the Deal

Moving ahead with the negotiation, Nichole said she wouldn't require a discount rate, which meant the Helium founders only had to negotiate one item: the **valuation cap**. Setting a valuation cap on a **SAFE** could protect Nichole's ownership from getting excessively diluted if Helium were to raise a giant amount of capital in their next **equity** round. Nichole explained that the **valuation cap** should be reasonable and enable her to convert to a meaningful ownership stake in line with the risk she had taken by investing in the company so early.

Helium's founders also needed to make sure that the **valuation** cap wasn't too low. A very low **valuation cap** could deter other investors if it appeared that **SAFE** investors were getting too good a deal. (The same logic applies to discount rates in **SAFEs**: setting the **discount rate** too high can scare off future investors.)

The Helium team proposed a $10 million **valuation cap** to Nichole, arguing this amount was merited based on their pipeline contracts and the valuations of other global healthcare technology start-ups. Nichole's team went to work building their own model and came up with a $4 million valuation cap. This was based on the fact that the company had contracts, but they were not yet signed, and on the heavy technical infrastructure that Helium would have to build. After some negotiation, the parties agreed on Nichole's valuation. It took three weeks for the deal to close. Not long afterward, Dimeji, Tito and Adegoke were off to Silicon Valley to participate in Y Combinator.

To YC and Beyond

Helium used **SAFE** agreements to close an additional $2 million in funding from Y Combinator, Tencent and Western Tech upon graduating from Y Combinator in September 2017. This funding enabled Helium to take its EMR system to market, secure its first state-wide contract, and ultimately establish its market dominance as the largest EMR provider in West Africa.

As Helium was building out their own business, Nichole was building hers as well. She spun out from GreenHouse Capital in 2019 and launched her own fund called Chrysalis Capital, which is a fintech-enabled fund looking to transform the education, renewable energy, healthcare, agriculture, security, and fintech ecosystems.

By 2020, Helium had launched several new products and the emergence of the global COVID-19 pandemic uncovered the value of the type of healthcare data and technology Helium had delivered to the West African market. The company closed a $10 million Series A round of funding co-led by Global Ventures and Africa Healthcare Masterfund (AAIC), with participation from Tencent, Ohara Pharmaceutical Co and VentureSouq. In this second round of funding, Helium Health had also managed to retain two of its original funders: Y Combinator and Nichole, who this time was investing via her new investment firm Chrysalis Capital.

This new Series A round of **equity** investment will enable Helium to expand its footprint and grow its customer base in Nigeria, Ghana and Liberia. It will also support Helium's launch into new markets in North Africa, East Africa and Francophone West Africa, as well as new areas of business that will enable it to monetize its data. For example, Helium is rolling out Helium Credit to help patients pay for their healthcare costs.

"It's all coming to fruition," explains Nichole when speaking about why she reinvested. "Everything that I thought they could do, three, four years ago is what they're actually doing now--literally because of that data."

Looking back, Dimeji believes the main value that **SAFEs** provide is "ensuring that time isn't wasted in the fundraising process, and that companies can move on quickly with the actual business, rather than expend a lot of time on terms with agreements and term sheets."

Is Equity Investment Right for You?

Founder

Let's take a look at some of the characteristics of equity to help you decide if it is an option that you want to pursue. In general, early-stage **equity** investors do not buy more than 50% **ownership** in a company during an investment round. This is because early-stage investors need to invest into many companies, and they do not have the time or expertise to manage all of these companies. Nevertheless, after multiple investment rounds, as a founder, you might find yourself owning less than 50% of the business, meaning you no longer control the company.

Early stage investing often relies on the "**back the jockey not the horse mentality**." Early equity investors find entrepreneurs that they believe in and invest in them, even if the business model still needs a lot of work. They believe that good entrepreneurs can pivot to build successful businesses.

Equity investors expect to be very involved in their investee businesses, providing **mentorship and valuable connections.** In an equity investment,[4] both the investor and the investee are incentivized to grow the business.

Equity investment capital is very **flexible** and, unless specified, it can be used for anything the entrepreneur wishes to use it for. As you'll see in the Term Sheet section of the online companion, there are some limits to this that are generally put in place.

Equity investors need to have an **exit** event to make their **return on investment**. Traditionally, VCs look for three different kinds of **exits**: a **trade sale**, a **secondary sale** or an **initial public offering (IPO)**.

A **trade sale** is when the entire company (otherwise known as the "target") is sold to another buyer. This buyer could be a corporate that is in the same industry as the target and is interested in acquiring them to grow their market share. It could also be a financial buyer such as a private equity firm that is interested in investing in the company to resell it again down the road.

A **secondary sale** is when the investor sells their shares in the company to another financial buyer such as a venture capital firm. A secondary sale is generally part of a larger raise that the company has completed where the new investors would prefer to buy the old investors out to make the ownership of the company simpler.

An **IPO** is a listing on a public stock exchange. It can also be called "taking a company public." An IPO involves selling shares of the company to the general public, by way of investment banks. This occurs only after many rounds of Venture Capital, and to be honest, often not at all, but despite its rarity, is generally the main goal of most VC investors.[5]

A common problem with **equity** investments is that many founders and funders structure their investments planning to make their return through a large **exit**, but statistically the likelihood of these **exit** events are much smaller than generally assumed. This is a problem both founders and funders face, particularly in emerging markets. Thus, while **equity** is often seen as the 'holy grail' for SMEs, in reality it is only designed for a very specific type of business: an aspiring **unicorn** pursuing **exponential** growth.

---

[4]The same is true for convertible debt investors that are expecting their investment to convert into equity, i.e., angel investors and VC.

[5]One last form of exit is called an acquihire. This is when a company acquires a target only to hire their staff, not to grow their product or service.

Let's talk quickly about **exponential growth**. The Oxford dictionary definition of **exponential growth** is "growth whose rate becomes ever more rapid in proportion to the growing total number or size." This means that growth continues to accelerate even as something becomes bigger. For founders, it is easy to imagine growing rapidly from your first customer to your 100th customer or even potentially to your 1,000th or 10,000th customer. But do you think you can continue that rate of growth to your 1,000,000th customer? To your 10,000,000th? There are a few start-ups that can build products that are so unique and useful that they can grow very quickly for an extended period of time, but even those businesses can't grow exponentially forever (or they'd take over the world). Most businesses need capital to start up and to reach profitability, but once profitable, don't grow exponentially.

As we discussed in this chapter, if you are looking to raise **equity**, you have a few different options around structuring. Firstly, you have **priced equity rounds**, where an investor buys a certain percentage of your company for a specific price based on a set **valuation** of your company at the time, i.e., 8% of your shares for $100,000. This provides a valuation of your company, in this case $100,000 / 8% = $1,250,000 post-money valuation and $1,150,000 pre-money valuation. These shares can be **common shares** or they can be **preferred shares** that come with additional rights for the investor.

Next, you have **convertible notes**, which can convert into **equity** in a subsequent round of funding and do not require a **valuation**. **Convertible notes** are the instrument of choice for most very early-stage investors. In essence, they are able to push the valuation of the company down the line for the next investor, likely when there is more information to base a valuation on. One of the reasons they are so popular is that it is very difficult to value very early-stage companies.

Finally, you have the **SAFE**,[6] which is an inherently founder-friendly instrument. It can be valuable when you are doing very small rounds of funding where time and legal fees could be detrimental to the deal and the business. That said, a new version of the SAFE, which is called the **Post-Money SAFE**, can require a **valuation** to be negotiated in the form of a valuation, which might take additional time. Additionally, investors, particularly those outside of Silicon Valley often add side letters to their **SAFE**

---

[6]There is another related option that we have not gone through in this chapter called a **Keep it Simple Security (KISS)**, an agreement that is a cross between a convertible note and a SAFE. It accrues interest at a stated rate and establishes a maturity date after which the investor may convert the underlying investment, plus accrued interest, into newly created preferred stock of the company.

agreements, which have many of the same considerations as a **convertible note**.

If you are an aspiring **unicorn** that plans to raise **equity** rounds, you'll want to closely evaluate your **equity** options before selling ownership in your company, unfortunately, that is not the focus of this book. There are many excellent resources for you online. Also, check out the book *Venture Deals* by Brad Feld and Jason Mendelson. The rest of this book can be helpful in explaining other types of financing you may need or want to consider alongside equity.

Funder

If you are a funder interested in providing risk capital to aspiring unicorns, then some sort of equity investment is likely the right option for you. That said, you probably have slightly different aspirations, as you have picked up *this* book instead of the dozens of other VC books available in the bookstore. So instead let's focus on the aspects of equity investing that can serve the needs of founders and funders such as risk-tolerant capital, alignment of incentives, flexibility and a long-time horizon. These characteristics are the building blocks for the "alternative" funding options that we'll discuss throughout this book, so it is important to understand some of the strategies of VC before we move on.

There are a couple of key considerations for investors choosing between **priced equity rounds** and **convertible note** agreements. The first is the level of **downside protection**, i.e., what happens when things go wrong. As a debt agreement, **convertible notes** come with **downside protections** for investors that are not available to an **equity** shareholder. How valuable these protections are when dealing with very early-stage companies that have little in the way of assets is certainly questionable, however.

Valuation is another consideration. One of the benefits of a convertible note is that early investors do not have to set a **valuation**, but can allow the next investor to do so when there is hopefully a bit more data to use. But that could be a drawback as well, particularly if the following valuation is large and causes the convertible note investor to end up with a smaller stake than they anticipated.

A **SAFE**, by comparison, comes with the benefits of speed and reduced structuring costs compared to a convertible note or a **priced equity round**. For very early-stage investors looking for a simple plug-and-play document that is founder-friendly, this can be a good option. It can help funders quickly deploy bridge financing to a start-up in a cash crunch, helping the start-up avoid raising a full funding round at a lower **valuation**. (In early-stage financing, this is called a "**down round**.").

There are some drawbacks to all of the **SAFE**'s advantages. **SAFE** investors have significantly fewer rights than investors using other types of equity contracts or **convertible note** agreements. Funders who are making significant numbers of **equity** investments will want to compare the benefits of a **SAFE** with other standard equity structures. To do so, I would recommend picking up one of those other VC books in the bookstore.

2

SOKO: Our Debt Financing Journey

Now that we have explored an equity financing journey with the Helium founders, let's take a look at what options you have for raising **debt financing** as a founder. **Debt** is when you **borrow** capital for your business and promise to repay this **loan**, generally with some amount of **interest**. Lenders often require **collateral** in the form of valuable **physical assets** that they can seize from your company if you **default**, i.e., stop paying the loan. **Debt** providers also look for a **credit history**, i.e., years of audited financials or a history repaying other loans. In this chapter, we will join Ella Peinovich on a debt funding journey in the creative manufacturing industry.

Beautiful Products, Ugly System

The artisan industry is one of the largest employers in most emerging markets. It is also one of the most disenfranchised. Most production is handled by women who work in small, informal workshops and sell their wares to tourists at the local market. The result? Artisans remain trapped below the poverty line, unable to create a sustainable living for themselves and their families.

This is especially true in parts of Africa where female artisans create hand-crafted goods using traditional techniques in order to support their children and extended families. In Kenya, where the unemployment rate hovers at over 10% and more than a third of the population lives below the international

© The Author(s), under exclusive license to Springer Nature
Switzerland AG 2021
A. Patton Power, *Adventure Finance*,
https://doi.org/10.1007/978-3-030-72428-3_2

poverty line, more than two million people depend on selling local arts and crafts for income.

Back in 2010, Ella Peinovich from Wisconsin, U.S., won a Legatum Center Voyager **Grant** to travel to Kenya to conduct primary market research for a creative manufacturing venture as part of her graduate studies at the Massachusetts Institute of Technology (MIT). Ella fell in love with traditional African artisanal products while in Kenya. She recalls returning to the U.S. with more suitcases than she left with, filled with handicrafts to sell at her family's art gallery.

Ella recognized the huge selling potential of Africa's artisanal crafts and felt frustrated that local artisans didn't have a way to compete in the international market, despite the evident demand. (The global creative manufacturing sector is projected to reach $1 trillion in sales by 2023.) As she prepared to return to Kenya to conduct field research at the University of Nairobi on localized design-manufacturing processes for her master's thesis, the issue of global distribution for local artisans weighed heavy on her mind.

Through her research, Ella began engaging with Nairobi's artisan communities. Not only did she recognize their skill and talent, but she also saw firsthand how difficult their working conditions were and the level of economic distress in the community. In the open-air markets where artisans sold their products, Ella recalls observing that they "were dealing in a lot of cash transactions, making them vulnerable to theft and assault." She also noticed the lack of toilets, or shade or water available. "They were producing beautiful products, yet the system for selling the products was ugly," she laments.

Ella says she became determined to develop a "system as beautiful as artisans' products." Back at MIT, Ella met Catherine Mahugu, a computer science student at the university, and pitched her an idea for a business that would disrupt the traditional African jewelry supply chain and, in turn, enable artisans across Africa to sell their handcrafted jewelry around the world. She also pitched it to designer Gwendolyn Floyd, and together the three women began working on the concept in their spare time.

Kuzindua SOKO

Ella, Catherine and Gwendolyn launched SOKO, meaning "marketplace" in Swahili, in 2011. The vision was to build a platform that would allow individual artisans to connect directly with consumers and manage their businesses directly from their mobile phones. The team scraped together early funding from various grants and student competitions. "It was with the first $10,000 we won from the Microsoft Awards, that I went off to buy a computer and a plane ticket to Kenya to focus purely on SOKO," Ella recalls. SOKO was no longer a part-time passion project.

But SOKO needed more money and a dedicated space to properly get off the ground. In 2012, the fledgling start-up joined one of the early MIT delta v start-up accelerator cohorts run by the Martin Trust Center for MIT Entrepreneurship. It also participated in the MIT Solve Inclusive Innovation Challenge and received seed grants from the Priscilla King Gray Public Service Center and MIT's Legatum Center for Development and Entrepreneurship. The founders launched their curated SOKO branded collection and online marketplace at DEMO Africa later that year.

SOKO went on to raise its first **equity** round in 2016, backed by Novastar Ventures. Ella had first met Novastar partner Niraj Varia at the Growth Africa and Village Capital incubator in Nairobi when he himself was a **social entrepreneur**. Niraj invited Ella to pitch SOKO's platform and progress to the other Novastar partners. Andrew Carruthers and Steve Beck shared an alignment to the mass reach of the social agenda of the business with the scale of commercial viability. They felt they could provide significant experience and support to ensure SOKO's commercial growth as a means of scaling its social impact. SOKO became one of the first investments in Novastar's East Africa fund, offering the company technical assistance in addition to equity investment. Novastar has reinvested in each of SOKO's subsequent rounds of **equity financing**.

Building a "Virtual Factory"

Novastar's initial **equity** capital enabled SOKO to build its "virtual factory,"—an innovative concept that changed the way artisans in Nairobi worked. The virtual factory was built on basic mobile connectivity, which most artisans had access to. Artisans could work in their own workshops on their own terms, rather than as employees working from a central factory. SOKO's virtual resource planning (VRP) solution matched product orders with the artisans using a machine-learning system built on metrics including artisans' reputation and performance. Artisans then managed **inventory**, arranged for deliveries to consumers and got paid directly through their mobile phones, using mobile money. The mobile-to-web system greatly reduced friction in the **supply chain** while cutting out the costly middlemen. SOKO's field workers also used it to track and quality-check production.

By 2016, SOKO's virtual factory was coordinating across a network of 1,400 independent artisans in and around Nairobi. This system aligned the efforts of the local artisan community with trends in the fashion world and enabled them to sell their ethically and sustainably created jewelry products worldwide. Through partnerships with international retailers like Nordstrom, The Reformation Inc and Urban Outfitters, Inc, SOKO's products caught the eye of the global fashion world. Larger and larger orders poured in. And with this increased demand, SOKO's business needs took another turn.

SOKO had proven that it could produce the goods, but its community of artisans needed help paying for their materials to satisfy SOKO's ever-larger wholesale orders. Many had until that point covered their **working capital** needs with **microfinance loans** from organizations like Kiva.org. But now artisans' own business needs were outgrowing **microfinance lenders**. SOKO needed additional capital to lend to its artisan community—as much as $5,000 per artisan per month—to cover the short-term gap between when clients' orders were received and when they were delivered and paid for.

Exploring Debt Options

Ella's first instinct was to apply for a **bank loan**. The type of **business loans** banks typically offer are known as **secured debt**, which requires borrowers to pledge something valuable as **collateral** for the loan. This way, if the borrower **defaults** on the loan (i.e., stops paying) the lender can seize the collateral and sell it to recover some of their loan. Traditional lenders like banks also typically require proof that a potential business borrower is **creditworthy** through audited financial statements, borrowing history, or evidence of orders for goods. **Secured debt** can be offered for any length of time, depending on the borrower's business needs. **Term loans** used for purchasing equipment, buildings and other income-producing assets tend to be longer-term, whereas **working capital loans**, which SOKO needed to cover day-to-day expenses, are shorter-term.

For an investor, a collateralized loan from a creditworthy borrower is a relatively low-risk investment, as the money is borrowed on condition that the lender will be repaid at a later date and there is valuable **collateral** that can be seized by the lender if it is not. But for SOKO, like many small businesses, **secured debt** wasn't an option. Lenders would want to see a track record of success, a proven business model, credit history and **collateral** to feel more secure about backing the business. Anecdotally, SOKO ticked all of those boxes. On paper, it didn't: while the company was growing significantly—64% increase in revenues from 2015–2016—its historical sales were not sufficient to fund current orders. For a traditional lender, this made the business appear risky. (Ironically, SOKO would have been more creditworthy to a bank if it wasn't experiencing such high demand.) Also, like most small and growing businesses, SOKO would struggle to make regular **interest** payments due to **cyclical cash flow** that fluctuates seasonally, which favored the end-of-year holiday season.

Since **secured debt** wasn't an option, Ella assumed SOKO would have to raise more **equity**, even though raising **equity financing** would mean selling shares in the company long term to finance short-term obligations. This would mean that Ella would have to **dilute** her, her co-founders and their equity investors' ownership in the long term in order to access **working capital** funding that was only needed for a very short period of time.

A Different Type of Growth Capital

Ella reached out to long-time contact Lilian Mramba from Grassroots Business Fund (GBF) to find out if GBF would be interested in becoming an **equity** investor. GBF is a global **impact investor** with operations in East Africa, Latin America, India and Southeast Asia that supports high-impact enterprises providing sustainable economic opportunities to people living in underserved communities. Lilian understood SOKO's immediate need for financing. "It was so obvious that they weren't going to walk into a bank and get a **working capital loan**," she says. "But it just didn't make sense for SOKO to use its equity to fund those types of needs." She asked Ella if she had considered **mezzanine financing**. Ella hadn't, so Lilian broke it down for her.

Mezzanine financing or "**mezz**" is a catch-all term for a broad group of debt instruments that are suitable for fast-growing companies. Mezzanine funding is a form of **quasi-equity**, which literally means it is a combination of equity and debt. Criteria for **mezzanine financiers** are typically based on the riskiness of the business's projected growth, not the collateral that a company can provide. Its terms often include a **kicker**, i.e., **upside** for the funder, as well as an interest rate.

Since they had previous **equity** investment from venture capitalists, SOKO qualified for a type of **mezzanine** financing called **venture debt. Venture debt** funders provide debt to fast-growing businesses that have been funded by equity investors, i.e., **venture-backed companies. Venture debt** investors typically base their willingness to lend on a company's financial projections as well as the reputation of its equity funders.

To meet early but fast-growing businesses' needs, **venture debt** usually has a **grace period**, wherein no repayments of principal are required, and does not require hard assets as **collateral**; rather, **venture debt** usually requires businesses to offer company shares as **collateral** or includes the right to buy shares (called **warrants**) as part of the deal.

SOKO fit the exact profile of the type of **venture-backed company** that **venture debt** was designed for: one that needed to access cash to meet its **working capital** needs, but which was too risky for bank financing. Ella asked Lilian if GBF would be willing to lend SOKO $700,000 in **venture debt** to enable SOKO to fulfill its clients' purchase orders.

Lilian was intrigued by the business and believed in Ella as an entrepreneur, but before she could make a commitment, she had to sell the idea to GBF's **investment committee**. Many of GBF's committee members had previously had negative experiences working with similar artisan platforms. Lilian worked hard to convince the committee to take a chance on SOKO by emphasizing the competitive advantage of the company's technology and operating platform. "It wasn't usually the type of company we liked to fund as it was just at a very early-stage," explains Lilian, "but we also knew that we wanted a seat at the SOKO table where we could learn about its model."

After about six months of conversation and due diligence, GBF committed to a three-year **revolving credit line** to fund SOKO's **working capital** needs.

To make use of the credit line, SOKO had to provide a list of returning wholesale clients and active orders. SOKO could draw down to 50% of the total order value for each order. This capital was then advanced to SOKO's artisans so they could fulfill the order and SOKO could deliver the goods before payment. SOKO continued providing a quarterly balance of all active orders from pre-approved vendors and requested more capital as needed. The company repaid the credit into a **Deposit Account Control Agreement (DACA)** account, over which GBF could obtain control if needed.

SOKO's Strategic Shift

As often happens with early-stage companies, SOKO's business model and their funding needs changed 18 months into the **venture debt** arrangement with GBF. The company was undergoing a major business pivot: it was shifting away from reliance on big-box retail distribution and started marketing directly to consumers. It launched its own e-commerce store and increased its presence on online retail platforms like Amazon Handmade and Goop. It also took on more specialty boutiques as clients that were able to better sell SOKO's story and convince customers of the value of the products they were buying.

The pivot ultimately gave SOKO more control over its brand messaging and enabled its buyers to learn more about the artisans making SOKO's products. In addition, it also meant that SOKO was generating fewer large wholesale sales and investing more in inventory. In light of the strategic change, SOKO and GBF, which was nearing the end of its **fund's life cycle**,[1] elected to wind down their funding agreement rather than accommodate the new business direction.

The **runway** from GBF's 18-month **venture debt investment** enabled SOKO to pursue more traditional **working capital** financing, in addition to new **equity** funding, to support its business growth needs. The company's virtual factory today supports a network of 2,300 independent artisans across Nairobi. SOKO has grown to $4 million in annual sales. And, it has been so successful marketing its brand that celebrities, from actress Nicole Kidman to the U.S.'s former first lady Michelle Obama, are buying and wearing its jewelry.

In Ella's perspective, "GBF's financing was instrumental to our growth. Like many fast-growing businesses we saw that with success, our challenges grew as well. The opportunity cost of not meeting the potential of our business outweighed any cost of financing."

Reflecting on this deal and the others that they have made in this fund, Lilian believes that funders who are interested in how they can play a catalytic role in growing early-stage businesses through **mezzanine** or other forms of **unsecured debt financing** need to be willing to be flexible and have a very steady hand. Her advice to funders is to "keep supporting the company, believe in the strategy and have a good amount of **dry powder**[2] available to continue supporting the company. Because oftentimes, it just takes a lot longer and it costs a lot more than any of us would ever imagine."

---

[1] We'll discuss why the fund life cycle can be significant for founders in Chapter 4.
[2] Capital that can be invested.

Which Type of Debt Options Are Right for You?

Founders

Nearly all forms of **debt** accrue **interest** and require the borrower to make **interest payments** of some kind. Generally, these **interest payments** are required at regular intervals (i.e., monthly) and are calculated as a percentage of the **principal** (the original amount borrowed) and can also be linked to national interest rates. Many small businesses struggle to be able to make **interest payments** at regular intervals due to limited cash flow in early stages of doing business or **cyclical cash flow** that fluctuates due to **seasonality** or consumer buying patterns.

Debt is considered a **self-liquidating** instrument. This means that it does not require a **third-party exit** event. The loan agreement states that the borrower will repay **interest** over time and by some date the **principal** borrowed. This means that the lender has a plan for when they will be fully repaid without relying on a separate event (like a sale of the company or an IPO).

Lenders often require companies (or individuals) to pledge something valuable to act as **security or collateral**. If a business defaults on the loan, i.e., stops paying, the lender can seize this and sell it to recover some of their principal. In addition to collateral, lenders generally require proof that a business is **credit worthy**. This can be in the form of audited financial statements, history of other borrowing or outstanding orders for goods.

There are quite a few options to consider when you are evaluating the kind of debt financing that is right for your company. Before we talk about some of the options, let's look at the two key factors that determine the cost and availability of debt: where the debt sits on the company's **capital structure**, and what kind of **security or collateral** is attached to the debt.

Your company's **capital structure** (or **capital stack**) is made up of various types of financing used for the business operations. This includes **external funding**, which is raised from **debt** and **equity** investors,[3] and **internal equity funding**, which is earned in the form of **net profits** or **retained earnings**. In other words, **external funding** is raised from investors and **internal funding** is earned through the profits from sales.

A **capital stack** is also called a **waterfall**, which is an apt way to think about how cash flows to funders and shareholders. Cash, revenues, profits, etc. first reach those at the top of the waterfall and then what is left progresses

---

[3] Or any of the other types of investors we speak about in this book.

down until it finally reaches those at the bottom, generally the **equity** investors. This "flow" happens during the normal course of business—for instance, interest payments to lenders are always paid before **dividends** can be paid to **equity** holders—and in the case of a **liquidity event**, where a founder sells the company or the company goes bankrupt.

The capital looks like the graphic below. Funders at the top of the capital stack are **senior** to those who sit at the bottom. Those at the bottom are **junior** (or **subordinated**) to those at the top. The more senior a funder's position in the capital stack, the "safer" they are. This is because the senior funders have the first claim to cash from the business. The more junior a funder is in the capital stack, the greater their risk and, likely, the more they need to charge to make up for taking that risk.

In general, **equity** funders are **subordinated** to **debt** funders. This is one of the main reasons that **equity** investors expect a much higher return on their investment than debt investors. With debt, junior lenders will typically charge higher rates than senior lenders to account for their riskier position. Mezzanine debt is likely to be subordinated to other types of debt and thus will be more expensive from an **interest rate** perspective (Fig. 2.1).

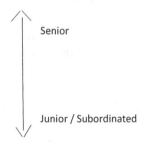

Senior

Junior / Subordinated

Fig. 2.1 Illustration of senior and junior debt in capital structure

Seniority of debt in the capital stack is just one element that determines price. **Collateral** is another. **Physical assets** are one type of **collateral** a company can provide, but there are quite a few other types as well. Recall that SOKO was able to use a combination of wholesale client orders and Novastar's support as an equity funder to ease the lending risk for GBF. **Senior secured debt** is the cheapest form of debt because it's the lowest risk for funders (Fig. 2.2).

But as you can see from SOKO's story and likely know from your journey, senior **secured debt** often isn't available to early-stage businesses. If it is, the repayment terms for traditional debt might not be the right fit for your business. This is why SOKO used **mezzanine financing** on its journey.

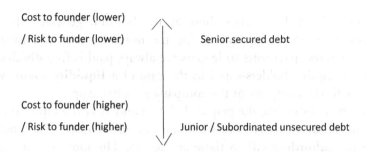

Fig. 2.2 Illustration of capital structure with cost and risk

Mezzanine financing combines elements of **debt** and **equity** to create funding that has more flexibility than pure **debt** and **equity**.[4] **Mezz funders** are willing to consider different forms of risk assessment, such as the presence of a **VC** funder (**venture debt**). They are willing to look at alternative forms of **collateral**, like SOKO's client orders. They are also willing to lend money that is completely **unsecured**, if necessary. As they are taking additional risk by funding earlier stage businesses or sitting **subordinated** to other funders, they look for higher returns than **secured debt** funders. These returns come from a **fixed interest rate** and some kind of upside opportunity in the form of a **kicker**.

There are two different kinds of kickers: **warrants**, which allow funders to buy small amounts of ownership in the business, and **cash kickers**, which trigger additional payments based on the performance of the company. **Cash kickers** are designed to give funders a bit more reward if a company does especially well, as a perk for helping the company succeed. For a founder, a **mezzanine** loan will be pricier than a term loan, but many mezzanine providers will offer lower **fixed interest rates** because they expect some additional upside from the **kicker**.[5]

Funders

Appropriately structured **debt** can be critical for early-stage businesses' survival and success. As funders, you'll need to evaluate what types of **debt** funding are the most appropriate for the founders that you are trying to

[4]Bennick, E. & Winters, R. *New Perspectives on Financing Small Cap SME's in Emerging Markets: The Case for Mezzanine Finance.* May 2016.
[5]Bennick, E. & Winters, R. *New Perspectives on Financing Small Cap SME's in Emerging Markets: The Case for Mezzanine Finance.* May 2016.

serve and how you can develop these funding options in line with your own **risk/return** requirements.

While lending to companies that have years of audited financials and significant **collateral** may be the lowest risk for you as a funder, you will be precluded from lending to most early-stage organizations. Similarly, requiring high levels of cash **interest payments** during the term of the loan may mitigate your risk, but will likely make **debt** payments unaffordable for early-stage borrowers with variable revenues.

By definition, **mezzanine** funders are willing to take additional risk by requiring little to no **collateral**. Instead of charging high cash **interest rates**, they pair together fixed interest rates and upside in the form of **warrants** or **cash kickers** dependent on the profit of the company. In this way, mezzanine financing can be a flexible funding alternative that can be molded to the varying financing and operational needs of funders.[6] By offering long-term growth financing with a higher risk tolerance, it can help to optimize the company's capital structure by efficiently bridging **equity** and **senior debt**. The flexibility of the various mezzanine instruments also means more complexity.[7]

Structuring **mezzanine finance** requires careful consideration. As mentioned above, a mezzanine finance provider ultimately takes more risk than a traditional loan provider, which means the financing costs of a **mezzanine** product are higher than those of a traditional term loan. If the mezz structure includes a kicker in the form of a profit-share, this will effectively translate into a higher **interest** rate as the company grows. This can lead to a high cash burden for the company. If you include **warrants**, this will add complexity to the company's **capitalization table**, which may prolong the transaction process. Lastly, **mezzanine structures** are relatively new in many markets, meaning that other **equity** investors, banks, lawyers, but also courts, tax authorities and policy makers sometimes have a lesser understanding of these structures.[8]

---

[6]Bennick, E. & Winters, R. *New Perspectives on Financing Small Cap SME's in Emerging Markets: The Case for Mezzanine Finance.* May 2016.

[7]*Mezzanine Financing for Access to Energy in Sub-Saharan Africa.* July 2020. Available at: https://triplejump.eu/wp-content/uploads/2020/08/TJ-EEGF-A2E-Mezzanine-Paper_Final-2.pdf.

[8]*Mezzanine Financing for Access to Energy in Sub-Saharan Africa.* July 2020. Available at: https://triplejump.eu/wp-content/uploads/2020/08/TJ-EEGF-A2E-Mezzanine-Paper_Final-2.pdf.

3

Powered by People and Equal Exchange's Trade Finance Journey

In the last chapter, we looked at **debt** options with different types of security or **collateral**. As a small business, you probably don't have a lot of physical assets that you can use for collateral. But mezzanine financing isn't the only type of debt that you can access without traditional collateral. In this chapter, we are going to explore **trade finance** options that allow you to use **customer orders** or **invoices** as collateral to access **working capital**.

Unlike digital products that can be sent to clients immediately, physical products take time to manufacture and ship to buyers. This means that if you're a small business making products, there could be a substantial gap between when you manufacture your goods and when your customers pay for them. That time can be expensive for you, if you have to fund all of the costs upfront. But this is the reality for all global supply chains, large and small. They are made up of millions of different businesses that need to access trillions of dollars of **trade financing** to cover the cost of getting products to market.

The World in a Cup

Let's start with one of the largest global supply chains: coffee. Equal Exchange is a U.S.-based fair trade coffee company that works with farmers in Latin America. It was founded in the 1980s by Jonathan Rosenthal, Michael Rozyne and Rink Dickinson. Jonathan, Michael and Rink saw pretty quickly

© The Author(s), under exclusive license to Springer Nature
Switzerland AG 2021
A. Patton Power, *Adventure Finance*,
https://doi.org/10.1007/978-3-030-72428-3_3

that the farmers they were working with needed access to **working capital** during their planting and harvesting seasons to be able to pay for the products, equipment and labor required to grow their coffee crops. Yet, farmers' options for accessing local funding were extremely limited and often unaffordable. So Equal Exchange's founders decided to use their own company balance sheet to try to help them out.

Jonathan, Michael and Rink decided that the best way to do this was to purchase coffee from farmers early. This means that Equal Exchange intentionally buys stock from farmer co-ops soon after harvesting, many months before it expects to sell the stock in the U.S. and stores the stock in its own warehouse facilities. This approach is distinct from traditional coffee companies, which purchase coffee beans on demand when they need to sell them. This on-demand approach keeps the large coffee companies inventory low but requires the farmers and farmer co-ops to bear the cost of storing the coffee and managing their cash flow while they wait for buyers to purchase their stock. Equal Exchange's approach shifts millions of pounds of inventory, and its capital burden, of off farmer co-**op's** balance sheets onto Equal Exchange's. (In Chapter 8 we'll discuss the innovative way they've funded their own capital needs.)

This type of transaction is called **supply chain financing**. It is a buyer-driven approach that provides access to **working capital** for small businesses by paying them early. In fact, many large companies have **supply chain financing** options for their suppliers. Different types include voluntary **early payment**, like Equal Exchange, or **dynamic discounting**, which allows small suppliers to secure early payment from buyers by offering a discount on their orders. For example, a small business might offer a 1.5% discount if the corporate client pays them within five days instead of 30 days, or 2% if they get paid immediately instead of within 60 days.

While **early purchasing** and **dynamic discounting** can alleviate small businesses' **working capital** burden by speeding up payments, both still require businesses to cover the cost of manufacturing their goods upfront and wait for payment. They also require buyers (typically large ones) that are willing to facilitate payments. So, they don't completely solve small businesses' working capital needs.

The Working Capital Conundrum

Ella (from Chapter 2) saw that the artisans she worked with at SOKO had this exact **working capital** problem and watched successful artisans turn down large, lucrative orders simply because they didn't have enough cash on hand to cover their upfront costs. In fact, most artisans had to wait on payment from one order to fund the next one. In the retail sector, where the standard is to have payment terms up to 90 days from delivery, this led to considerable downtime and lost income for the makers.

But just as SOKO did not have the required **collateral** to access **secured debt**, the artisans did not have collateral to access **working capital** lines of credit that would help them smooth out their cash flow issues. Also, as many worked in the informal cash-based economy, they did not have historical business statements or other paperwork to prove their **creditworthiness**.

Ella wanted to find an alternative way of looking at credit scoring—one that didn't depend on financial history or cash flow. Instead, she wondered whether it was possible to build an affordable and accessible credit product around factors like, "have you delivered this product before and at this scale?" and "have you had successful transactions with this same buyer or similar types of buyers?" Because she knew the creative manufacturing sector, she believed it was possible to develop financing products for artisans. So, in 2019, she stepped away from SOKO and launched Powered by People, a technology platform for artisans, providing **purchase order financing** against market transactions.

Order, Ship, Invoice

Purchase order financing is a way for businesses to use orders from customers as a form of **collateral** to secure a loan. In **purchase order financing**, a business owner will take their customer's purchase order and sell it to a third-party financier, in this case Powered by People. The third party then handles payment collection from those customers to recoup its costs for paying the producers early. For business owners, this type of transaction provides the upfront cash they need to buy raw materials to fulfill their orders and meet other **working capital** needs.

Purchase order financing is a type of **factoring**, or a loan that uses invoices or purchase orders as **collateral**. It is similar to **supply chain financing**, except that **factoring** is initiated by the producer/supplier and requires an external financier to make the loan. (In fact, another name for supply chain financing is **reverse factoring**.)

Factoring is an ancient practice that has been traced to Phoenicia and the Roman Empire, when farmers and merchants would obtain financing from lenders based on their future harvests or shipments. **Purchase order**

Table 3.1 Types of factoring and their characteristics

Purchase order financing	Shipment financing	Invoice factoring (Receivables factoring)
Goods ordered by buyer	Goods shipped to buyer	Goods delivered to buyer
Purchase order issued	Shipping Bill issued	Invoice issued

financing allows businesses to receive payment when an order has been placed, but not yet delivered to the customer. While convenient as short-term **working capital** for producers and suppliers, it can be risky for funders, as the goods have not yet been made or delivered. Because of the high level of execution risk, **purchase order financing** can be difficult for many start-ups and small businesses to obtain.

There is another type of **factoring** that reduces some of the risk for funders: **invoice factoring**. With **invoice factoring**, also called **receivables factoring**, financiers buy a business' invoices for goods that have been delivered. For producers, this means they can get paid on a more predictable schedule, directly after issuing an invoice, rather than having to wait 30, 60 or 90 days. Additionally, **shipment financing** can be used after the goods have been shipped and a shipping bill has been issued. Below is a table that describes the stage at which each type of factoring occurs (Table 3.1).

Factoring can be an excellent option for short-term financing, but it can be an expensive one, as businesses typically have to sell their **purchase orders** or **invoices** at a discount. How steep the **discount** is represents the cost of the financing. So, for example, if a company sells a purchase order for 95% of the total amount, the cost of the financing would be 5%.

The Gems and Stones of Factoring

Now let's go back to Powered by People and understand how its **purchase order financing** model works. Say one of Powered by People's artisans had a $20,000 jewelry order from a large department store for the Christmas season. To have the cash needed to complete the order, the artisan offers to sell 50% of the purchase order to Powered by People, i.e., $10,000 of the order.

Powered by People offers to pay $9,500 for the **purchase order.** If the artisan agrees to this price, Powered by People enters into a tri-party agreement with the buyer and artisan and would transfer the $9,500 to the artisan. Because the artisan is receiving 500 *less than the* 10,000 future payment from the customer, the cost of the financing for the artisan is 2.5% per month for 2 months (500 = 5% of 10,000). When the department store receives

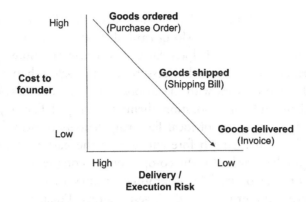

Fig. 3.1 Cost and risk of factoring options

the jewelry items it ordered in a couple of months' time it will pay Powered by People the full $20,000, per the tri-party agreement. Powered by People will remove the $9,500 advance and fees of $500 and will pay the remaining $10,000 to the artisan. If the financing was only for two months that would be the equivalent of 30% annual **interest rate** (2.5% × 12 = 30%).

The amount of the **discount** at which businesses have to sell their **purchase orders** and **invoices** is usually set by the financier to reflect the level of risk they have to take on. **Factoring** financiers take into account the risk that the producer will not get the product finished and delivered, and the buyer will not pay. Thus, the farther the product is from delivery and payment, the higher the chance that the goods won't be produced, or the order will be cancelled or that there will be shipping issues, etc. More risk equals more expensive financing (Fig. 3.1).

Solving for Affordability

One of Ella's foremost concerns in launching Powered by People's finance offering was ensuring that **factoring** was affordable and suited to the artisans she wanted to serve, while also being financially sustainable. To achieve that, she developed a technology platform that uses alternative ways of evaluating the risk of the transaction by looking at the creditworthiness of the buyer and the historical performance of the borrowers to reduce the risk of Powered by People's lending. By measuring the borrower's delivery times, production quality, order growth and recurring customers Powered by People is able to generate a historical picture of the business operations and efficacy by which to evaluate the business' ability to fulfill an order and therefore the risk of financing it.

The founders of Equal Exchange made a similar discovery to Ella about their coffee farmer co-ops' **working capital** needs. While Equal Exchange's advance coffee purchases helped farmers get capital more quickly after harvest, farmers often needed access to capital *before* harvest. So Equal Exchange decided to work with the co-ops to help them access **factoring**.

Rather than building a solution themselves, Equal Exchange's founders helped develop a network of local **factoring** lenders to help farmer co-ops access affordable financing before and during the harvest. Equal Exchange provides a purchase order for the co-op's coffee, along with a 25% **payment guarantee** on the order. The **guarantee** ensures that regardless of what happens during the growing and harvest seasons, Equal Exchange will pay a portion of the order. That lessens the risk for the purchase order factoring lenders and enables the farmers to get cash before the harvest, when they need it the most.

Same Same, but Different?

Factoring and Supply Chain Financing are similar in that both strategies facilitate early payment to help businesses better manage their **working capital** or cash flows. Where they are different is that **factoring** is a **loan** with the **receivables** counting as **collateral** for an external funder and **supply chain financing** is a prepayment program created by a buyer. Below is a table that lays out the characteristics of the two different types of trade financing (Table 3.2).

Table 3.2 Comparison of factoring and supply chain finance

	Trade finance	
	Factoring	Supply chain finance
AKA	Receivables financing, invoice factoring, shipment financing, purchase order financing	Reverse Factoring
Initiated by	Supplier (small business)	Buyer (large business)
Description	Loan with receivables as collateral	Prepayment of receivables
Transaction	Debt on supplier's balance sheet	Off-balance sheet transaction (payment of accounts receivable)
Parties involved	Supplier, Factoring Financier, and Buyer	Supplier and Buyer
Risk assessment	Execution and delivery risk, and buyers' ability to pay	Buyers' ability to pay

Is Trade Finance Right for You?

Founders

At a foundational level, **factoring** is primarily a source of cash flow for a business that can be used for its short term operational needs. It does not really solve core financial issues that a business may find is affecting its balance sheet or long term cash flow.

As this is short-term financing, often only a few weeks or months, this can be expensive for the business when calculated on an annual rate. In the example above with Powered by People, the annualized cost of the loan would be 30%. Due to its cost, **factoring** should be evaluated based on opportunity cost and used to bridge a cash gap or allow companies to maximize production capability to scale, not to survive month to month over a long period of time. Finally, some funders might ask for a **personal guarantee** for **invoice factoring**, so founders will need to evaluate the risk that this presents to them when they consider signing an agreement.

In addition to formal **supply chain financing** programs that your large customers set up, you can ask your customers to pay for their purchase orders early or to pre-pay at a discount. As consumers, we often do this for companies. Think about the last time you were offered a cheaper rate to purchase a yearly subscription rather than paying monthly. If you chose to pay for the yearly subscription upfront, you helped that company fund its ongoing **working capital** needs. As an entrepreneur, if you have large customers with whom you have a good track record, you could ask them to pre-pay their **invoices**, potentially even at a discount, to avoid looking for **working capital** from external funders.

Funders

Although factoring can present many benefits to organizations from a short term cash flow perspective, when you are evaluating **invoice factoring** as a funding option, you do need to be careful as you are shifting how companies receive their payments, which means they might not be able to cover their costs in a given month if they have not budgeted properly. The sophistication of the finance department of the small business is also an issue. The business has to be able to do more sophisticated forecasting and planning to be able to account for the variations in cash flow. Finally, this creates additional complexity from a tax perspective in many jurisdictions.

Lendable started out doing **invoice factoring** for off-grid solar providers in Africa and Asia. Instead of taking the risk of large customers (such as Nordstrom or John Lewis in Powered by People's case), they were taking the risk that hundreds of thousands of customers that were paying for solar panels on a **pay as you go (PAYGO)** basis would continue to pay. They stopped utilizing the factoring method of financing as they realized they were shifting around the timings of the cash flows for these small businesses. They found that this created additional risks for their clients around being able to pay future fixed expenses (such as salary or rent). If small businesses shift their payments forward, they might not be able to cover their costs in a given month in the future. So Lendable shifted to a more traditional **term loan debt** structure. They consider their debt secured, but instead of physical **collateral**, they use the cash flows from the thousands (or hundreds of thousands) of users as the collateral.

Another issue with **factoring** is that it doesn't allow businesses to recycle or reinvest the capital that they are lent. In other types of **debt**, companies can use the cash they have borrowed to spend on inputs, products, services or research and when they turn those products or services into revenue, they can use the earnings to spend it on something else and so on until they owe the lender the principal of the loan back. Although the company may owe **interest** and even a portion of **principal** along the way, they are able to use most of the money in whatever way they choose during the term of the loan. With **factoring**, the lending is directly related to one particular order, so the company only has access to the amount they need for that specific order.

4

Unpacking Our Self-Evaluation

Alright, before we go any further, let's circle back to that checklist that I gave you at the beginning of the book and unpack each set of questions in turn. If you are brand new to the world of early-stage finance, you probably have quite a few questions based on the last few chapters, so it's a great time to pause and go through some of the basics. If you are a seasoned pro who is just interested in all the cool funding instruments that I promised upfront, feel free to skip ahead! (Table 4.1)

Table 4.1 Founder's self-evaluation checklist

Who are we?	How is our company registered?
	How do we make money? Who are our customers?
	What stage company are we?
	What are our growth projections?
How mission driven are we?	How embedded is our mission in our company?
	Do we have an impact track record?
What are our funding needs?	How much funding do we need?
	What do we need to spend it on?
	How do we want to pay it back?
	What are our ownership expectations in the short/medium term? Long term?

(continued)

© The Author(s), under exclusive license to Springer Nature
Switzerland AG 2021
A. Patton Power, *Adventure Finance*,
https://doi.org/10.1007/978-3-030-72428-3_4

Table 4.1 (continued)

	How involved do we want our funders to be?
What type of funder is right for us?	What types of funders are there?
	What kinds of resources can they provide?
	What level of risk are they comfortable with?
	What kind of return do they require, and when?
	Who are their stakeholders? How does funding get approved?

Who Are We?

How Is Our Business Registered?

As a founder, you are building an organization to create value. While the legal structure of your organization does not determine the value that you are creating, it can set guidelines for how you engage with **internal** and **external stakeholders**. This book is written for **founders** of any kind of organization, so to start out, let's discuss a few common legal structures and how each one affects an organization's ability to access different types of capital.

If you are a non-profit organization, it means no one can own shares in your business, but there will be individuals that make decisions about your every day operations and your strategic direction. These decision makers will generally be some combination of management and a **board of directors**. As a non-profit, you can borrow and repay loans, but you cannot issue dividends, since you cannot have shareholders in your business. This means that all earnings and "profits" remain within the entity. Non-profit organizations are generally tax-exempt, although different jurisdictions have varying requirements.

If you are a for-profit company, you can have any number of owners who participate in the growth and success of the business. These shareholders can include the founders, employees, external investors or some combination of all of these. Your company's ownership can also change over time, depending on who acquires company shares. Ownership of shares is generally connected to governance, so if an external investor owns shares in your company, then that investor will have voting rights and an opportunity to nominate member(s) to the board of directors. A for-profit company can choose to distribute profits as dividends to its shareholders or retain profits and reinvest them into the business. This decision will depend on the contractual obligations of the company to its shareholders and investors (such as external financing). For-profit organizations also need to pay taxes on profits that they make.

Social enterprises are a relatively new category of business, originating from a confluence of traditional business and philanthropy. Rather than relying on public or grant monies, **social enterprises** are businesses that strive toward a social or environmental mission by generating and reinvesting revenues. Some countries have a legal registration category for **social enterprises**, but many do not. Examples of legal structures that blend profit and purpose include **Public Benefit Corporations, Limited Liability Companies (L3Cs)** in the U.S., and **Community Interest Companies (CICs)** in the UK In some jurisdictions, certain **social enterprise** legal structures limit how **dividends** can be issued.

Hybrid organizations have two different types of legal structures i.e., a for-profit and a non-profit.

Co-operatives (co-ops) are partially or completely **employee-owned** companies. There are a wide variety of legal structures in different jurisdictions that govern employee-owned companies.

How Do We Make Money and Who Are Our Customers?

For any of the financing options that we discuss in this book, it is vital for you to have a sense of how you are going to sustain, and hopefully grow, your operations. This is necessary regardless of whether you are a non-profit or a for-profit company. You can think of your **revenue model** as your internal financing model. Being able to clearly articulate your internal financing projections will help you understand whether you need external funding and if so, how much you need. It is also important to be able to clearly articulate your business model to potential funders.

Your **revenue model** is likely based on some combination of the following:

- Selling or renting products or services to end users,
- Having third parties (like donors) pay for your products and services,
- Selling access to your end users,
- Selling data collected through your operations.[1]

---

[1]If you are selling data collected through your operations, this raises issues around data privacy and exploiting end users. It is important to carefully consider how you structure this.

You also need to be able to answer critical questions about the types of users or third parties that drive your revenues by purchasing or renting your products and/or services.

Who are they? To answer this, think of how you would segment your customers by age, geographic location, preferences, or other criteria.

Are they individuals or businesses? Selling to individual end users is referred to as a business to consumer (B to C) strategy, versus a business to business (B to B) strategy.

Why are customers incentivized to spend money on what you are offering? Funders will want to understand how your offering compares to others in the market.

For more information on defining and building your business model, I highly recommend using the Lean Canvas or the Social Business Model Canvas. These resources and more are available in the online companion to this book.

What Stage of Company Are We?

See Table 4.2:

Table 4.2 Stages of a company's growth

Concept stage	Early stage	Growth stage	Scaling	Established
You generally have an idea, but not necessarily a **minimum viable product (MVP)** or a **proof of concept**	You may have an **MVP** or **proof of concept** and you may even have started protecting your **intellectual property (IP)** legally, but you still only have a small number of paying customers, if any	You have defined your product or service offering and have a base of paying customers. You are building your internal infrastructure to grow	You have a large and growing customer base, have built your internal infrastructure, and are in the process of scaling up your operations and potentially adding new products or services	You have a steady base of paying customers and a successful business track record

What Are Our Growth Projections?

Next, you'll need to look at your **business growth projections**. You'll want to examine both your revenue, as well as your free cash flow projections. If you are a not-for-profit, you'll want to look at your fundraising projections as well as any earned revenue. Questions you need to answer here include:

How large is the market of addressable customers? You'll need to have a good understanding of the size of the market of potential customers for your product or service.

How scalable is your product? If your product is a physical good (or a service that must be done in person), then you'll need to factor in your ability to physically produce your product and distribute it to end users. If you offer a digital product or service, your ability to scale is significantly easier because you lack physical limitations. You will also want to consider scalability in terms of replicability in other contexts or geographies.

Helium Health's founders had always planned to build an **exponential growth** business. In the start-up world, we call these aspiring **Unicorns**, which are working toward a valuation of $1 billion. As aspiring **Unicorns**, the Helium founders were projecting **exponential growth**, expecting to raise many additional funding rounds and were willing to sell ownership in their company. In the medium to long term, this might mean losing control of the business, but they wanted to build a multi-billion dollar business around healthcare data, so **equity** financing worked for them. If you are reading this book, you likely aren't a **Unicorn**, so what are you? Well, you might be a **Zebra**.

Zebras are businesses that come with many different stripes, representing the diversity of their founders and the problems they are trying to solve. They are collaborative but feisty, building companies with impactful solutions while also taking care of their workforces, communities and environments. **Zebras** are also both black and white, which represents striving for both profit AND purpose.[2] Here is an overview that creators of the **Zebra** framework came up with to describe the difference between **Zebras** and **Unicorns** (Fig. 4.1).

Zebras are a very broad category that speaks more to philosophy than specific growth specifications and types. And they are just one of the many types of animals that are used to describe start-ups. You might also hear about camels, gazelles, oxen and potentially even others! In this book, we are going to use the below classifications that were developed by Dalberg, the Omidyar Network, the Collaborative for Frontier Finance,[3] and adapted by Zebras Unite, Village Capital.[4]

High growth venture—as a high growth venture, you have a disruptive business model, large addressable markets, high growth projections, ability to scale quickly and are quite risky. These are often referred to in the start-up world as Gazelles.

Category pioneer—as a category pioneer, you have disruptive products and services, new markets that are likely large, have variable growth and the potential to scale.

Niche Enterprise—as a niche enterprise, you have an innovative product or service, niche markets and customer segments and are projecting steady to high growth.

Dynamic enterprise—as a dynamic enterprise, you are in an established industry and sector, you have existing products that are tried and tested, a proven business model and are projecting steady growth.

Livelihood enterprise—as a livelihood enterprise, you are a family run, highly localized business that is driven by local opportunity and are projecting limited future growth.

---

[2]The Zebra framework was created by four U.S.-based founders (Jennifer Brandel, Astrid Scholz, Aniyia Williams, and Mara Zepeda) who in 2016 found themselves frustrated in their own capital-raising journeys. They had each founded for-profit tech-enabled companies with purpose and then found that these companies seemed unfundable in the unicorn-obsessed VC world. When they approached social impact investors, they realized that the investors often didn't understand the industries that they were developing products for. If they did understand the industries, these technologies-enabled system interventions did not fit into their theories of change. A brief history of Zebras Unite is here. The 2017 "manifesto" from which the table is reproduced is here. Brandel, J., Zepeda, M., Scholz, A. & Williams, S. (2017, March 8). "Zebras Fix What Unicorns Break." Available at: https://medium.com/zebras-unite/zebrasfix-c467e55f9d96.

[3]Hornberger, K. & Chau, V. The Missing Middles: Segmenting Enterprises to Better Understand Their Financial Needs, the Collaborative for Frontier Finance (Omidyar Network/Dutch Good Growth Fund [DGGF]). Available at: https://static1.squarespace.com/static/59d679428dd0414c16f59 855/t/5bd00e22f9619a14c84d2a6c/1540361837186/Missing_Middles_CFF_Report.pdf.

[4]Need to ask Astrid how to cite the frameworks.

	UNICORN	ZEBRA
THE WHY		
purpose	exponential growth	sustainable prosperity
end game	exit, liquidity event, 10x	profitable, sustainable, 2x
outcome	monopoly	plurality
THE HOW		
worldview	zero sum, winners and losers	win-win
method	competition	cooperation
natural model	parasitism	mutualism
resources	hoarded	shared
style	assertive	participatory
seeks	more	enough, better
THE WHO		
beneficiary	private, individuals, shareholders	public, communities
team composition	engineer heavy	balanced: community managers, customer success, engineers
user pays	with attention (opaque)	for value (transparent)
THE WHAT		
growth direction	hockey stick	regenerative growth
metric	quantity	quality
priority	user acquisition	user success
obstacle	product adoption	process adoption

Fig. 4.1 Comparison of Unicorns and Zebras

How Mission Driven Are We?

How Embedded Is Our Mission in Our Company?

Whether you are a **social entrepreneur** who has established your business to create social and/or environmental impact, or a founder that doesn't identify as a social entrepreneur but is motivated to create a **sustainable business**, it is important for you to be able to clearly articulate your **mission statement**. A clear **mission statement** sets a foundation for your company strategy. It can also help you to recruit and onboard new staff by helping them understand (and identify with) what your business is trying to achieve. And it establishes your desired social and environmental impact to potential funders, which can positively affect the type of funding you can secure, whether from foundations, governments, development institutions, private investors and interested in advancing your social and environmental impact.

As you go down your funding journey, you will likely engage with some funders that completely understand and support your mission. You may also encounter funders that are interested in your business but see your mission as secondary to, or even a hindrance to, your growth. It is therefore important for you to evaluate how you want to feature and articulate your **mission statement** in your funding journey to reduce the risk of mission drift, i.e., moving away from your social and/or environmental mission.

Do We Have an Impact Track Record?

If you are interested in accessing funding from **impact focused funders**, you'll likely need to provide evidence that you are operating in an under-served, inefficient or untapped market. If you're a financial services company, for example, this might mean presenting data on the socioeconomic status or gender of your target customers that demonstrates how low-income customers and women are inadequately served by existing market players. You'll also need evidence that the product or service you are providing has a significant impact on these relevant datapoints.

What Are Our Funding Needs?

How Much Do We Need?

In order to assess the total amount of funding you need; you must start by calculating how much cash you make each month and subtract the amount you are currently spending every month. If the difference in this calculation of debits and credits is a positive number, then it is the amount of **free cash** you are generating each month. If it is a negative number, then that is called your **burn rate**. It is important to note that this calculation requires you to understand how much cash, not how much revenue, you are bringing in each month. If it takes 30 days or 60 days or several months to turn revenue into cold, hard (or electronic) cash, that may mean you have significant sales, but you still cannot cover your monthly expenses.

Next, you'll need to look at your projections to identify significant milestones. Milestones could include when you create your **minimum viable product (MVP)**, **break even** on revenue, or reach certain number of customers. You'll then need to account for all of the various costs that you incur to reach your growth targets. Founders often underestimate how much it will actually cost to create the growth that they project.

Finally, you'll need to calculate the **total amount of cash** that it will take to achieve each milestone by taking the **total sum of your revenues** and subtracting the **total sum of your expenses**.[5]

Then, when a funder asks you how much cash you need, you can tell them the **total amount** it would cost you to reach a specific milestone. The number of months that you can realistically sustain your business based on the cash you have available is called your **runway**.

What Do We Need to Spend It on?

Proof of Concept—this is cash required to test your product or service in the market or build your initial **MVP**. Proof of concept can relate to your first product, a new product, or expansion into a new market.

Growth capital—this is cash needed to hire people, invest in product development, put systems in place, and pay for marketing that helps you build your business.

Working Capital—this is cash required to run the day-to-day operations of your business and buy inputs, inventory or materials required for your product or service.

Assets—this is money needed for physical or intangible investments for your business, such as buildings, equipment and brands.

How Do We Want to Pay It Back?

If you secure funding from external funders to cover your business's spending and growth needs, there are three ways to repay your funders. The first is repayment through a **third-party exit**. Basically, this means that you expect

---

[5]If your projections are seasonal, you'll want to make sure that these totals don't conceal any large swings in cash available. If there are large cash swings, make sure that the total amount you are raising is larger than the biggest deficit.

to repay your funders sometime in the future, either by selling your company or listing it on a stock exchange.

The second strategy is repayment from **internal cash flows**. In this case, you plan to repay funding based on cash that your business generates while your funding agreement is in place.

The third strategy is to **use future funding** to repay your financial backers. For this strategy, you may use funding in the early stages of your business, or in the short-term, to build a credit history and track record that allows you to access better, less expensive funding with which to repay your initial financial supporters.

Technically, you have a fourth option, which is not to pay it back, but unless it is a grant that doesn't have any repayment requirements, that isn't a great plan.

What Are Our Ownership Expectations?

From an ownership perspective, you need to evaluate your current status, as well as your plans for the near, medium and long term. Do you want to continue on at the helm of your business in the future? Or do you want to sell your business to someone else or transition ownership to your employees?

How Involved Do We Want Our Funders to Be?

If you are looking for a funder to help shape your business, you'll need to be willing to provide incentives for them to do so. Generally, this means offering some kind of upside, or return, if the business does well, and this calculation would need to be considered in your evaluation of different funding options.

You'll also want to understand the priorities and capabilities of potential funders to determine what kinds of incentives and terms are appropriate. That requires doing active due diligence to understand what kind of funder can get involved and deliver the value-add your business needs.

What Type of Funder is Right for Us?

What Types of Funders Are There?

Throughout this book, we'll be exploring options that involve all different kinds of funders. Here is a quick of who you should keep in mind while you are reading this book (Table 4.3).

Table 4.3 Types of funders

Finance provider	Definition	Typical investee lifecycle stage
Angel investor	Individuals or networks with resources who invest in very early start-ups and provide advice	Concept
Business accelerator/incubator	Institutions that help ventures define and build their initial products, identify promising customer segments, and secure resources	Concept Early-stage
Government agency	Government institutions established for the specific purpose of promoting economic growth and development through variety of direct or indirect support mechanisms	Concept Early-stage Growth Established
Non-profit/social enterprise	Typically impact-oriented organizations that have as a part of their mission to support SME growth primarily through capacity building	Concept Early-stage Growth Established
Private equity fund	Medium- to long term finance provided to an investee company in return for an equity stake in potentially high growth, unquoted companies	Established

(continued)

Table 4.3 (continued)

Finance provider	Definition	Typical investee lifecycle stage
Venture capital fund	A subset of private equity that specifically invest in start-up companies and provide advice and other non-finance resources	Concept Early-stage Growth
Debt & mezzanine fund	Pools of capital that invest in businesses through mezzanine and debt instruments	Growth Established
Commercial bank	Financial institution that accepts deposits, offers checking account services, makes business, personal, and mortgage loans to individuals and small businesses	Early-stage Growth Established
Microfinance institution	Formal institutions whose major business is the provision of financial services and insurance products to low-income individuals and micro and small businesses	Concept
Non-bank financial institution	Institutions that provide certain types of banking services but do not have a full banking licenses (e.g., credit unions, CDFIs, fintech, etc.)	Concept Early-stage
Development finance institution	Specialized development banks or subsidiaries setup to support private sector development in developing countries	Concept Early-stage Growth Established
Foundation	Independent legal entity setup solely for charitable purposes, often drawing on the resources of a single individual, family, or corporation	Concept Early-stage

(continued)

Table 4.3 (continued)

Finance provider	Definition	Typical investee lifecycle stage
Endowment	Donation of money or property to a non-profit organization, which uses the resulting investment income for a specific purpose	Early-stage Growth Established
Family office	Private wealth management advisory firms that serve ultra-high-net-worth investors	Early-stage Growth Established

Adapted from Hornberger, Kusi, "Enterprise Segmentation Project Supply Side Literature Review", March 2018.

What Kinds of Resources Can They Provide?

In your self-evaluation, you'll want to consider what kinds of support, financial and otherwise, your business needs to make sure that the funders you partner with can provide those resources. Here are some of the different resources that funders may be able to offer (Table 4.4):

Table 4.4 Types of resources

Type	Description
Creditworthy collateral	Assets that have significant value
Debt capital	Capital that can be lent out
Distribution channels	Ability to distribute products or services through proprietary or shared channels
Equity capital	Capital that can be used to purchase ownership
Fundraising support	Support, advice and connections for future funding
Financial management[d]	Help develop financial management capabilities, financial and accounting systems
Geographic knowledge/presence	Knowledge of or presence in the geography targeted

(continued)

Table 4.4 (continued)

Type	Description
Grant capital	Capital that does not expect a financial return
Governance support[b]	Support to develop board of directors, strengthen governance systems
Human capital support[c]	Connecting you to talent for hiring, helping to strengthen existing management
Impact strategy	Support developing theory of change and impact measurement and management strategies
Outcomes/industry knowledge/experience in issue areas	Experience working in the identified social and environmental outcome areas
Purchasing power	Ability to commit to purchasing products/services
Social capital	Influence and/or trust as an entity or individual with relevant people/communities
Strategic support	Business model development, business planning
Technology experience	Ability to use and build relevant technology
Visibility	Ability to disseminate information to large numbers of relevant people

[a]Boiardi, P. & Hehenberger, L. (2015). *Adding Value Through Non-financial Support—A Practical Guide*. European Venture Philanthropy Association
[b]Boiardi, P. & Hehenberger, L. (2015). *Adding Value Through Non-financial Support—A Practical Guide*. European Venture Philanthropy Association
[c]Boiardi, P. & Hehenberger, L. (2015). *Adding Value Through Non-financial Support—A Practical Guide*. European Venture Philanthropy Association

Some of these resources will be applicable at a firm level, i.e., the funding organization as a whole can provide you and your business. Others may be at a personal level, meaning you'll want to evaluate who at the organization you would ideally want to work with. This is a particularly important consideration for specific individuals that may take a seat on your board.

What Level of Risk Are They Comfortable with?

In Part VI, we'll go through an evaluation of different kinds of risks that funders consider when underwriting investment and funding opportunities. For now, let's just think about risk in terms of the stage of your company. Very early-stage companies require funders that are willing to take significant risks by stepping into unknown or unvalidated territory, while more established companies can work with funders that have a lower risk tolerance. To pick the right type of funder for your needs, you'll need to make sure they are comfortable with the risks that you present.

What Kind of Return Do They Require, and When?

Many funders will be looking for a **risk-adjusted financial return**. This means that they will design the funding based on their evaluation of the investment risk and set their upside expectations to compensate them for taking on that risk. When funders say they are looking for a **market-rate return**, they mean they are looking for returns similar to other investments with a comparable risk profile.

Some mission aligned funders *might* be willing to trade some financial return for social or environmental impact achievements (i.e., impact returns). It is important not to assume that just because a funder is impact or mission-focused, they do not also seek **market-rate returns**.

Funders, like foundations, that primarily offer **grant** capital will be most concerned with a beneficiary's impact achievements; any financial upside is likely to be secondary in their return's calculation.

A final point of consideration: you'll need to understand a funder's time frame for backing your business. Are they looking for returns within a year? Two years? Ten years? You'll need to ask both when they expect you to *start* paying them back, and when they expect to be *fully repaid*.

Who Are Their Stakeholders? How Does Funding Get Approved?

In order to understand funders' opportunities and limitations for disbursing capital, you'll need to look at who their key stakeholders are and how their funding gets approved. Many funders have **external stakeholders**, such as investors or donors, and have obligations to those stakeholders. If their

external stakeholders are investors, then they will likely have defined parameters on the types of businesses they can invest in, their return requirements, the level of risk they can take, and the timeline for generating returns. If their external stakeholders are donors, funders will likely have specific impact goals and restrictions around the types of businesses they can fund.

Funders that are accountable to **external stakeholders**, like venture capital firms who are accountable to their own investors called **limited partners (LPs)**, are likely to be less flexible in how they structure their funding and with the types of resources they can provide. That doesn't mean that they cannot be innovative, but you should recognize that their ability to raise their own capital in the future is dependent on achieving certain results for their external stakeholders.

Funders like **family offices** and endowed **foundations**, meanwhile, may not be beholden to **external stakeholders**, but they will still have **internal stakeholders** to whom they have obligations. These funders may be more flexible in their ability to structure deals and the types of resources that they can provide, but their commitments must nevertheless meet internal criteria for success.

A final point you'll want to consider is how funders get approval for their capital (or resource) commitments. Some may have an **investment committee**, a **board**, or a **senior management committee** that determines which deals get approved. All will have different timeframes for approving and disbursing capital. The amount of time it takes to close a deal with an individual funder will depend on the type of financing and how much due diligence documentation is required.

5

Reflections on Debt and Equity

Okay, now that we've walked through **equity** and **debt** journeys, introduced the concept of **quasi-equity, mezzanine** financing and **trade finance**, and unpacked the checklist of self-evaluation questions, let's recap the last four chapters.

In our current funding landscape, we use **venture capital equity funding** to mean **risk capital**. This means we assume that equity is the only way to get capital that is:

- Flexible—can be used for anything,
- Patient—doesn't require payments initially,
- Risky—willing to invest in early-stage companies without any collateral and very little intellectual property (IP),
- Hands-on—includes mentorship and alignment of incentives around growth.

While **equity capital** from commercial VC investors does give us all those things, it also:

- Requires **exponential growth**—investors expect to **exit** an equity investment at a significant multiple to their original investment.

© The Author(s), under exclusive license to Springer Nature
Switzerland AG 2021
A. Patton Power, *Adventure Finance*,
https://doi.org/10.1007/978-3-030-72428-3_5

- Expects the founder to keep raising additional equity by means of funding rounds until the sale of the company to another investor (**Secondary Sale**) or a listing on a public market (**IPO**).
- Is expensive—founders have to sell ownership in their business in each equity financing round.
- Creates a strong possibility founders will lose control of the business over time.
- Doesn't work for non-profits or co-ops.

Dimeji, Tito and Adegoke from **Helium** (Chapter 1) needed to raise **equity capital** from **angel investors** and **VCs** to propel them forward on their **exponential growth** path. They ended up using **SAFEs** as well as **priced equity** during their **pre-seed, seed** and **Series A** rounds. Below is a table that maps out a traditional equity fundraising process and the investors involved (Table 5.1).

As we discussed in the last chapter, most of you reading this book, aren't aspiring **Unicorns**. So, if **equity** isn't the right instrument for most companies, what are the other options? Let's turn to **secured debt** from banks. As we saw in **Ella's** case with **SOKO** (Chapter 2), bank debt often might not be the best option for many early-stage organizations either.

Firstly, it isn't always accessible due to small businesses' risk profiles. **SOKO** wasn't able to access a **working capital** facility from a bank because they didn't have a long enough **credit history** with consistent revenues. They also didn't have **collateral** to act as security. Not only do most start-ups and small businesses not have enough assets to put up as **collateral**, the possibility of losing those precious assets if you do not make the payments as required, could be disastrous for your business.

Additionally, most **debt** also requires consistent payments regardless of earnings. As a founder, you may have very seasonal revenues like **SOKO**, which would make traditional bank payment terms difficult.

Finally, bank-financed debt is generally an "arm's length transaction" that doesn't involve mentorship. This means that you might not get the help and partnerships that you need to grow your business (Table 5.2).

Here is an overview of the pros and cons of equity and debt financing:

Table 5.1 The equity funding lifecycle and players by company stage

Concept stage	Early stage	Growth stage	Scaling
You generally have an idea, but not necessarily an MVP or a proof of concept.	You may have an MVP or proof of concept here and you may even have started protecting your IP legally, but you still only have a small number of paying customers, if any at all.	You have defined your product or service offering and have a base of paying customers. You are building your internal infrastructure to grow.	You have a large and growing customer base, have built your internal infrastructure and are in the process of scaling up your operations and potentially adding new products or services.

Pre-Seed	Seed	Series A	Series B	Series C	Series D...

Friends, Family and Fools (the 3Fs) provide investment to build prototypes and start a business

Angel Investors, often high net-worth individuals (HNWI) or Angel Networks of HNWIs, put capital into fledgling businesses to help them develop IP and attract customers to prove their business model

Accelerators and Incubators work with companies at these stages as well to help them become investment ready. Some will invest capital as well.

Venture Capital funds (VCs) invest in companies to help them scale.

Later stage equity investments are made by **Private Equity firms (PE)** using what is called growth capital.

Table 5.2 Comparison of debt and equity

	Pros	Cons
Debt	Can be relatively cheap (compared to other options)	Consistent payments required
		Collateral needed
	Lenders don't take ownership or get involved in decision making	Need to be creditworthy and have operating track record
	Self-liquidating, doesn't require an external investor to exit	Arm's length transaction - generally no mentorship involved
Equity	Flexible	Requires exponential growth and exit scenario
	Patient	
	Risk tolerant	Expensive (sell ownership in the business)
	Investor and investee are incentivized for growth	Investors are involved in key decisions and veto rights
	Hands on: access to mentorship and partnerships	Potential to lose control of business over time

Mixing It Up with Mezz

Ella had used a **convertible note** to raise **equity capital**, but then needed to access **working capital** to address short-term funding needs due to the seasonality of the business. Accessing **mezzanine finance** gave her the cash that she needed without selling more ownership in the company.

Lilian from **Grassroots Business Fund** (Chapter 2) uses **mezzanine financing** to be able to fund early-stage, fast-growing businesses that are in need of **debt capital**, but do not have the **credit history** or **collateral** to qualify for bank financing.

Mezz funders are generally subordinated to other funders. They are willing to make loans that are **unsecured** or are partially **secured** by alternative forms of **collateral**, like **personal guarantees**.

Mezz funders are willing to use innovative types of risk assessment to allow them to lend to early-stage, high growth organizations. For instance, **Venture Debt**, a type of **mezz**, is lent to companies that have a reputable **VC investor** in their **capital stack**.

In addition to **interest** on the loans, they use **kickers** in the form of **profit sharing (cash kickers)** or **warrants** to participate in the upside of the business's growth.

In the next section, we'll dive a bit deeper into **quasi-equity** structures like **mezz**.

Trading Invoices for Cash

Equal Exchange (Chapter 3) buys coffee from their farmer co-ops directly after it is harvested, using **supply chain financing** to reduce the **working**

capital needs of the farmers. They also help to facilitate **working capital** funding for the farmers from local **invoice factoring** companies by guaranteeing payment on a portion of their order.

Ella from **Powered by People** (Chapter 3) created a product for artisans that uses **invoice factoring** and **purchase order financing** to give them access to working capital.

Invoice Factoring, Shipment Financing or Purchase Order Financing are short-term funding options that allow you to borrow against your invoices, shipping bills or customers' orders to finance your working capital. This funding is likely more expensive than many other types of financing but can be useful for early-stage and/or seasonal businesses that are looking to build a **credit history** to access other types of debt.

Supply chain financing uses pre-payments from your customers to help finance your working capital needs. Some suppliers have established supply chain financing programs that you can participate in. If you have good relationships with larger, regular customers, you can initiate conversations with them outside of formal programs as well.

Below is a simple table that can help you understand what options you have based on key characteristics (Table 5.3).

Table 5.3 Summary of options by criteria

Do I...?	If yes, then my options include:
Mission / Impact	
Have Unicorn aspirations? Am I committed to trying to grow exponentially and willing to give up control of my businesses over time?	Equity (Convertible Note, SAFE, Priced Equity Round)
Have a verifiable social/environmental track record	
Have physical assets and a credit history?	Secured debt
Have invoices / purchase orders / history of fulfilling orders?	Invoice factoring, purchase order financing, supply chain financing
Have venture capital funding?	Venture debt
Have none of the above?	Mezzanine financing, unsecured working capital facilities, credit cards

Comparing Your Options

See Table 5.4.

Table 5.4 Comparison of debt and equity options

	Equity (priced equity, SAFE, convertible debt)	Secured debt	Mezzanine debt	Venture debt	Factoring (invoice factoring, shipping financing, purchase order financing)	Supply chain financing
Description	Purchase of ownership or the future right to ownership in a company	Loan that is secured by collateral	A loan that is paid back with a fixed interest and has upside through kickers such as warrants or profit share	Loan made to fast growing venture-backed companies	Short-term funding option that allows you to borrow against your invoices/shipping bills/purchase orders	Uses pre-payments from your customers to help finance working capital
Business registration	For-Profit, Social Enterprise	Non-profit, For-profit, Co-op, Social Enterprise	For-profit, Social Enterprise		Non-profit, For-profit, Co-op, Social Enterprise	
Revenue model	May not be determined yet	Consistent or mildly seasonal	May have some seasonality		Likely seasonal or highly variable	
Company stage	Concept, Early-stage, Growth	Growth, Scaling, or Established	Early-stage, growth or scaling	High growth	Early-stage, growth, scaling or established	
Business growth projections	Unicorn aspirations or High Growth Venture. Some Category Pioneers	High growth venture, Category pioneer, Niche venture, Dynamic enterprise, Livelihood enterprise	High growth venture, category pioneer, niche venture	High growth venture, category pioneer	High growth venture, Category pioneer, Niche venture, Dynamic enterprise, Livelihood enterprise	
Embeddedness	If you have high mission embeddedness, you will want to seek out impact funders for your equity partners	Not exceptionally relevant	If you have high mission embeddedness, you may want to seek out funders that are mission driven		Not especially relevant	If you and your buyer/customer have high mission embeddedness, you may find your financing goals are aligned as well

	Equity (priced equity, SAFE, convertible debt)	Secured debt	Mezzanine debt	Venture debt	Factoring (invoice factoring, shipping financing, purchase order financing)	Supply chain financing
Track record	You may not yet have an impact track record, but you can build a comprehensive IMM plan	Unless you have social or environmental milestones in your debt agreement, this will not be relevant	Impact investors may look for an impact track record for later stage companies		Not especially relevant	Unless you are dealing with a mission aligned buyer, this will likely not be relevant
Spend funding on	POC or Growth for long term	Working capital, assets, growth capital	Growth capital, Working capital		Working capital	
Assets for collateral	None required	Physical assets and credit history	Some mix of physical assets and alternative types of collateral. Some funders may be willing to be completely unsecured	Venture capital funding and potentially some level of collateral	Invoices, shipping bills or purchase orders	Customer goods
Planned payback source	Third party exit through sale, IPO, merger or secondary	Internal cash flows or external borrowing	Internal cash flows for interest rate and cash kicker, if warrants are included then also a third party exit		Customer payment	NA
Ownership	Willingness to dilute control of business over time	No impact on ownership	If payback is interest + cash kicker, it is not necessary to be willing to dilute ownership. Warrants will require willingness to dilute ownership	Willingness to dilute control of business over time due to VC funding	No impact on ownership	

(continued)

8 A. Patton Power**

Table 5.4 (continued)

	Equity (priced equity, SAFE, convertible debt)	Secured debt	Mezzanine debt	Venture debt	Factoring (invoice factoring, shipping financing, purchase order financing)	Supply chain financing
Funding in future	Mix of equity and debt	Can be used alongside any type of future funding	Can work with both equity and debt funding in future		Can create credit history for future debt funding	No impact on future funding
Funder involvement	Financial upside focused. High ongoing involvement including board seats, significant voting rights and information rights	Financial downside focused. Low ongoing involvement based on covenants in the debt agreement	Both upside and downside focused. Will have ongoing involvement. Covenants will act as downside protection, and voting rights and information rights may be used as upside involvement		Focused only on specific transaction(s) that are financed	Must initiate the transaction
Most likely funders	VC fund, Private Equity Fund, Angel Investor, Incubator, Accelerator, Development Finance Institution, Family Office	Bank, Development Finance Institution, Debt fund, Non-Bank Financial Institution	Debt Fund, Mezzanine Fund, Bank, Non-bank Financial Institution		Mezzanine Fund, Non-Bank Financial Institution	Customer

Part II

What If: You Want to Redesign Risk Capital?

In this part of the book, we are going to follow some pioneering funders and founders who have adapted traditional **risk capital** models to better suit the needs of founders by creating structures that blend together equity and debt.

These funders and founders have built **structured exit agreements**. Expanding on the idea of **mezzanine financing**, structured exit agreements take the best parts of **equity** (flexibility and patience) and mix them with the best parts of debt (**self-liquidation** and cost) to create **risk capital** funding that doesn't require **exponential growth** and force the eventual sale of your business to satisfy investors. Although the language for these types of structures is very unsettled, I've chosen to refer to this category as **structured exits** for the rest of the book, as this seems to be the most descriptive and widely used term by both founders and funders.[1]

A **structured exit** refers to a risk capital agreement where founders and funders contractually agree on a plan for the funder to fully (or partially) exit the investment. Unlike **equity** funders, who have an open-ended agreement that relies on exponential growth and an unknown future buyer or listing on a stock exchange, structured exit funders have a specific, achievable plan for how they are going to receive their return through dividends, profit sharing, redemptions or a combination of different types of payment.

---

[1]Another term you might hear is **contingent-payment debt instruments**. It doesn't easily roll off the tongue! But the term is technically correct, as the payment of these instruments is contingent on some kind of revenue or cash flow calculation. Another term that you might hear is **self-liquidating instruments**, which means the agreements don't require an external exit event, like a sale. This is a bit confusing, since all debt is self-liquidating. In later editions of this book, perhaps the market will have finally decided what these structures are, and then I can delete this whole discussion!

Like **mezzanine financing**, these structures fall into a large group of **quasi-equity** funding options, which, as we discussed in Chapters 3 and 5, means they're a bit like equity and a bit like debt.

While **structured exit** agreements can take many different forms,[2] it would be overwhelming to try to cover all of them in this book. So, to make the concept as clear as possible, I've created a handy framework for understanding different categories of structures. We'll unpack this a bit more in the last chapter of this part (Table 1).

In Chapter 6, we are going to use Aner Ben-Ami's journey to explore what kind of companies need **structured exit financing**. In Chapter 7, we are going to follow myTurn's journey to see how **redeemable equity** can be used to allow early-stage founders to repurchase ownership as they grow. In Chapter 8, we'll see another option for redeemable equity in the form of a **preferred stock** offering from Equal Exchange that includes a **mission lock**, which protects the company's mission.

In Chapters 9 and 10, we'll walk through **convertible revenue-based financing (Convertible RBF)** instruments, which are growth capital agreements with variable payments and the potential for funders to convert into equity, through the experiences of Provive and Maya Mountain Cacao. Finally, in Chapter 11, we'll see how VIWALA and GetVantage are using technology to extend **revenue-based financing (RBF)**, a working capital option that allows founders to repay their **debt** through revenue (or cash flow) based payments.

---

[2]It is important to note that there are almost limitless combinations of terms that you can pair together to build a new type of **structured exit agreement**. If you really want to geek out on the technicalities of structured exits, the online companion goes deep into the term sheet options and tax and accounting considerations.

Table 1   Types of structured exits

Categories	Structured Exits			
	Mezzanine Debt	Redeemable Equity	Convertible RBF	Revenue-based Financing (RBF)
Basic description	Loan that is paid back with a fixed interest and has upside through kickers such as warrants or profit share (cash)	Purchase of shares that can be redeemed at a pre-agreed multiple or mutually agreed price	Loan that is repaid as a percentage of future revenues or cash flows with an option to convert to equity	Loan that is repaid as a percentage of future revenues or cash flows
AKA	SME risk capital, venture debt	Redeemable preferred stock, performance aligned redeemable convertible preferred stock, equity redemption, Indie.VC, variable VC, flexible VC, preferred stock	Revenue-based debt, demand dividend, variable dividend, revenue-based investing, subordinated variable payment debt, revenue-based mezzanine debt, shared earnings agreement, royalty financing[a]	Revenue share agreement, cash flow financing, royalty financing[b]
Featured in:	Chapter 3	Chapters 7 and 8	Chapters 9 and 10	Chapter 11

[a]It is important to note that there are almost limitless combinations of terms that you can pair together to build a new type of **structured exit agreement**. If you really want to geek out on the technicalities of structured exits, the online companion goes deep into the term sheet options and tax and accounting considerations

[b]The term **royalty financing** is used quite often to describe revenue-based financing, even though it is technically its own type of financing. A royalty agreement acts like a scheduled percentage of revenue calculation, but only applies to a specific revenue stream such as an identified product or service. Examples of this are revenues derived from specific intellectual property (IP) assets, oil wells and mines. It is particularly common in IP heavy industries such as movies, tv, music and healthcare. Although many types of structured exits have been called royalty financing in the past as for short, a true royalty agreement uses the associated IP as security for the agreement and would take ownership of that IP in the case of default

6

Candide Group: Our Structured Exit Journey

As an aspiring Unicorn, Helium needed to follow the traditional equity path in order to raise the **risk capital** they needed to fund the growth of their business. But what if you are in need of **risk capital**, but know you aren't going to be a **Unicorn**? In this chapter, we will meet an investor who came into early stage investing and found that there were very few good answers to that question. Like a good innovative financier, he decided to help build some better options for the world's venture **Zebras**.

Learning the Ropes, One Step at a Time

In 2012, Aner Ben-Ami had experience as a management consultant with the Boston Consulting Group, but no investment experience when he started working with one of the members of the Pritzker family to develop a strategy for investing her wealth with a purpose. His broader business background, but relative newness to investments was actually one of the reasons she hired him. The woman and her family were also new to impact investing, and to investing in general, and so instead of a guide with insider knowledge, they wanted to take the journey with someone from the outside who was learning too.

© The Author(s), under exclusive license to Springer Nature
Switzerland AG 2021
A. Patton Power, *Adventure Finance*,
https://doi.org/10.1007/978-3-030-72428-3_6

As with all journeys, Aner started from the beginning and emphasized building his network. He joined **investor groups** and **networks** such as Investor Circle and Toniic and reached out to accelerators such as Impact Engine and Unreasonable Institute. He went to all of the **pitch events** and **investor demo days**, trying to meet with as many entrepreneurs as possible. He was keen to build a strategy from the bottom up by understanding what these entrepreneurs needed. One of the first things that struck him was the diversity of the companies he met, both in terms of the problems they were solving and their business models. There were money transfer companies trying to make remittances cheaper; bricks-and-mortar retail companies creating jobs and sustainable products; platforms connecting global artists to buyers and brands, service-based businesses specializing in vegetable garden landscaping; and on and on. And yet all of them seemed like they were trying to sell themselves as a Y Combinator-like start-up that needed **equity** capital for **Unicorn** style growth.

Aner realized that the reason all of these businesses were forcing themselves onto an **equity financing** path was because they didn't know of any viable alternatives. Yet **VC** investors often turned down many of these businesses with innovative business models because they didn't fit the VC "boom or bust" mindset. He also saw dedicated **social entrepreneurs** get pressured into a "growth at all costs" approach to their businesses that resulted in significant mission drift or deemed failures for not successfully growing at **exponential rates**. "Why weren't there risk capital models for non-**Unicorns**?" he wondered.

The Exit Requirement

To begin answering that question, he first sought to understand why **equity** wasn't a suitable financing option for many of the companies he met. He realized that for most companies, it came down to the requirement for an investor to get his or her money back through an **exit**.

When an investor buys **equity** in a company, the company does not make a promise to pay back the investor[1]; rather, the investor's expectation is that

---

[1] In a convertible debt agreement, investees agree to pay the debt back if it doesn't convert, but generally investors expect to convert the debt into equity.

the company will grow in value and that someday, the investor will recoup his or her investment plus a sizable profit when the company is **acquired (trade sale)** or goes public (**IPO**), or when the investor is bought out by another investor (**secondary sale**). Often, you will hear **VC** investors talk about **10×** **returns**, meaning they are looking for an **exit** where they get repaid *ten times* the amount of money that they put in.

In the **equity** contract, there are terms that specify what percentage of the proceeds the investor and investee will receive in the event of different kinds of **exits**, but no firm commitment or requirement to pursue one versus the other. Realistically, many investors wait years (sometimes decades) for an **exit** with a successful company. For investors and **VC** fund managers, this means that although their investment portfolios may look incredibly valuable on paper, they cannot actually access, return or reinvest any of the capital they have committed until there is an **exit event**. For founders, it means that they must continuously try to raise more and more cash, while sustaining high enough growth to qualify for some kind of **exit**.

Baseball, Cricket, the Olympics, and Portfolio Construction

A traditional angel/VC portfolio is built with the understanding that the possibility of an **IPO exit** is quite small. So, for every ten investments, an angel/VC expects one investment to be a home run (achieving 10× returns or more); three to be "doubles" or "triples," giving them some smaller return on their capital; four to be "singles" (just getting their money back); and three to be zeros (losses). If these terms sound completely foreign to you, they are actually baseball terms, which perhaps make sense in Silicon Valley, the birthplace of VC, but don't necessarily translate well in other parts of the world where baseball isn't a common sport. Here's a handy chart I've prepared with comparisons to other sports terminology (Table 6.1).[2]

Let's switch over to the world of poker for a minute. Investors recognize that getting a Royal Flush is a rare event, but they still need every hand that they bet on to have the *potential* to be a Royal Flush. If it looks like it could only be a Pair or a Full House, it isn't worth the bet. This means that companies that aren't submitting Royal Flush/Home Run/Gold Medal/Hat Trick projections won't get an angel/VC investor's capital.

---

[2]This original baseball analogy table was adapted from: Libes, L. (2016). *The Next Step for Investors: Revenue-based Financing.* Lunarmobiscuit Publishing.

Table 6.1 Traditional angel/VC portfolio construction, by sport

# of deals	Baseball	Cricket	Olympics	Poker	Soccer/Football	Cash on Cash (CoC) Return[a]
1	Home run	Six	Gold Medal	Royal Flush	Hat Trick	>10×
3	Double/Triple	Four	Silver/Bronze	Full House	Goal	2–5×
4	Single	Single	Finisher	Pair	Assist	1×
3	Strike out	Wicket	Doesn't qualify	Fold[b]	Own Goal	0×
10 Total						Average 2.9×

[a]Cash of Cash (CoC) refers to the amount of money returned to investors in relation to the amount invested. If you invested $100,000 in a company and got $1,000,000 back, you'd have a 10× return
[b]Technically this would be folding post-flop, which would mean that you lost the blind

Aner had two advantages as he was learning about how traditional VC start-up fundraising works. One, he was working for a family office, which meant his emphasis was on seeking long term, consistent value versus raising and returning capital on the traditional 10-year cycle of a VC fund manager, and thus didn't have to adopt a traditional **equity** funding approach or portfolio construction. Two, because he was an outsider, he maintained a healthy level of skepticism of the entire model.

From this point of view, he identified an innovation gap between investors and founders. While founders were coming up with innovative models using market solutions to address social challenges, investors were using the same set of tools that were designed to fund Silicon Valley start-ups for decades. He realized this meant he might need to evaluate each business individually and decide what type of funding made the most sense.

A Bumpy Start

Swimming against the **equity** tide proved to be extremely difficult. Despite his misgivings, Aner's first few deals were in fact traditional **convertible note** agreements or **preferred equity** agreements. He says, in reflection, that he lacked the confidence then to say, "let's do this differently." Also, as these were the family office's first few deals, they wanted to test the water with smaller check sizes and invest alongside others, which made going along with the traditional equity herd the path of least resistance.

Aner didn't give up, though, and in 2013, he got a chance to try things differently. The **family office** opted to invest in a company called Big City Farms using something called a **revenue share agreement**.

Big City Farms was a greenhouse farming operation in Baltimore, Maryland that employed previously incarcerated people. Because it was a young, seasonally dependent business, Big City Farms wasn't a good fit for traditional **debt** and its growth profile made it a poor fit for **equity**. Aner invested money in the business looking for his return through payments based on a percentage of the revenues in the future.

Unfortunately for Aner and Big City Farms, the company hit a run of really bad luck, in spite of its solid business model and great management team. Everything that could go wrong for this company, went wrong. First, they lost their largest farming site when a corporate giant bought the land and kicked them off. Then, their back-up land proved to be contaminated. And finally, the coldest winter in decades hit Baltimore and destroyed most of their crops. Big City Farms was forced to close its doors.

Aner wasn't deterred by the early failure. He continued to see a gap in the funding market for purpose-driven companies that weren't a good fit for traditional **equity financing**. But to try more innovative models, the family office would need to either "**lead the round**" with a large check or bring a bunch of other investors to the table to assure founders that they had a group of investors they could count on, even if they chose a non-traditional path.

Joining Forces for Justice

Also in 2013, Aner met Morgan Simon, an experienced impact investor and social justice advocate who was the founding CEO of the impact investor network Toniic. Aner and Morgan joined forces to start an impact investment firm called Candide Group, expanding beyond one family office to more broadly serve families, foundations, athletes and other influencers who wanted to put their wealth to work for social justice. The additional clients and capacity gave Candide access to more capital to lead deals and more confidence to advocate for alternative terms.

As part of this new firm, Aner decided they needed to build a community of funders who were interested in alternative funding models to **equity**, so he began convening a working group of like-minded investors. Each month, one investor would present to the group a deal that had used an alternative structure, and the group would discuss the learnings and ways to collaborate on future deals.

One of the first opportunities for collaboration came in late 2013, when Jim Villeneuva from Eleos brought forth a deal with Maya Mountain Cacao (MMC), a premium cacao producer based in Belize. As we'll see in Chapter 10, Aner participated in the consortium of investors trying out a unique profit-sharing agreement called a **demand dividend** for the first time. This agreement promised to deliver returns to investors through payments from MMC's cash flows instead of a conventional VC exit.

Other members of the working group included **revenue-based mezzanine debt** providers like Adobe Capital, who we'll meet in Chapter 8, and **redeemable equity** providers like Village Capital, who we'll meet in Chapter 23. The investment options these funders were using enabled founders to repay, or redeem, their funders' investments over time, instead of requiring a **sale, merger** or **IPO**.

As Aner collaborated with these funders, he began to see how adopting investment agreements that provided an **exit** strategy upfront addressed many of the shortcomings of traditional equity. For many founders, **structured exit agreements** provided clarity for both parties and set reasonable expectations for the course of the funding relationship in a way that open-ended equity contracts didn't.

If you are feeling overwhelmed by the number of options in this chapter, don't worry! We'll be going over the different types in the coming chapters.

What he also learned from **structured exit agreements** was that although portfolio construction can look very different to a traditional VC portfolio, the financial outcome can nevertheless be quite similar. In other words, if you are investing in more "singles" and "doubles" and fewer failures and home runs (feel free to translate that to your sport of choice!), you can create portfolios that mirror the actual portfolio-level return that VC investors target.

Selling Broccoli in a Candy Store

As Candide Group expanded, Aner and Morgan continued to experiment with **structured exits**. The firm has led investments in Organically Grown Company,[3] Firebrand Artisans and Berrett Koehler that include a form of

---

[3]Fun fact: Aner met the founders of the Organically Grown Company at the Zebras Unite conference called Dazzle Con (a group of Zebra are called a Dazzle) in 2017.

profit-sharing or **dividend payout structure**,[4] and in Tanka Bar, Solar Holler and Ultranauts using an internal buyout option[5] where the companies buy back **equity** from their investors. As of late 2020, Candide Group has supported investments in more than 90 companies and funds. Significantly, more than half of these companies are led by women and people of color.

Looking back on his **structured exit** journey, Aner borrows a phrase from his friend Bryce Roberts, describing the early years he spent convincing founders and funders to try out **structured exits** like "selling broccoli in a candy store." Nonetheless, he believes that this is changing with the emergence of founder-led movements like Zebras Unite, who advocate for more aligned and flexible capital, and like-minded investors like Collab Capital, Purpose Ventures and Earnest Capital.

Aner believes the "next frontier" is combining **structured exits** with ownership structures that have a strong emphasis on workers and other stakeholders, like Candide did with Firebrand, Berrett Koehler and Organically Grown. These types of deals will create multi-stakeholder profit distribution waterfalls that can facilitate wealth creation among larger groups of individuals, creating situations where entire communities reap the rewards of sustainably run businesses.

Are Structured Exits Right for You?

Founders

As a founder, you will be in a much better position to grow your business if you have access to funding that is (1) flexible enough that it doesn't restrict your business strategy, (2) patient enough that it doesn't weigh on your short-term cash flow, (3) risky enough to fund your company without **collateral** or large amounts of IP, and (4) hands-on enough to provide the mentorship and connections that you need.

Structured exit agreements give you access to this kind of **risk capital** in forms that are not as **dilutive** as traditional **equity** and that are accessible if you are not projecting **exponential growth**. In general, **structured exits** can be designed for all types of companies.

If you raise money through a **structured exit** agreement, you may not necessarily require additional **risk capital** in the future; rather, you could

---

[4]See Chapters 10 and 12 for more detail.
[5]See Chapters 7, 8 and 12 for more detail.

focus on reaching profitability, establishing your cash flows and building a **credit history**. Contrary to traditional **debt**, these agreements offer flexible payment schedules and initial **grace periods** well suited to early-stage and growth stage enterprises.

Funders

First and foremost, funders need to understand that **structured exits** were not created with **Unicorns** in mind. This is not to say that they can't work for high-growth companies. Indeed, there are interesting examples of high-growth companies using revenue-based financing (**RBF**) alongside VC, or using **redeemable equity** as a way to preserve founder ownership and delay VC **dilution**. Nevertheless, structured exits were designed for the needs of the 99% of companies that do not fit the VC paradigm, and therefore necessitate a completely different way of looking at companies and portfolio construction. Designing portfolios that target lower but more realistic returns with a greater number of liquidity events may mean completely changing your perspective around how you allocate capital. Many **structured exit** investors actually have a similar mindset to traditional **debt** investors, albeit with the willingness to create more flexible contracts for early-stage and growth entrepreneurs.

Going back to the baseball analogy, Aner describes **structured exits** as the *Moneyball* approach, from the Michael Lewis book. In the statistics-driven Moneyball management approach, the coaches worked toward optimizing for on-base percentages, rather than swinging for home runs. A similar analogy in cricket would mean that you are consistently looking for runs instead of "waiting for sixes," or in rugby, "consistently kicking for poles" and taking the points when you get a penalty instead of "going for the try." The bottom line is that you are developing a completely different portfolio strategy when you use a structured exits approach.

To successfully implement a **structured exit** strategy, you need a lot more visibility around a company's financial and growth projections than you would with traditional **equity**. To this end, many **structured exit agreements** borrow and repurpose concepts from traditional debt financing models, such as **factoring** and **receivables financing**. This is not to say that you can't create options within **structured exits** for earlier-stage companies and even build in some upside opportunity in case they do go to the moon, but the main focus of these structures is to give more entrepreneurs access to capital that allows them to grow sustainable businesses on their own terms.

From a **liquidity** perspective, this type of approach can be advantageous for funders used to having their **risk capital** locked up for a decade or more in traditional VC funds. Essentially, **structured exit** investors trade some of their upside on individual deals for greater certainty around liquidity. So as a funder, if you are interested in building portfolios that have a clearer **liquidity** path, **structured exits** are good options for you to consider.

7

myTurn: Our Redeemable Equity Journey

In this chapter, we are going to join Gene Homicki and Luni Libes on myTurn's **redeemable equity** journey. Unlike traditional equity, **redeemable equity** contracts have specific instructions around how founders can (or must) repurchase equity in their companies in the future.

The Emerald City

Gene and Luni's journey starts in Seattle, during a hackathon for social enterprises hosted by Hub Seattle,[1] an impact co-working space in historic Pioneer Square. Hub Seattle was the brainchild of Brian Howe, who had a vision for cultivating Seattle's budding impact ecosystem in a shared space for entrepreneurs, investors and others looking for access to networks and business resources. Luni, a serial entrepreneur, met Brian in 2011 and together they worked on a business plan for launching a **social enterprise accelerator** in the Hub. As part of that effort, they were curious to find out if there were enough **social entrepreneurs** in Seattle to support such a program and they decided to host a **hackathon** to find out.

#Socent Weekend kicked off in February 2012, based loosely on the then-new Start-up Weekend model. Seventy-two entrepreneurs bought tickets. Brian and Luni felt the electricity in the room as everyone convened. As they

---

[1] Later branded Impact Hub Seattle.

© The Author(s), under exclusive license to Springer Nature
Switzerland AG 2021
A. Patton Power, *Adventure Finance*,
https://doi.org/10.1007/978-3-030-72428-3_7

listened to founders present their ideas, they were particularly impressed by Gene, who pitched an idea for an online service that could be used to manage community lending libraries. Gene was a software engineer and had designed a program (later renamed myTurn) that could streamline the sharing of power tools and other DIY equipment within communities, since this can facilitate access to affordable equipment regardless of income levels. Though he didn't win the pitch event, Luni made a mental note to follow up with Gene.

For the **hackathon**, Luni and Brian were pleased with the turnout and impressed by the entrepreneurs. They decided there was enough market activity to support a dedicated accelerator program. Luni took on the initiative and built a program that he later named Fledge. He was confident that Fledge could provide the acceleration support early-stage start-ups needed, but he knew they needed capital support too, and he wasn't quite sure how to design an investment model around social entrepreneurs who had little desire to sell or exit their businesses. That meant that traditional VC **equity**, which depended on generating returns through an **exit**, wouldn't work. He needed to find another approach.

Finding a New Approach

It was in helping Brian tackle his own fundraising challenges for Hub Seattle that Luni got the idea of using **redeemable equity** as a solution to social start-up investing. At the time, Brian had found investors who were interested in backing Hub Seattle, but neither **debt** nor **equity** were the right fit for the company or for investors. (This was way before co-working companies like WeWork had come about, attracting swarms of VC.)

Luckily, Luni remembered a story from one of the board members of his previous start-up company about an investment firm called Lighter Capital that was making **revenue-based loans** to tech companies. The terms seemed like they might also be suitable for Hub Seattle. Through Lighter's co-founder, Luni was connected to Thomas Thurston, a former assistant to Clayton Christensen at Harvard Business School who had introduced the Lighter Capital team to the idea of **revenue-based financing**. Thomas had been advocating for the use of revenue-based financing for start-ups and explained to Luni the idea of using a **redeemable equity** structure instead of debt for start-ups. With this structure, Brian would be able to buy back the equity shares in Hub Seattle over time. This would mean he could access the financing he needed, while giving his investors a pathway to **exit** from a business model that was promising but unfamiliar at the time.

The model also sounded like the ideal solution for Fledge and its investments in start-ups.

The First Cohort

Gene and his software start-up were first on Luni's list when he began recruiting his first cohort for Fledge just a few months later.

Gene was an experienced entrepreneur, having built a software consulting company serving high profile customers like the *Economist*, ABC News, the National Science Foundation and Sega, but he was passionate about sustainability and curious about **social enterprise**. He got the idea for software that could manage a tool lending library through work with a local non-profit, where he saw firsthand how useful these tool sharing resources were for communities.

Gene wasn't looking for investment into the idea at the time. He was also skeptical of angel investments and VC, because he had seen other founders get pressured into the "growth at all costs" model. He was, however, drawn to the idea of being a part of a **social enterprise** cohort, so when Luni raised the prospect of **redeemable equity**, this piqued his interest.

What Luni presented was a deal where Fledge would purchase shares in myTurn, which myTurn could buy back from Fledge at a later point in time using a percentage of their revenues. This structure meant that Gene wouldn't have to **exit** to a third party or pursue **exponential growth** to satisfy the investors' return expectations. Also, since myTurn was still pre-revenue at the time, the redeemable equity deals wouldn't require Gene to begin the repurchase process until the company had income coming in.

The Nuts and Bolts

For the specifics of the deal, Luni offered to invest $20,000[2] in myTurn, plus two months of training at the accelerator, in exchange for 50 shares, or 6% ownership. myTurn would then be obligated to redeem half (25 shares) through quarterly payments set at 3% of myTurn's revenues. The redemption price of the shares would be $3\times$ their original price, which meant that myTurn would pay 3% of its revenues to Fledge until it had paid back $30,000. The company would be able to redeem the remaining 25 shares

---

[2]Hypothetical figures for illustrative purposes.

after seven years. The **redemption price** of those shares would be based on **fair market value**, which Fledge and myTurn would mutually agree upon at the time of redemption.

Gene and the myTurn team were at first a bit concerned about having to pay out 3% of the company's revenues instead of investing that cash back into the business. But they loved the idea of being able to repurchase their equity, and they did understand the need for Fledge to make a fair return.

What's more, the opportunity to be part of Fledge's first cohort was the "forcing function" Gene says he needed to actually build myTurn from a piece of software into a company. So, although the early myTurn team would be giving up a percentage of the company at a very low value, they believed they would get a lot more out of the deal both for the company and by being part of a community of socially conscious entrepreneurs in Seattle. Or as he puts it: "Ninety-four percent of something is worth a lot more than 100% of nothing."

Gene and myTurn agreed to Luni's offer.

Changing Tack

As happens in a business accelerator, every aspect of myTurn's business prospects was questioned. It was clear that Gene's software was valuable, but the financial viability of building a business around tool lending libraries was not. Luni and the other Fledge mentors asked myTurn if community tool libraries were the right addressable market. Why not apply the software more broadly, to any rentable item? The team began looking into it, and building out the capacity of the system, even though they didn't find many examples of tracking software to guide them.

One day, after the **accelerator**'s program ended, a call came in from a representative at the healthcare company Kaiser Permanente. The representative said that they had ultrasound machines and other healthcare equipment across their entire network of facilities and that they needed a better way to keep track of the machines. They asked if myTurn's software could do that for them. This marked a turning point for myTurn, when the company began building custom-made tracking software to fit different customer needs.

Seven years later, myTurn has more than 1,000 customers in 15 countries. The company has successfully repaid the original investment from Fledge, repurchasing the first half of its shares over seven years, and then repurchasing the second half in year eight. More significantly, myTurn hasn't had to raise any additional capital because it has been able to finance its growth through its own revenues and profits.

The "Negotiation"

Gene and Luni both remember the negotiation around the final share **redemption price** as surprisingly simple and quick. It played out something like this (with different numbers):

Luni: You did $500,000 in revenue last year. If I offered you a check right now for $500,000 to buy your whole company, would you sell it to me?

Gene: No, not a chance..

Luni: What if I offered you $1 million for the company? Would you give that a second thought?

Gene: Maybe. A little..

Luni: What if I wrote a check right now for $2 million?

Gene: Yes, I think I'd sell for that.

Luni: Great, so 1× revenues is too little, 2× is interesting, and 4× is too high. Let's find a multiple that works for both of us. How about 1.5×? That would mean the company is worth $750,000 ($500,000 × 1.5). I'll sell back the remaining 3% of myTurn's equity for $22,500.

Gene: That sounds reasonable, but I don't have $22,500 in the bank I can use right now. I do have $20,000. So if you want $22,500, we can continue the 3% revenue share or I can write you a check today for $20,000.

Luni: I'll take the check.

In this hypothetical calculation, Luni would have received $30,000 from the first half of redemption payments and $20,000 from the second half. In other words, Fledge would have made a total of $50,000 from a $20,000 investment, or 2.5×. That translates to roughly an 18% **internal rate of return (IRR)**. IRR is more or less the **return on investment** if the investment had been a traditional loan, paid annually. In the above example, Luni put in $20,000 in 2012 and then got payments for several years equaling $30,000 and then a payment in 2019 of $20,000. Even though these payments were in different time periods, the IRR calculation gives a smoothed out return as if Luni got a similar amount of cash each year, in other words, an 18% return each year.

Looking back, Gene says he would do the deal again. He knows that myTurn wouldn't have gotten started without a push from Fledge and its

Table 7.1   myTurn illustrative capitalization table

	Shares	% ownership	Value
Gene	783	94%	$313,200
Luni	50	6%	$20,000
Total	833	100%	$333,200

accelerator program. But he felt he maybe should have negotiated better on the **redeemable equity** contract.

Luni, meanwhile, continued to refine the **redeemable equity** contract with his Fledge cohorts. He has lowered the share **redemption multiple** from 3× to 2×, but now includes the value of the accelerator in the contract. Since launching in 2012, Fledge has made more than 100 investments in two dozen countries through its accelerator programs and has built a network of partners that use similar terms.

Is Redeemable Equity Right for You?

Founders

In equity redemption agreements, you sell equity to investors that you can redeem in the future. Thus, equity redemption models can be useful for high growth, **early-stage companies** that are either interested in being able to repurchase shares before a future raise, so as to limit **dilution**, or that need **risk capital**, but do not want to be forced down the traditional VC path.

The three major considerations around a redeemable equity agreement are *cost, affordability and future financing plans*.

When considering the *cost*, you'll need to ask *how much do I owe?*

In this agreement, Luni bought shares 50 shares of the company for $20,000.[3] This equaled 6% of the company, giving them a **pre-money valuation** of $313,200 and a **post-money valuation** of $333,200. This equates to $400 per share ($20,000 / 50 = $400) (Table 7.1).

Gene agreed to repurchase 50% of the shares (25 shares) for 3× their original price. The other half he would repurchase after seven years at a mutually agreed upon price. So, at the time of the contract, he knew that he owed $30,000 to Gene over the next few years and another undetermined amount after seven years.

---

[3] Hypothetical figures for illustrative purposes.

In deciding whether this cost makes sense to you, you'll need to evaluate your alternative **risk capital** options, the other terms of the agreement, and the value that the funder brings to the table in addition to cash. For Gene, in addition to being able to repurchase the shares, the incubation program that Luni offered was a major selling point in taking the investment.

For *affordability*, you'll need to look at *When do I owe it? And how do I redeem the shares?*

For Gene, he owed $30,000 to Luni as a quarterly dividend that would be calculated as 3% of revenue. The important thing to note is that in most jurisdictions, **dividends** can only be declared when the company is solvent. This means that you can't bankrupt your company by declaring a **dividend**, so the **dividends** would only be paid when the company could afford to pay them (i.e., has enough cash to do so). From a tax perspective, as these payments are considered dividends, they do not reduce your tax liability like **interest payments** do.

For the outstanding 25 shares that Gene needed to repurchase after seven years, he knew he would need to negotiate with Luni at that time. The contract states that if they cannot come to an agreement on the value of the shares, they will need to employ the services of an outside valuation firm. When Luni requested the redemption of the shares and they agreed upon a price, Gene could choose to repay as a lump sum or on a similar schedule to the first 50% (i.e., dividends calculated as a percentage of revenue).

Thus, Luni has contractually obligated Gene to repurchase all of the shares in the agreement; the first 50% on a predetermined schedule and the second 50% at a later date. After seven years, this means that 100% of the redemption payments for this contract are scheduled (or mandatory). In other contracts you might also have **elective payments** and/or **residual stakes**, which are explained below (Table 7.2).

In general, for **redeemable equity** contracts, repayment can be **internal**, i.e., using a percentage of revenue or cash flow to repurchase the shares, or **external**, i.e., borrowing money to repurchase the shares or using another investors' cash during an equity round.

For future financing plans, you'll need to ask *What happens if my company raises additional funding? What happens if my company is sold? What rights will the funders have?*

Many **redeemable equity agreements** have language that deals with what happens if there is an additional round of financing. In some cases, there is a clause that allows some or all of the shares to be repurchased (generally with similar terms to the **change of control** clause below).

Table 7.2 Comparison of types of structured exit repayments

Type of payment	Scheduled or mandatory[a]	Elective	Residual stake
Description	Payments that are scheduled over a defined period of time or at the request of the investor. In other words, dividends equaling 3% of revenues until 25 shares are repurchased at 3× the original purchase price. Or redemption after seven years at a mutually agreed upon price	Optional payments that can be made in addition to scheduled payments to reduce the number of shares outstanding. The decision to make these payments lies solely with the investee	Shares that cannot be redeemed except through a change of control (sale of the company) or a liquidation event (i.e., IPO or bankruptcy)

[a]When referring to structured exits, these are also called mandatory payments, but in the case of redeemable equity, dividends can only be paid when the company is solvent and able to do so

In general, the terms in **redeemable equity** agreements with regard to future rounds depend on the mindset of the funder. If a funder has designed their portfolio with the idea that their return will come mostly from **scheduled** or **elective payments** from the entrepreneur, they may be willing to be paid out by funders in a new funding round. If they believe their returns will come from a **residual stake** in the company when it makes it big, then they will be less willing to allow future funders to repurchase their shares. You will need to be in alignment with your funder around your future plans to make sure that you both have the same vision for the company.

In the event that myTurn was sold (**change of control**), Luni would receive the greater of the amount he was due according to the redemption schedule (3× the original purchase price for 50% of the shares and the current purchase price of the remaining shares) or the current purchase price of the shares. If Gene sold the company for $1.5 million (or $1800 per share) and he hadn't yet redeemed any of Luni's shares, Luni would get $90,000 ($1800 × 50 = $90,000). Whereas if Gene sold the company for $900,000 (or $1080 per share), Luni would get $57,000 in total [($1200 × 25) + ($1080 × 25) = $57,000]. This is fairly standard in **redeemable equity** agreements.

We'll discuss investor rights in future chapters and in the online companion to the book. You'll want to evaluate what rights a **redeemable equity** holder has with regard to voting and governance, and the right to participate in future rounds.

Funders

As we discussed in the last chapter and as you've seen in this journey, **redeemable equity** agreements were not created to cater to the needs of unicorns. Redeemable equity agreements were created to make **risk capital** more accessible for the 99% of companies that do not fit the VC model. Equity redemption offers an interesting option for early-stage funders who are interested in **pre-revenue** companies that may not be on the traditional VC path. For some investors, there will be significant tax considerations around **redeemable equity**, which we will discuss in the online companion to this book.

Some VC-like funders like to have their cake and eat it. This means that they use **redeemable equity** in a way that allows for upfront **liquidity** and greater certainty of some return through **scheduled payments** AND still keep some upside in the case of potential high growth companies through a substantial **residual stake** (sometimes greater than 50%).

Others create a hybrid instrument by combining elements of a **SAFE** (the right to buy equity in the future) with a right to a percentage of equity. Thus, they aren't quite equity holders (like Luni) and aren't debt holders (like we'll see in the coming chapter on convertible RBF). Instead, what is being redeemed is a right to equity, as opposed to equity itself.

If you decide that a **redeemable equity** agreement is appropriate for the types of companies you are funding, it is important not to be too overwhelmed by the complexity of creating a deal structure. One reason that early-stage investing using agreements such as **SAFEs** or **convertible notes** or **priced equity** agreements are considered standard is the funders have used them many times and have many templates available. Creating templates for new approaches to investing is, unfortunately, not an easy or simple process, so the transaction costs for funders attempting these types of investments for the first time in a jurisdiction can be high. It can be common to find lawyers and accountants who are not familiar with redeemable equity and thus try to talk you out of it. Hopefully, you can use the contracting chapter at the end of this chapter and the online companion to help reduce that complexity and cost. Another reason traditional templates are standard is because they are designed for a very specific subset of companies—the 1% of companies that fit the VC mold. Such companies tend to be tech start-ups that are growth-oriented, asset light and plan to be repeatedly financed by third parties. While these investment structures can be transferable to other types of businesses that do not fit this typology, doing so can result in untoward consequences in the future due to their fundamental misalignment. **Structured exit** agreements, on the other hand, can and should, be considered for funding broad categories of businesses due to your ability to adapt them for different contexts and funding needs.[4]

A lack of understanding of the appropriateness of **redeemable equity** from the founder side can be another obstacle to closing a deal. It is important that each party starts with an understanding of **structured exits** or a commitment to climb a steep learning curve quickly. If one party is trying to convince the other skeptical party about the merits and the technical details of the deal, it can get contentious quickly and potentially cause the deal to fail.

From a returns perspective, it is important to remember that while **structured exit agreements** generally schedule repayment terms, they often don't fix the investors' actual **IRR**, due to the repayment flexibility and variability.[5] So, this will need to be explained to **investment committees, boards** or potential **asset owners** investing in a fund.

Fundamentally, **redeemable equity** agreements may present an opportunity to create funding that is better tailored to the underlying needs of entrepreneurs as well as your own **liquidity** needs as funders.

---

[4]Brian Mikulencak, Revenue-Based Financing for Impact Investing (draft available upon request).
[5]Brian Mikulencak, Revenue-Based Financing for Impact Investing (draft available upon request).

8

Equal Exchange: Our Preferred Stock Journey

In this chapter, we are going to dive into the history of Equal Exchange, the worker **co-op** that we met in Chapter 3, to understand their unique offering of mission locked **preferred stock**, a type of **redeemable equity**. Investors who hold these shares earn a yearly dividend from Equal Exchange and they can sell back their shares to the company, at the purchase price, after holding the shares for five years. This **stock offering** was created to help Equal Exchange access equity growth capital when they were first founded. As they have grown into a mature, scaled company, they have continued to turn to their community of investors for flexible, values-aligned capital in this form, and have helped others create similar offerings.

Deja Brew

You'll recall that Equal Exchange was started in the 1980s by three founders, Jonathan Rosenthal, Michael Rozyne and Rink Dickinson, with the goal of helping Latin America's coffee growers achieve higher incomes. The global food system was undergoing a major shift at the time (much like today). In the U.S., where Jonathan, Michael and Rink were based, family farms were being displaced by industrial-scale, corporate-run agribusinesses. A counter-movement was also forming, with a proliferation of consumer food co-ops

© The Author(s), under exclusive license to Springer Nature
Switzerland AG 2021
A. Patton Power, *Adventure Finance*,
https://doi.org/10.1007/978-3-030-72428-3_8

offering local and organic produce as an alternative to the mainstream products commercially farmed with heavy duty chemical fertilizers and pesticides. High-quality specialty coffee was in high demand.

Jonathan, Michael and Rink met each other working for a co-operatively owned food distribution company in New England and shared a passion for changing the public's relationship to food and who grows it. It took three years to craft their ideas into something tangible. They launched Equal Exchange with a vision of being:

- A social change organization that would help farmers and their families gain more control over their economic futures;
- A group that would educate consumers about trade issues affecting farmers;
- A provider of high-quality foods that would nourish the body and the soul;
- A company that would be controlled by the people who did the actual work;
- A community of dedicated individuals who believed that honesty, respect and mutual benefit are integral to any worthwhile endeavor.

The three founders bootstrapped Equal Exchange with their own money and investments from friends and family, whom they warned would likely never get that money back. They sourced a not insubstantial $100,000 in start-up capital and began building, focusing first on coffee and coffee growers.

A Tough Cup of Joe

Things didn't go well to start. For three years, Equal Exchange, with its utopian notions, non-profit mentality, and for-profit, worker-owned business model, struggled and lost money. It was in part because the founders lacked experience with, or knowledge of, working with small-scale coffee farmers in Latin America. They faced a steep learning curve trying to identify democratically-run farmer groups, understand the internal structure of farmer co-ops, and determine product quality—and to do all of that in Spanish. But they held firm, and by their fifth year—1991—they had gained some traction with coffee farmer co-ops in Latin America and Africa. They also joined the Fair Trade network in Europe, where the conscious food movement was about a decade ahead of the U.S.

As a Fair Trade specialty coffee company, Equal Exchange offered food co-op customers a full line of coffee beans, roasts, and even flavored coffees. The organization cultivated a strong following of loyal customers, who helped

Equal Exchange reach another important milestone in 1991: its first $1 million in sales.

The organization had a challenging, capital-intensive business model, however, which was proving limiting to its capacity and growth. As we discussed in Chapter 3, Equal Exchange supported coffee growers by **pre-paying** for their harvests, many months before that coffee would ever be sold. They also **guaranteed** a portion of their purchase agreements to help the farmer co-ops secure outside financing. Both its **pre-payments** and **guarantees** offered a safety net for farmer co-ops, and thus formed a key part of Equal Exchange's social impact work. But they were also very costly to the organization, and Equal Exchange seemed to be in a perpetual scramble for cash as a result.

From Dedicated Sippers to Preferred Stock Owners

The Equal Exchange founders knew they needed to find a sustainable way to access growth capital, but they didn't want to sell ownership to investors who would push them away from their mission as a company. They struggled to get banks to understand their co-op model, particularly the fact that the company paid above market price for their coffee inventory. To be fair, the founders were equally skeptical of commercial banks and the type of agreements that they would be required to sign to access **debt**.

What Equal Exchange did have was a dedicated and passionate customer base, who believed in their mission and in the company. So, in 1989, the founders decided to create an opportunity for these customers to become investors in the company in a way that would align with the company's mission. In order to do this, they created a **preferred stock offering** with the following terms, which remain in place today during capital raises.

- A fixed stock price;
- A five-year minimum holding period;
- No voting rights for investors (those are reserved for workers);
- A modest, targeted (but not guaranteed) **dividend** of 5%;
- And a **"no exit" clause**.

The terms it offers are strict, and, on the surface, not particularly inviting. Normally **preferred stock** (or **preferred shares**) is a type of **equity** ownership that gives investors special rights and options over common stockholders.

Equal Exchange's preferred equity effectively does the opposite: it limits the rights and options of its non-worker-owners.

What the **"no exit" clause** means is that if Starbucks or Nestle, for example, wanted to acquire Equal Exchange, the company's bylaws require Equal Exchange to repay investors only what they invested, and to give all net proceeds from the sale to another Fair Trade organization. Simply put, there would be no upside for investors if some deep-pocketed competitor dangled a large acquisition check in front of Equal Exchange.

Daniel Fireside, who has overseen the preferred stock program at Equal Exchange since 2010, says the **"no exit" clause** removes any potential financial temptation or pressure to sell out. "Preemptively taking this little devil off our shoulder has several effects," he explains. "First, it assures outside investors that they aren't being taken for suckers by agreeing to forgo the potential of windfall profits. Second, it frees us from worrying about making decisions based on how we're viewed by speculators with no connection to our mission."

Without the clause, for example, worker-owners might not have voted to invest in developing a Fair Trade organic banana business, where margins are razor-thin and the politics is… fraught, to say the least.[1] Instead, notes Daniel, "Our investors give us full backing to expand our Fair Trade model into other ventures like olive oil from co-ops in the West Bank of Palestine, and sugar from small farmers in Paraguay."

Equal Exchange's **"no exit" clause** reflects the company's fundamentally different conception of company ownership. The company was founded to promote egalitarian and democratic workplaces and change how trade is conducted and perceived. The clause ties Equal Exchange to that mission. It also disentangles "ownership" from "capital." Investors may provide most of the **equity financing** for Equal Exchange, but they are just one part of the broader company pie, and therefore do not enjoy any special advantages over other essential stakeholders, like farmers, whom Equal Exchanges needs to produce high-quality goods. Nor do they enjoy advantages over workers, who commit their time, energy, and skills. Land, buildings, equipment, packaging, electricity and any number of other utilities, services and infrastructure are also seen as critical to running the business day to day.

---

[1] For more on this, start with: "The Economist explains: Where did banana republics get their name?".

A Latte of Progress

All in all, Equal Exchange set its preferred equity investment terms to be "pro profits but anti excess capital gains." The founders were practical enough to recognize that they would need investors—both **equity** and **debt** investors—but they didn't want their capital needs to drive their mission. And while they no longer tell their investors that Equal Exchange will likely lose their money (to the contrary—the company has paid **dividends** every year since 1989), they guarantee that none of their investors will get rich off of Equal Exchange either.

If it sounds like an odd sales pitch, it's been compelling enough: Equal Exchange has raised more than $17 million in **preferred stock** sales through **private placements** over the past 31 years. Most of those investors have been attracted by the company's mix of social mission and profitable business model. Along the way, they have also attracted **debt** providers who are aligned to their mission, giving them access to a mix of mission aligned debt and **equity** capital.

Today, Equal Exchange's Fair Trade model is thriving, buoyed by a broader movement that has grown to more than 400 coffee buyers and countless other buyers of other types of agricultural products.

This story isn't all silver lining though. Equal Exchange's founders recognize that the Fair Trade movement of which they are part of, faces significant challenges. The acceptance of large plantations and corporations such as Nestlé into the Fair Trade labeling system has resulted in skepticism in the certification system. Also, in spite of Equal Exchange's own success, it has had only a modest impact on smallholder farmer incomes at large; most of the world's hundreds of millions of small farmers continue to live in poverty.

As Daniel reflects on the preferred stock offering, he says, "For us the whole idea was, we don't mind paying a price for capital. But we're committed to the idea that everything we do should further our goal of shifting the economy and shifting supply chains, we want that **interest payment** or those **dividends** to be part of that shift."

Is Preferred Stock Right for You?

Founders

The **preferred stock agreement** that Equal Exchange has created blends together many elements that we have discussed already in this book. It uses

preferred shares, which give investors the right to a **dividend**, if the company decides to issue one. And it also allows for the redemption of those shares at a pre-agreed price, if the investor elects to redeem them (after 5 years). But, unlike the **redeemable equity** that we discussed in the last chapter, the investors will only be able to redeem the shares at the same price that they purchased them for, plus any accrued **dividends**. This is a great example of founders taking the traditional terms of **equity** and making them work for the company. When Equal Exchange was a start-up, these terms were a difficult sell, as the promised return did not seem to match the risk. It took early investors who believed in the mission of the company, including many faith-based organizations, to help it grow.

If we look at this agreement through the same lens we applied to the previous agreement, we can see that from a *cost* and *affordability* perspective this is a very founder-friendly document. The 5% target **dividend** is at the discretion of the company and 1× **repurchase price** is very inexpensive for the company. This is part of the reason that it was quite difficult for Equal Exchange to raise money at the beginning of their journey using this structure. In general, this structure is better suited to companies with a longer track record of profits, steady growth and access to potential investors who are passionate about the goals of the company.

From a tax perspective, the 5% **dividend** is more expensive to the company than a 5% interest payment as the dividend is taken out of post-tax profits, instead of pre-tax earnings.

From a *future financing perspective*, the **"no exit" clause** means that there would be no upside for the shareholders if the company were to sell. The employee owners also do not have an upside and thus, no motivation to look for an external buyer for the company.

In the past 11 years overseeing the **preferred stock** program, Daniel has found that many other founders seek him out to better understand how they could use similar terms to raise capital that works with their mission-driven organization. His advice?

- Be very cautious about accepting conventional VC or other funding with terms that essentially require to put investor returns above the mission.
- There are tradeoffs with any capital strategy. The calculus will change over time during the course of your company's development.
- Mission aligned financing is fundamentally about relationships rather than financial returns and term sheets. Although the capital is generally much cheaper and founder friendly, the company needs to invest resources

into sustaining the relationships and building an engaged community of supporters.

- Developing a capital strategy that enhances, rather than undermines, the social mission of a company will take time and experimentation. But it will provide a much more stable and lasting foundation than conventional bank or VC financing.

Finally, it is important to mitigate the downside of **preferred stock**. One of the ways to do this is not to be blinded by the potential capital but to seek and understand the terms of the agreement from an independent third party or advisor, as well as to ensure that the business meets its milestones and that it meets and exceeds its competitor benchmarks or industry standards.

Funders

For funders, it is important to realize that at the heart, this type of contract is a preference share structure with restrictions that may be negotiable. What you really need to consider is what is important to you, where the investee company has flexibility and why the investee company has proposed the restrictions. For Equal Exchange, communicating the rationale behind the voting restrictions, the redemption price and the **"no exit" clause** are part of their story as a company.

If you are a mission-aligned funder, this type of mission lock may make it easier to convince your **board or grant committees** to be more comfortable with an investment as opposed to grant since the investee has this mission lock, consistent with their charitable objectives.

9

Provive: Our Revenue-Based Mezzanine Debt Journey

For our next journey, we are going to head to Mexico where Provive and Adobe Capital join forces to tackle the issue of affordable housing through a **revenue-based mezzanine debt** agreement. This type of agreement falls into my categorization of a **convertible revenue-based financing (Convertible RBF)** agreement because it features a **variable payment** based on revenue or earnings, but also has the option of converting to **equity**. **Convertible RBF** allows funders who are taking **equity-like risk** to create contracts that provide additional upside if the founders decide to raise additional capital or have a **liquidity event**. They're also founder friendly, as they don't require a company to achieve **exponential growth** and provide a path for long-term ownership.

Location, Location, Location

When it comes to housing and property, there is one truth that always wins: location, location, location. For thousands of families in Mexico, location can be an insurmountable issue for those trying to move up the economic ladder. Take Cañadas del Florido, a low-income neighborhood in Tijuana, the northernmost city in Mexico. The neighborhood faces a number of problems, including high rates of crime, drug addiction, and trash accumulation. Whole areas of the neighborhood have been abandoned as a result, and the

© The Author(s), under exclusive license to Springer Nature Switzerland AG 2021
A. Patton Power, *Adventure Finance*,
https://doi.org/10.1007/978-3-030-72428-3_9

quality of services like schooling and mass transport is poor. The issues residents of Cañadas del Florido face impact nearly three million households across Mexico.

Antonio Díaz founded Provive because he saw an opportunity to tackle these challenges. The social impact enterprise aims to improve housing and rebuild underserved and neglected neighborhoods in Mexico by purchasing foreclosed, uninhabited homes, refurbishing them, and helping community members purchase the restored properties.

Antonio, a mathematician with an MBA and a Wall Street banking career, got the idea for Provive when America's housing bubble burst in 2008. Watching the housing market crumble in the U.S., Antonio realized there was an opportunity to use his knowledge of the finance world to uplift Mexico's low-income neighborhoods. He launched the enterprise with co-founders Clemente Villegas and Rene Medina in 2009 and acquired Provive's first six houses with money borrowed from friends and family.

It didn't take long before the founders realized the strength of the communities they were supporting. The interaction with the neighbors and a survey of community perception made them realize that the key instrument to secure the purchase of the houses was building communities around them. It wasn't just a matter of bricks and mortar; it was a matter of people and communities. Like every family, low-income families in Mexico seek safe neighborhoods that are close to work where kids can play freely in the streets. They realized that was what motivated them to buy a house from Provive.[1]

Show Me the Money

Buying up properties at scale is an expensive undertaking, especially for a new company, and Provive was in need of significant financial support. In 2011, Antonio and the team secured an initial MX$44 million ($3.4 million) in start-up **equity** from Mexican impact investment fund, IGNIA. That helped the company grow its revenues from MX$60m to MX$565 million (from $3 million to $28 million) over the next three years. But despite its growth Provive was caught in a cash crunch. In need of a cash infusion, the founders went back to IGNIA. IGNIA said it couldn't commit to a follow up **equity** transaction as the fund had spent down its capital, i.e., used up all of its available cash.

---

[1]Otegón, L.S. "Abandoned Houses Prove Golden Opportunity in Mexico." 31 July 2014. Available at: https://www.americasquarterly.org/blog/abandoned-houses-prove-golden-opportunity-in-mexico/.

Meanwhile, Provive was in a perilous situation for another reason: its source of housing, government-run foreclosure auctions, had stopped. Mexico had just undergone a change in government and the new government had halted the sale of homes without any timeline for restarting them. Antonio was worried that Provive would not survive the year without a significant cash investment.

Antonio set off to raise funding at the Latin American Impact Investing Forum (FLII).[2] It was here that he was introduced to Rodrigo Villar and Erik Wallsten, the co-founders of an early-stage impact investing fund called Adobe Capital. Adobe's mission was to address a capital gap in Mexico and Latin America for entrepreneurs with innovative, profitable and scalable business models addressing the most pressing social and environmental challenges. The firm sought to do this with alternative financing options, which Rodrigo and Erik believed better served founders.

Social Mezzanine?

Rodrigo was especially familiar with the shortcomings in Mexico's start-up finance ecosystem, having had a similar experience to Aner from Candide Group (Chapter 6) in realizing that traditional venture capital was often not right for green and social entrepreneurs. There were very few examples of **exits** and **IPOs** from VC-backed companies in Mexico, which made the space unattractive to traditional venture capital funds. Also, many of the enterprises looking for investment capital needed much smaller checks than VCs were willing to write. In all, Rodrigo felt the market lacked the right type of start-up capital for impact enterprises.

Rodrigo and Erik launched New Ventures in 2010, and with support from the Kellogg Foundation, developed Adobe Capital Social Mezzanine Capital Fund I, an early-stage investment vehicle that would deploy both traditional **equity financing** as well as **mezzanine** options that would return money to the fund faster. Rodrigo and Erik saw the fund as an opportunity to prove two things: one, that alternative financing mechanisms in developing countries were a good strategy for investors[3]; and two, that a fund investing in ventures delivering basic services to Mexico's low- and emerging-middle classes "could

---

[2]FLII, which was started by Rodrigo, has been instrumental in building the impact investing ecosystem in Latin America, you'll see it referenced several times throughout the book.
[3]Pothering, J. "Adobe Capital, IGNIA Exit Mexican Home Rehab Start-up Provive". 11 April 2019. Available at: https://impactalpha.com/adobe-capital-ignia-exit-mexican-home-rehab-start-up-provive/.

provide equal or better returns than other funds." They succeeded in raising $20 million by 2012.

As Rodrigo and Eric evaluated each deal for the fund, they tailored the type of investment structure to the needs of the entrepreneurs. They used traditional **equity** for companies in mature industries where they saw a viable path to an **exit**, including healthcare, financial institutions and mobility ventures. As these were all industries where mergers and acquisitions were common, a **trade sale** or sale to a financial buyer (**secondary sale**) was a strong possibility. They used **mezzanine structures** for companies that were earlier stage, close to cash flow positive, and unlikely to raise subsequent **equity** funding in the future.

For Provive, Erik and Rodrigo noted that the company had fast-growing revenues and was close to cash flow positive. But they weren't clear on what kind of buyer would be interested in Provive down the line and didn't want to **dilute** the founders' ownership any further, so they decided to offer them a **revenue-based mezzanine debt deal**.

A Good Offer?

Antonio was initially perplexed by Adobe's offer. He had assumed that Adobe's investment would be **equity** based, like IGNIA's; he didn't have a good grasp on how this financial structure would work. So, in one very long conference call, Erik walked Antonio through the deal.

Convertible Revenue-based financing (Convertible RBF) is a loan that is repaid as a percentage of a **return variable** until the **total obligation** is fulfilled. In Provive's case, this meant that it was a **loan** that they would repay monthly as a percentage of their earnings before tax, amortization and depreciation (**EBITDA**) until they had repaid 2.5× the original amount.

As you can see, the **return variable**, which dictates how the repayment is calculated, isn't always revenue as the name suggests.[4] The **return variable** can be a single line item like revenue or gross margin or EBITDA or it can be a calculation using a combination of line items. In the next chapter, we'll look at some different types of calculations that can be used.

The total amount that must be repaid to the investor is called **the total obligation**, which is calculated as a multiple of the original loan amount (the "2.5×" in Provive's case). Multiples typically vary from 1.1× to 4.0× and are set based on the length of the agreement and the riskiness of the

---

[4]Don't blame me! I didn't make up this language and I also find it a bit confusing, to be honest.

investment. Seed investments generally require a higher multiple (above 2.5×) than growth-stage investments (closer to 2.0×) because of the risk factor.

The length of time that a **convertible RBF** agreement is valid depends on the financial model and the funders' own capital constraints. In Adobe's model, the firm does not include a **maturity date**, so its contracts continue until the amount is repaid in full.

Erik also proposed a **convertible clause**. That meant that if Antonio decided to later raise an **equity** round, the amount Provive still owed Adobe could convert to **equity**. In such a case, the conversion would be at Adobe's discretion—i.e., Adobe would decide whether or not they wanted to **convert** or continue getting paid back according to their agreement.

Finally, the offer featured a **grace period** at the outset of the loan, in which payments are not required, in order to give Provive time to put the new capital to work and grow its operations and revenues. **Grace periods** in **convertible RBF** agreements can be time-based, i.e., with payments starting after three months or one year, or they can be milestone-based, i.e., with payments starting after three months of positive net profits. In Provive's case, Adobe offered a time-based grace period of 18-months.

Signing the Deal

Once he understood the terms, Antonio quickly grasped that Adobe's **convertible RBF** was likely going to be the only option available to Provive, as he just couldn't find other **equity** funders interested in the business. In essence, they were the iconic example of a "**missing middle**" company: too small for big investors and too big for small investors. What Adobe was offering was expensive financing, to be sure, but it was also much more flexible than traditional **debt** and satisfied the amount of capital Provive needed. Antonio felt the deal made sense for the company in a market where traditional **equity** investors were scarce.

IGNIA was less convinced. Looking at the 2.5× repayment terms, IGNIA pushed back against what they saw as a very expensive deal. "The **mezzanine structure** was an expensive one, but as an entrepreneur, I knew that the most expensive money out there is the money you don't have," recalls Antonio. "We needed between MX$40 and 50 million ($2–2.5 million), without it, our dreams would have died."

From his banker's lens, Antonio also felt the terms were fair. He pushed IGNIA for four months to get them to see it that way too, and finally succeeded, accepting Adobe's investment. Rodrigo joined the company's board, and Adobe also offered acceleration support through its New Ventures platform.

Within a couple of months, it became clear that Adobe's capital was absolutely critical to helping Provive survive the abrupt stop in government foreclosure auctions.

Back to the Negotiating Table

In 2017, two years into the deal and just after Provive's **grace period** expired, Antonio realized that there was a significant problem with how Provive's monthly payments had been structured. Provive's monthly payment amount was determined based on the company's *projected* performance (EBITDA) from the previous calendar year, rather than the management team's *actual* performance. Unfortunately, even though revenue performance was fairly good, EBITDA performance was not, and that translated into higher monthly peso repayment as per the Adobe terms and conditions. Thus, Provive was saddled with a payment amount that the company could not afford based on its current cash flows.

Antonio realized that what Provive should have negotiated was payments based on revenue targets, instead of EBITDA targets. He pitched the change to Adobe, but Adobe rejected the idea, so Antonio then found himself in the unenviable position of having to choose whether to pay Provive's taxes or pay Adobe. He ultimately decided to pay the taxes, and Adobe didn't receive payments from Provive for several months.

With Provive's survival Antonio's only concern, he headed back to Adobe once again with his cap in his hand to ask Eric and Rodrigo to grant Provive some breathing room on their **debt** payments. It took two months to convince Adobe that this was the only way forward but, in the end, it granted Provive a **grace period** of three months. Adobe also agreed to reset the terms based on Provive's revenues.

The Golden Years

Adobe's flexibility enabled what Antonio affectionately calls Provive's "golden years." The company started growing consistently, reaching an EBITDA level of MX$90 million ($4.4 million) in 2018. In the years that followed,

Provive restored more than 10,000 homes and housed more than 40,000 individuals—an almost 4.5× increase in the time since Adobe had invested.

This growth ultimately resulted in Provive accepting long-term debt financing from Credit Suisse, which enabled it to consolidate all of its short-term debt and buy-out IGNIA's majority **equity** control. Provive also used the capital from Credit Suisse to repay Adobe's **loan** in April 2019. Because the company was paying off the debt earlier than anticipated, Antonio was able to negotiate a **prepayment discount**, which meant Provive only had to repay 2.2× the amount of the original loan.

In reflection, Antonio says it is important for founders to understand two things about convertible revenue-based financing. "First, this is not equity. And also, this is not debt," he says. "[Convertible RBF investors] are running the risk of your performance, and they are completely subordinated to your other creditors," meaning that the cost of convertible RBF agreements reflects the level of risk that your funders are willing to take on.

Second, he explains, "It's not just about the money," with a **revenue-based debt** investor, "just like with an **equity** investor, it's your partner. It's your ally. It's the contacts. It's the ideas. It's who they know. We experienced that with IGNIA and we experienced that with Adobe. We've not experienced that with our creditors."

For funders who are considering **convertible RBF** investments, Rodrigo from Adobe Capital has this advice: "If you are going to invest in this way, do a deep dive into the needs of the entrepreneur, understand their cash flows and their capital needs."

"And remember," he adds, "this doesn't work for every entrepreneur."

Is Convertible RBF Right for You?

Founders

Revenue-based mezzanine debt falls under my **convertible RBF** category and it is best suited to **post-revenue, early stage to growth-stage enterprises** that are unable to access **secured debt** financing. While **convertible RBF** agreements are **risk capital**, they are generally not appropriate for early-stage companies that are **pre-revenue**. In order for funders to be able to correctly calculate the pay-off period for this instrument, the business needs to have revenue projections that are based on verifiable assumptions. This is much simpler if you already have revenue that you have earned from selling your product or service.

Similar to **redeemable equity**, there are three key advantages for founders over traditional **equity financing**:

- Maintaining control and ownership;
- Sharing the volatility risk of future revenues; and
- Facilitating long-term independence because investor **liquidity** is not tied to an "**exit**."[5]

An additional advantage to founders is that payments[6] on **convertible RBF** agreements are likely to be treated as **debt** payments i.e., as **interest** payments, thereby reducing your tax liability.

From a *cost* perspective (*how much do we owe?*), the total amount that needs to be repaid to the funder is called the **total obligation**. Sometimes this is explicitly stated as an amount and other times the multiple is stated and you have to calculate the total obligation by multiplying the amount of money the investor is investing by the multiple they are requiring. In this case the 2.5× the ~$2 million that Adobe invested (i.e., a total obligation of around $5 million).

From an *affordability* perspective (*When do I owe it?*), the **mandatory payments** required by Adobe were monthly (**frequency**) and had a **grace period** of 18 months before the payment began. Most **structured exit** funders include some sort of **grace period** in their contracts and design them around the needs of the founders to make sure the capital creates some growth before payments are made. A well-designed grace period makes sure that the founder has enough time to put the cash to work to see the results from the investment before having to begin payments.

How do I repay it? The **return variable** used in the repayment calculation was quite complex (EBITDA performance versus management projections) and Antonio and Adobe ended up simplifying it to a percentage of revenues. As a guide, revenue repayment percentages are often a single digit value (1–9%). As we discussed in Chapter 6, there are several different types of payments in **structured exits**. For Provive, their entire total obligation was due in mandatory monthly payments, but in the end, they used an **elective payment** to settle the amount with the cash from Credit Suisse (Table 9.1).

Unlike **redeemable equity, convertible RBF** payments are generally classified as **interest** payments, so they are on the **income statement**. Like we saw with Provive, although these are variable, they can still be unaffordable

---

[5]Brian Mikulencak, Revenue-Based Financing for Impact Investing (draft available upon request).

[6]Payments made above the principal amount. We'll discuss how this calculation can work in the final section of this book.

Table 9.1 Comparison of types of structured exit repayments

Type of payment	Scheduled or mandatory[a]	Elective	Residual stake
Description	Payments that are scheduled over a defined period of time or at the request of the investor—i.e., repayments of 4% of revenues until the total obligation is fulfilled	Optional payments that can be made in addition to scheduled payments to reduce the total amount outstanding. The decision to make these payments lies solely with the investee	*Generally not relevant for convertible RBF agreements*

[a]When referring to structured exits, these are also called mandatory payments, but in the case of redeemable equity, dividends can only be paid when the company is solvent and able to do so

if the company does not have high enough **gross margins** to support the payments. In general, **convertible RBF** agreements do not work well for low margin companies.

In order to create a realistic **convertible RBF** agreement, you'll need to have a firm understanding of your revenue and/or cash flow projections. This will be different from presenting a rosy set of projections to a potential **equity** funder. You will need to be pragmatic about what you can achieve to make sure that the loan is actually affordable. You'll need to play around with your revenue and cash flow model to understand what type of payment would be feasible for you.

What if I default? If you miss **mandatory payments** in a structured exit agreement, you risk defaulting on the agreement like Provive did in the Adobe contract. If you are found to be in default of the agreement, then the **total obligation** becomes due. However, as we saw in Provive's case, Adobe did not use the default to force the company to pay the total amount due, rather they renegotiated the deal to work for both parties. This is common in **convertible RBFs**, particularly where the founder and funder are **mission aligned**. Many funders take the view that a default is an opportunity to come back to the negotiating table to understand what is happening at the company and how the funder can help.

For ***future financing plans*** (*What happens if my company raises additional funding?*), some funders will prefer to repay the **total obligation** at the time of an **equity** funding round. We saw this in Provive's case when Credit Suisse decided to use their cash to fulfill the total obligation owed to Adobe. Often this willingness to pay off the amount owed is due to **equity** investors not wanting to have a variable cash payment owed to another investor. The other option in the event of an equity raise is that the **convertible RBF** funders **convert** into shares at the same price (or a **discount**) to the new equity investors. This option to convert will only apply to the **total amount outstanding**. The total amount outstanding will be calculated by subtracting the **total payments made** from the **total obligation**. Often this is a "one-way option", i.e., it is up to the **structured exit** funder to be able to choose whether or not they convert. If you are planning to raise additional **equity** in the near term, you'll want to carefully evaluate signing a **convertible RBF** agreement as the **convertible RBF** funder may be able to buy a sizable number of shares due to a large total amount outstanding.[7]

As far as new **debt** goes, **convertible RBF** funders may stipulate that written permission or approval is needed for the company to take on additional **debt** obligations. This is a relatively standard lender protection and is referred to as a "**permitted indebtedness**" clause. As a founder, you might be concerned that your ability to raise debt funding will be hampered by this clause. Ideally, if the funder has requested this, they plan to be a partner in the business going forward and will help you continue to build the correct **capital structure**, including taking on more **debt**, if needed. If you are worried about their ability to partner with you to do this, then you may want to flag this clause.

What happens if my company is sold? If your company is sold, **convertible RBF** funders will likely require a payment of whatever is greater: the total amount outstanding or the amount due, based on ownership.

What rights will the funders have? The role of the funders in a **convertible RBF** agreement will vary. As we saw in Adobe's case, they took a seat on the board and were very involved with the company during the term of the investment. You'll need to have a frank conversation with your potential **convertible RBF** funder prior to the investment around your expectations of their involvement. It is important that you are on the same page in this regard.

Funders

Convertible RBF agreements can be useful for funders who are willing to take equity-like risk on post-revenue, early and growth-stage companies. Like **redeemable equity**, this option was created for companies that require **risk capital**, but are outside of the traditional VC typology. This type of funding

---

[7]In the online companion, you'll find examples of how different contracts affect valuation and the total cost to the company.

may also be useful alongside VC funding, as we saw in Provive's case, as more of a **mezz-like** or **venture debt-like** offering. There are many different ways to structure these agreements so that they fit the entrepreneurs' needs as well as the funders' requirements around risk, return and **liquidity**.

Convertible RBF agreements look quite different to **equity** agreements. Nevertheless, most **convertible RBF** investors target a comfortable range of **IRRs** based on reasonable expectations of the company's performance, and safeguard against the possibility of zero-return by providing for payments shortly after funding, though often after an initial **grace period**.[8] If the company grows faster than expected, the repayments will be made sooner and the **return on investment** will be higher. Thus, even if they do not convert into equity, **convertible RBF agreements** have upside potential. All also have downside potential as most have no more than a **personal guarantee** to underwrite the risk and sometimes do not even require that.

One thing that does not change from traditional **debt** or **equity** investing is the focus on the entrepreneur and the team. If the entrepreneur is not aligned with the investor to build a sustainable company that can pay off this loan, then there will be considerable friction that no number of covenants can fix.

That being said, as a funder, you'll also have to be willing to come back to the table to renegotiate the terms of the agreement if there are changes that necessitate it. Alejandra, a portfolio manager from Adobe Capital, said that they have had to renegotiate 60% of their outstanding **revenue-based debt agreements** and they haven't been invested in the other 40% long enough yet to trigger a renegotiation. This discussion may be around a **grace period** or a change in terms, but similar to the original agreement, should be based around the needs of the company and a win-win situation for the founder and funder.

Most founders will not be familiar with the concept of a **structured exit** and might not have a robust enough financial model to do the projections required. For some funders, this means that they have to help entrepreneurs build out a financial model to understand what is affordable for them. For any scheduled repayment this means asking questions like how recurrent are the revenues? Does the company sell once-off goods or services, does it sell subscriptions, or does it enter into long term purchasing contracts? Does the company have impending capital needs?

---

[8]Brian Mikulencak, Revenue-Based Financing for Impact Investing (draft available upon request).

When you are evaluating the affordability of a contract, you need to balance (a) your return with (b) not starving the company of much needed cash for operations and reinvestment.

As a funder, if you are worried about extracting cash from a founder when they need it most, i.e., when they are growing their company, it is important to stress this affordability factor. For companies that have a very low margin, it might be very difficult to make this type of deal affordable. For those with a healthy enough margin to make the model work, it still might be prudent to make sure there are covenants or triggers around profitability designed to make sure that the plan makes sense for both of you. Some options include triggering repayments through specific levels of EBITDA or net profitability or using a ratcheted **interest** rate, which increases over time, to put less pressure on founders upfront.

10

Maya Mountain Cacao: Our Demand Dividend Journey

In this next journey, we'll join Emily Stone and Alex Whitmore as they search for the right type of early-stage capital to support their sustainable cacao sourcing venture in Belize. Just like Antonio, they were looking for capital to be able to expand their early-stage company and stay true to its social mission. Their journey features the use of a **demand dividend**, which is a **convertible revenue-based finance (convertible RBF)** agreement, and a lot of lessons about the complexities of **cash flow-based convertible RBF** investments.

A Cacao Way of Life

Cacao is a way of life for people in the Toledo district of Belize. The cultivation and processing of cacao is a family tradition passed down from generation to generation, often with few changes made to the ancient practice.[1] Despite this rich history, Toledo is one of the poorest districts in Belize, with more than 79% of the population living below the poverty line.

The persistence of poverty in Toledo exasperated Emily Stone, an energetic social and environmental activist, who had worked as a shareholder advocate for Green Century Capital Management, an investment advisory firm, and had experience in Fair Trade certification and sustainable corporate

---

[1] Sniffin, T. "How to Cacao in Toledo." 29 April 2016. Available at: https://mybeautifulbelize.com/how-to-cacao-in-toledo/.

© The Author(s), under exclusive license to Springer Nature
Switzerland AG 2021
A. Patton Power, *Adventure Finance*,
https://doi.org/10.1007/978-3-030-72428-3_10

supply chain development. She knew firsthand the power of well-run cacao collaboratives in fighting poverty.

In 2010, Emily met Alex Whitmore, owner of Taza Chocolate, a Boston-based organic chocolate company. He was looking to source high-quality cacao from Belize. At the time, most of the Toledo district's smallholder cacao farmers sold their harvests to a single dominant buyer: the Toledo Cacao Growers' Association, which supplied exclusively to Mondelez for the Green & Black's brand. Alex saw the potential for competition.[2]

A Sweet Opportunity

Emily and Alex joined forces to launch Maya Mountain Cacao (MMC), which would be a sustainable, fair-wage, ultra-premium cacao-sourcing venture. MMC's business model was straightforward: provide farmers with the tools they need to grow eco-friendly, high-quality cacao, and then pay them a premium rate for the product. The venture would work along the entire value chain, helping farmers develop organic growing and harvesting techniques; arranging access to **micro-loans** to help them finance equipment and training; and building processing facilities for the cacao fruit.

Each piece of this value chain was important from a business and an impact perspective for MMC. Without access to finance, farmers would be unable to afford the equipment or training needed to improve their crops. Without the sustainable growing and harvesting techniques, the farmers would not achieve commercial-scale production capacity. And without a centralized processing plan, farmers would not likely be able to maintain the cacao beans' quality, which was necessary to pay them premium rates and increase their incomes. Most smallholder farmers in Belize did not have access to such facilities and had to complete the two-week-plus cacao fruit fermentation and drying process themselves, then travel hours to the market with their crop (often on public transportation) all of which compromised the quality of their product and increased the risk that they would not be able to sell it.

While all of these components were essential to build the type of high-impact business Emily and Alex wanted, they were also very expensive. The founders managed to get through the first few years mostly by self-financing the company, along with a $75,000 investment from Taza and pre-harvest financing from an agricultural trading company. But by 2013, MMC needed some investment capital to support plans to expand beyond

---

[2]Case adapted from: Pothering, J. "Sweet Deal: How One Company Found a New Way to Support Cacao Farmers." 9 December 2014. Available at: https://www.entrepreneur.com/article/240624.

Belize. The issue was, MMC was not a good candidate for traditional **equity financing**, because it didn't have the high-growth financial projections most equity investors look for, nor did it offer a clear path to **exit**. Emily and Alex also knew the company was not a good candidate for traditional **debt**, because MMC needed growth capital that would be sensitive to the seasonal nature of its revenues making traditional debt repayment schedules difficult.

Emily was trying to figure out what MMC's investment options were while on a program retreat in Nicaragua with the Agora Partnerships Accelerator Program. There she met Jim Villanueva, executive director of the Eleos Foundation, a small foundation based in Santa Barbara, California, and the two sat together for lunch one day to talk about a potential collaboration. Jim, who was exploring financing options that would give young social ventures better chances for success, listened as Emily told him about the issues that MMC was facing and together, they began brainstorming.

Still in discussion, Jim and Emily walked into a presentation by John Kohler, a former venture capitalist and a senior director of the Miller Center for Social Entrepreneurship at Santa Clara University. John was presenting on a financing idea he had been working on since 2009—something he called the **demand dividend**.

A Demand What?

The **demand dividend** agreement is a type of **convertible RBF**. It's similar to the one we explored with Provive in the last chapter, except that instead of paying off **debt** over time as a percentage of revenue or **EBITDA**, the **return variable** is set around a company's **free cash flow**. This means the loan payments are calculated from a company's available cash, rather than its revenues or even income. As with Provive's **convertible RBF**, the **demand dividend** includes a **grace period**, a **multiple of cash invested** that caps repayments, and a **conversion clause** that allows investors to convert the amount outstanding into ownership shares, generally at the next **equity** funding round. Significantly, **demand dividend** agreements typically include a powerful renegotiation clause, if payments fall significantly below expectations. They also generally do not include **personal guarantees**, meaning that if the founder fails to pay, the funder cannot come after their personal assets.

John began exploring the idea for such a financial structure after spending years as a start-up **equity** investor. At the Miller Center, as he engaged with **social entrepreneurs**, he realized that there were significant differences between the goals of **social entrepreneurs** and traditional VC-backed companies that were unaccounted for in standard **equity financing**. The **social entrepreneurs** he was meeting had positive environmental and social benefit embedded in the fabric of their business models and wanted to ensure that growth and impact remained aligned. Also, most weren't serial entrepreneurs looking to build big companies and sell as quickly as possible. Finally, they weren't building businesses in countries where an **IPO** was likely.

If a traditional **exit** was unlikely for many **social enterprises**, John began to consider what kind of financing would help these companies grow. He first considered **venture debt**, but quickly realized that the type of capital **social entrepreneurs** needed had to be even more flexible from a repayment perspective, and potentially more affordable.

John spoke further about the **demand dividend** in a private conversation with Jim and Emily after his presentation in Nicaragua, and almost immediately, clear synergies emerged. Emily felt that it could be an appropriate tool for financing MMC's expansion into northern Belize and Guatemala, while also addressing the financial seasonality of agriculture. John felt that MMC could provide a great test case for the **demand dividend**. Jim agreed and so he offered to arrange the financing.

A Rocky Road

Because MMC was the first company to accept a **demand dividend** investment, it had to go through the pains of first-time deal structuring. Through Eleos, Jim recruited 14 investors to participate in the $200,000 deal, John Kohler being among them. But to aggregate all of those investors' interest, Jim had to first create a limited liability company (LLC). Then everyone had to go through the painstaking process of thinking through the deal structure and terms. In all, it took six months to finalize MMC's **demand dividend** investment, which closed in July 2013. One of the issues that held up the negotiations was the calculation of cash flow. This continues to be one of the most complicated components of a **demand dividend** agreement, as the calculation of cash flow affects investors' future repayments and thus represents a significant risk to investors. The investors in MMC remedied this in two ways. First, as part of the agreement, MMC had to submit an approved business plan, which could only be amended with the written consent of investors. Second, they came up with a very specific calculation for MMC's free cash flow, which was written into the agreement. It was as follows:

> Specific elements of the calculation for the purposes of this Financing shall be negotiated between the parties and included in the Business Plan. In

general, Free Cash Flow shall be calculated as gross sales, less discounts, cost of goods sold, operating expenses approved under the Business Plan, and periodic payments of trade financing obligations due within the reporting period (current quarter).

In addition to the cash flow complexities, another reason the deal took so long to finalize was its tax implications, which actually almost derailed the deal entirely.[3] In the end, they had to rename it a "**variable payment obligation**" so that the U.S. tax authority had no confusion about it being **debt** and not **equity**.

In the end, the final terms of the deal gave MMC, though its parent company Uncommon Cacao, a $200,000 cash infusion, which the company was expected to repay at 2×—a total of $400,000—over the next six to seven years. The terms gave MMC a two-year **grace period** to begin repayment, after which payments were scheduled for every six months. The amount of payment required was based around the 50%[4] mark on the company's free cash flow, but payments could be higher if MMC's cash flows exceeded targets, and lower if they fell below a certain threshold.

MMC used the capital to first expand its farmer training and cacao seedling initiatives, with the goal of increasing volumes to achieve economies of scale for MMC. It also supported MMC's growth into neighboring Guatemala, for which Emily set up a sister company, Cacao Verapaz. Because of the **demand dividend**'s flexible terms, MMC was able to capture the benefits of these new initiatives before it had to begin making payments on the **debt**. They also ensured that MMC as a whole wouldn't be jeopardized if its producers had a bad growing season.

Another Round, Please

Three years after closing the **demand dividend**, Uncommon Cacao raised a $1.575 million round of Series A **equity** investment, led by Morgan Simon of Candide Group (who we met in Chapter 6) on behalf of Pi Investments Innovation.[5] It was a significant but complicated milestone for the company because, by that point, Uncommon had yet to make its first payment on the **demand dividend**. That meant that Emily, with help from Jim as the leader

---

[3]We'll discuss the tax implications a bit more below.

[4]Usually this number is between 20 and 30%. MMC was a holding company structure, so Jim set the repayment to half of the cash flowing up to the holding company after operating costs.

[5]The story of this investment is chapter 8 of Morgan Simon's book *Real Impact*.

of the syndicate, had to convince all of the demand dividend investors to convert the outstanding **debt** to **equity**, per the terms of the agreement. In the end, all but one of the investors agreed to convert their debt to equity in the new round. The one investor that did not was paid out their remaining **total obligation** by the Series A investors.

Today, the Uncommon Cacao group has grown into a successful company both in terms of its commercial returns and impact. Uncommon sources cacao from 16 origins (in nine countries). There are 5,428 smallholder farmers now in its network, of which 3,750 are certified organic, with 1,738 registered female farmers amongst these numbers.

Reflecting on the deal, Emily says that despite the headaches, including the long delay in closing the transaction, she wouldn't have been able to build the company to where it is today without the **demand dividend** investment. The financing reflected the company's early-stage phase, as well as the requisite repayment flexibility needed to support the company's growth and impact.

John observes that since many social enterprises are driven by agrarian economies and fluctuating income patterns, even if they are not themselves agriculture companies. They will also, at best, have regional growth aspirations. Thus, there are many solidly performing companies like Uncommon that would benefit from growth capital in the form of a **structured exit** like the **demand dividend**, in order to increase their capacity to serve unmet demand.

Jim, for his part, plans to continue making **structured exit** investments, but now feels that **revenue-based structures** are more straightforward than **cash flow-based financing**. "The primary reason we do not intend to make cash flow-based structured exit investments is that it requires a very high degree of trust," he explains. That's because it can be easy to manipulate cash flows in accounting practices (a practice known as "**Hollywood accounting**"). It's not that Uncommon wasn't trustworthy, he adds, rather, "the level of trust required is difficult to achieve when making initial investments, almost by definition."

Is Convertible RBF Right for You?

Founder

As a Convertible RBF, a **demand dividend** works for **post-revenue for-profit** companies. These post-revenue for-profit companies can range from **early-stage to growth stage to established companies** that aren't able to obtain more traditional **debt financing** because they lack **collateral** or the ability to make consistent payments.

From a *cost* perspective (*how much do we owe?*), MMC had a **total obligation** amount as an amount of invested capital that it needed to repay. For Emily, she compared this cost to **equity** funding, as opposed to **debt financing** as MMC didn't have the **collateral** or credit history to access debt financing.

From an *affordability* perspective (*when do I owe it?*), MMC had a two-year **grace period** and after that had payments due every six months. When you are negotiating the **frequency** of payments, one of the things to keep in mind is how time consuming and costly it will be to process the payments. For agricultural enterprises like MMC, the minimum length should be the time between harvests to allow for sufficient cash flow. The term of this agreement was seven years.

How do I repay it? The **return variable** was **Free Cash Flow**, which was defined in the agreement. If you are using some form of cash flow in the repayment calculation, you need to be able to project, and appropriately calculate, cash flow. Compared to a Convertible RBF based on revenue, cash flow-based repayments can ensure that payments are affordable, but they can also add complexity. As discussed below, this complexity translates into risk for funders. There are ways for the funder to reduce their risk in this regard, such as a MMC's pre-agreed business plan and cash flow calculation, but these may lead to a reduction in flexibility for a founder. Thus, you might not be prepared to trade-off control for the additional affordability considerations of a **demand dividend**.

What if I default? In this case, a default could be triggered by a few different situations, including MMC's revenue or cash flow being 60% below the business plan, the company declaring bankruptcy or a *force majeure*[6] that prevented the company from normal business. Lastly, the company could trigger default if the **total obligation** had not been paid within the seven years and they were unable to agree on a business plan going forward. In the case of default, the remaining **total obligation** would become due and payable immediately.

Obviously, if MMC were in any of the above situations, it would be very difficult for them to repay the **total obligation**. As with the Provive case, the Eleos investors would be looking for MMC to come back to the table and work with them on how to fulfill the payment obligation.

---

[6] A force majeure clause means unforeseeable circumstances. These clauses were important for many businesses globally during the COVID-19 pandemic to help them delay payments or cancel contracts.

For *future financing plans* (*What happens if my company raises additional funding?*): As we discussed in the previous chapter, if you are planning to bring in traditional VC investors down the line, you need to be aware of the complexities of the agreement (and potential ramifications around ownership). There is always the possibility that this might dissuade investors from investing in your company or create a significant amount of work to transfer the **demand dividend** investors over to the new terms. We saw this when MMC decided to raise **equity financing** from Pi Investments: Emily needed to convince her investors to convert into this new round of financing. This took a series of negotiations and added time to the transaction.

What happens if my company is sold? Similar to our discussion in the previous chapter, if your company is sold, convertible RBF funders will likely require a payment of whatever is greater: the total amount outstanding or the amount due based on ownership.

What rights will the funders have? Eleos was very engaged in MMC during the term of the investment, including having a seat on the board. They also had a significant number of covenants that required the company to seek their written approval to undertake major decisions such as raising additional debt or equity, amending bylaws and more. They also requested the unaudited financial statements every quarter in their **information rights**. Finally, in their **participation rights**, they were able to participate alongside new equity investors. This meant that in addition to converting the total amount outstanding, they would have the right to buy new shares along with investors, if they chose. To learn more about these term sheet terms, please see the online companion.

Funders

Like other Convertible RBFs, **demand dividends** offer **equity**-like benefits to investors without the need for a third party **exit**. As a funder deciding on the **return variable**, it is important to recognize the risk that lies in the complexities of defining cash flow. For instance, in the MMC **demand dividend**, there was a separate negotiation over a business plan as well as over a definition of **free cash flow**. This requires a level of sophistication around forecasting and accounting ability, which might not be present in all potential investments.

Regardless, no definitions of cash flow are immune to manipulation, whether nefarious, strategic or unintentional. Although there is a difference between fraudulently adjusting reporting to keep from paying cash to the investor and legitimately managing cash flow to grow your businesses before announcing **dividends**, the bottom line is that sometimes it may be in the company's best interest to delay payments and founders might be tempted to do so legally. While this does come down to the trust between a founder and funder working towards similar objectives, the opportunity for disagreement between the founder and funder over the disbursement of cash flow is exceptionally high, even if they are aligned.

In the online companion, you'll find more information about the tax implications of **convertible RBF**, but in general, most jurisdictions treat **RBF** repayments to investors as loan repayments, which means they are ordinary income. This means that, unless you are a tax-exempt entity, RBF investing may not be as tax efficient as **equity** investing and that must be taken into account when calculating your fund economics. In addition, in the U.S., considerations such as **original issue discount (OID)** accounting and required debt amortization schedules, which caused headaches at the end of the MMC investment process, can add complexity to a deal.

11

GetVantage and VIWALA: Our Revenue-Based Financing Journey

Next, we head to Mexico and India to experience the journeys of two different entrepreneurs who have committed to making it easier and faster for founders to access unsecured debt financing by using tech-enabled **revenue-based financing (RBF)**[1] platforms. Although many of the terms are similar, **RBF** funders act quite differently to **convertible RBF** funders. The easiest way to think about it may be that **convertible RBF** funders act more like **equity** investors providing **risk capital** and **RBF funders** act more like debt or mezzanine funders providing **working capital**. This means that **Convertible RBF** funders do deep due diligence on potential investments and engage extensively with their investees, requesting board seats and multiples on their investments over long periods, while **RBF** funders use historical revenues to make quick decisions about creditworthiness, engage in arm's length transactions and look for their money back over shorter time frames with returns more comparable to debt than equity. Let's start with Bhavik's story in India to better understand the motivation for this type of financing.

From Mumbai to Silicon Valley

Bhavik Vasa was born and raised in Mumbai by a family of entrepreneurs. He had the opportunity to attend university in the U.S. and "stumbled" into

---

[1]Confusingly in the development finance world, RBF also refers to results-based financing. Throughout this book, we will use RBF to mean revenue-based financing.

© The Author(s), under exclusive license to Springer Nature Switzerland AG 2021
A. Patton Power, *Adventure Finance*,
https://doi.org/10.1007/978-3-030-72428-3_11

banking and financial services with a campus placement at Wells Fargo Bank in 2005. That placement just happened to be in Silicon Valley, where the entrepreneurial bug bit him quickly. He joined a small tech firm called ISTS as a founding member in 2006 and hustled his way through the early wave of mobile payments and mobile wallets.[2] In 2010, he decided he wanted to help launch digital payments back in India, so he moved home and began building some of the earliest digital cash and digital wallet companies.

One of those companies was ItzCash, which Bhavik helped scale to a team of 450 people, processing over $2 billion in transactions with annual revenues of $40 million. In 2017, Ebix Group bought ItzCash at a $150-million-dollar **valuation** and Bhavik decided it was time for a career break. He wanted to take time off to focus on his growing family and to reflect on the past decade of his fintech journey.

One of those reflections: having raised millions of dollars in **equity** funding, Bhavik realized he had experienced a lot of "personal pain" in the fundraising process. Even at the height of ItzCash, when it had $40 million in revenue and strong connections with traditional lenders and banks, it was difficult for the company to secure **working capital**. Banks would ask for **collateral**, such as a piece of land or physical assets, which a digitally based business like ItzCash simply didn't have.

Frictionless Fundraising?

Bhavik knew this issue was not unique to ItzCash, because he experienced the same problem with another venture: Via.com, India's third largest travel booking site. Via's largest company expense was digital marketing through channels like Google and Facebook, which typically cost upwards of $250,000 per month, or more during the holiday travel season. Even though Via was well funded, the company had a cash flow problem because of its digital marketing expenses.

What Bhavik heard most from the market was that businesses needed to raise **equity** to resolve their cash flow problems. But Bhavik didn't think that equity made sense as a solution to a short-term financing need (much like it didn't make sense for Ella and SOKO in Chapter 3). He also believed that forcing founders into the Silicon Valley venture capital model of prioritizing users and scale above revenues, and equity rounds above profitability, had a number of problems. Moreover, he knew that, if they wanted to take

---

[2]The company was eventually sold to Clear2Pay in 2011.

on equity, emerging market entrepreneurs struggled to access venture capital because most VCs weren't based in emerging markets nor had experience with, or knowledge of, the local market conditions. In short, most VCs were influenced by (biased toward) their own worldview and didn't look far outside of what they knew in Silicon Valley. Together, these issues created friction in the venture funding ecosystem and resulted in many worthwhile entrepreneurs being unable to get the cash that they needed to grow.

Bhavik decided that for the next stage in his entrepreneurial journey, he wanted to design a "frictionless way of raising capital" for fast-growing, post-revenue, digital start-ups in emerging markets. He knew he could leverage his experience in fintech to develop a tech-focused solution, but what kind of financing model made sense for entrepreneurs?

Kicking Dilution to the Curb

As Bhavik explored, he came across the idea of **revenue-based financing (RBF)**, through which companies were offered loans based on their recent revenue numbers and repayment was based on a percentage of future revenues. He was taken with the idea immediately as a model for offering funding to start-ups that needed short-term advances and **working capital**. He started speaking to friends in the founder community in India to test out interest. The reception was enthusiastic: Founders understood the concept of trading a percentage of future revenues for the capital they needed to grow their companies. They were also excited by the flexibility of RBF payments versus traditional bank **debt** payments and loved that they didn't have to give up **equity** like traditional venture capital.

In 2019, Bhavik launched GetVantage, a tech-focused **RBF** company that targets fast-growing digital businesses that need capital to finance their marketing and development costs. GetVantage offers companies financing based on their monthly revenues, for a fixed fee. It has a unique under-writing model built around data points that are relevant to digital businesses. As companies access capital and GetVantage gains better visibility over their financials, companies' cost of financing goes down. The platform also manages capital disbursement and payment collections.

Within a few months of launching, hundreds of Indian founders applied for funding. The company also saw numerous requests from outside of India. Bhavik believes this proves that companies are hungry for **non-dilutive** capital options that allow founders to focus on boosting revenues, operating margins and profitability.

GetVantage's loans typically range from $20,000 to $250,000 for a flat fee of anywhere from 6% to 9%. Terms are adjusted to an individual company's needs. Borrowers then repay the entire loan as a share of future revenues. This percentage varies based on the monthly revenues of each company; however, it is typically in the range of 5% to 25%.

For the company to be able to provide this kind of financing, GetVantage must itself have access to capital to lend. It has proven difficult and time consuming to educate lenders on how to forecast repayments and calculate risk for a company with such variable earnings. But lenders are beginning to warm up to the idea, Bhavik says, as they question whether **collateral**-focused fixed **interest rate** loans are suitable for digital start-ups. That maturing of the funding ecosystem in emerging markets like India is encouraging, he adds, because the number of options available to founders needs to expand and become more accessible. **RBF** is one such tool with which to achieve that.

From India to Mexico

Nearly 16,000 km away in Mexico, the founders of New Ventures saw a similar opportunity to employ technology to unlock **RBF** for early-stage start-ups and small businesses.

Eric Wallsten, Rodrigo Villar and Armando Laborde had more than a decade of experience using **revenue-based debt** to invest in growth-stage companies through their investment fund, Adobe Mezzanine Fund (from Chapter 9). This work had exposed a huge gap in access to **working capital** for Mexico's business owners, particularly small companies with revenues of around $100,000 per year and which needed loans of about $20,000 to satisfy their working capital requirements. Eric, Rodrigo and Armando knew that Adobe's funding model, which included deep due diligence and involvement with portfolio companies wouldn't work for loans of that size from a cost perspective: It was too expensive to do such small deals. So, they set to work on an underwriting and lending process that could make sense.

First, they spent the time trying to understand the founders of the companies that needed this capital. They discovered that the founders were often serving in most or all of the core roles of their business. They were the saleswoman, the operator, the CEO and the CFO. Also, despite founders' business acumen, many didn't have the knowledge or capability to create reliable financial projections. And lastly, they needed the money today—not tomorrow, not in three months…

The typical founder that Eric, Rodrigo and Armando wanted to serve was in the midst of a pilot for a large company like Walmart, selling their product in five stores. When that founder got a call from Walmart saying that they wanted to go national with their product, their company would need the cash to deliver on that contract immediately.

As founders of an **impact investing** firm, Eric, Rodrigo and Armando also wanted their new firm to have a meaningful impact through its lending activities. One issue that continuously re-emerged through their discovery process was a gender gap in small business financing. Across Latin America, female founders face a $98 billion credit gap.[3] The partners decided that in addition to targeting small businesses that had a more traditional social or environmental impact, they would focus on investing with a gender lens.

Light Touch and Lightning Fast

In 2018, Rodrigo, Eric and Armando hashed out the idea for VIWALA, a new fintech venture that would be launched out of their early-stage start-up accelerator, New Ventures. The idea was to accelerate and reduce the cost of small business revenue-based financing by doing three things.

First, by automating most of the back end underwriting and lending processes, i.e., substantially cutting down the costs of lending, while still being personal enough to screen companies for social and environmental impact potential. Second, by designing an accessible and easy-to-complete application for founders who were time constrained or had low levels of financial literacy; and third, by developing a light-touch **due diligence** process that focused on verifying past monthly revenues as opposed to future projections. All combined, VIWALA would aim to be a lightning-fast lender for small businesses. The founders gave it the slogan "momentum capital!".

Eric, Rodrigo, Armando and the rest of the New Ventures team gave VIWALA a test run at a financial innovation contest held by USAID. VIWALA won and was awarded $200,000 to build out the concept. With this seed capital, they reached out to Karla Gallando, a former associate at the New Ventures accelerator, and asked her to be VIWALA's CEO. Her first task was cultivating demand for VIWALA's solution from both entrepreneurs and other capital providers.

---

[3] "*Opportunities for Gender Finance in Latin America: What Can Banks and MFIs Do to Service Women Entrepreneurs Better?*" 6 December 2019. Available at: https://www.fmo.nl/news-detail/64eefb1c-2091-4f84-b4ce-536425e0b7a2/opportunities-for-gender-finance-in-latin-america-what-can-banks-and-mfis-do-to-service-women-entrepreneurs-better.

Show Me the Money

Like Bhavik, Karla found that selling VIWALA's offering to entrepreneurs was easy. Small business founders intuitively understood the concept of borrowing against your future sales and repaying based on a percentage of those sales. But when she approached investors for VIWALA, most of the questions they asked focused on borrowers' historical revenues and the affordability of the loans. They were also skeptical of founders' ability to accurately report their revenue. Karla eventually found an investor—a **family office** in Mexico—that had more flexibility than traditional investors or financial institutions and was willing to invest $800,000 for VIWALA's initial lending phase.[4]

The $1 million VIWALA raised has enabled the fintech start-up to make 19 loans while building up its capabilities and further streamlining its **due diligence**, disbursement and collection processes.

Recently, the Mexican government, like several others in Latin America, mandated **electronic invoicing** for all businesses, which has been a boon for **fintechs** capturing data to build out new financing products. The availability of this data enables VIWALA to develop a technology that integrates with the Mexican tax office, verifying businesses' monthly sales and cash flow. In turn, VIWALA is now able to process an **RBF** application within two days and disburse approved loans within 10 days.

VIWALA does have some firm guardrails in place to mitigate portfolio risk. For instance, it will only lend up to 20% of a borrowing company's previous annual sales. This is based on internal analysis VIWALA has done around loan affordability. When they lend more than $30,000 to a company, they ask the entrepreneur for a **personal guarantee** against the loan. In all cases, its loan terms are 36 months with a repayment multiple of 1.5x.

For Karla, "in order to close the credit gap the women led SMEs have in Latin America we need to create 360º solutions that include an innovative financial product, an easier and faster process to have access to it, moreover we need to align potential investors to this new financing model."

As Bhavik reflects on his journey thus far, he says, "The VC model has too much pressure on entrepreneurs to grow fast, build fast, disrupt. That's taken away a lot of attention from building businesses for the right reasons, with the right fundamentals and the right balance. The **RBF** model…is a more balanced, structured and stepwise approach. In the future, I believe more

---

[4]As we saw in the last chapter with Aner, family offices operate without external funding, so they can make decisions based on the criteria and priorities of internal stakeholders. This means that they can often be quicker and more risk tolerant than traditional institutions. As they often have a small staff complement, they can be more difficult to get in front of and are also subject to the changing priorities of the family members.

entrepreneurs will use this approach, rather than raising tons of capital and trying to burn their way to scale."

Is RBF Right for You?

Founders

RBF is most suitable for **post-revenue, early-stage to growth-stage enterprises** that need to access **working capital** and **growth funding**. You may be unable to access secured **debt financing** due to a lack of **collateral** or you may need to access funding that is more flexible than bank financing. Having an additional option for working capital beyond traditional bank **debt**, or credit cards, can be a useful tool in your toolkit.

From a *cost* perspective (*how much do we owe?*), the **RBF** contracts in this chapter demonstrated two different types of pricing. For VIWALA the agreements look similar to Adobe's with a **total obligation** that is calculated by a multiple of cash loaned. This multiple is lower than we saw in the Provive cash and reflects the shorter time frame as well as the lower level of involvement that VIWALA will have with the company. In other words, both the cost and the involvement look more like a **debt** transaction. GetVantage is similar, in terms of cost and involvement, except that their product is a fee calculated as a percentage of the total amount raised (6–9%). These loans are even shorter than VIWALAs, likely paid back over the course of months.

From an *affordability* perspective (*when do I owe it? How do I repay it?*), both companies evaluate potential borrowers based on their ability to repay the loans within a relatively short time frame. Simplicity, transparency and affordability are paramount to GetVantage and VIWALA's successful. Unlike **convertible RBF** funders, Bhavik and Karla cannot create bespoke contracts for each borrower. They need to have a set of terms that the borrowers can choose from and calculators that show them how much they can afford and what their payments will look like. Using technology to automate this process is essential. If you are considering an RBF agreement from a **fintech**, you'll need to have a solid understanding of the affordability of the capital offered, both from a percentage of revenue and from a total repayment amount. For this you'll need to compare the cost of the deal with other viable alternatives. The comparison should be based on total cost to you as an entrepreneur as well as the flexibility that the funding provides.

What if I default? Many funders, including GetVantage and VIWALA, require **personal guarantees** for larger loans, so if your company **defaults**, you may personally be on the hook for repayment.

For *future financing plans* (*What happens if my company raises additional funding? What happens if my company is sold?*), **RBF** contracts are pretty simple: Either the payments will continue similar to other **debt** payments or there will be a clause that allows the total amount outstanding to be paid in full. This is the same if your company is sold.

Funders

As a funder, you need to determine your own priorities around how to apply **RBF** in different situations, geographies and types of companies. As VIWALA has found, just because RBF agreements are not suitable for early-stage, **pre-revenue** companies, it does not mean that they are not suitable for very small companies. But in order to create access for smaller companies, the cost of diligencing and distributing the loan needs to make sense, which is where technology becomes essential.

Using the same tech-enabled approach, GetVantage has identified another market: **post-revenue** tech start-ups in emerging markets that need to access non-dilutive capital to fuel marketing and development spend. This is particularly true of companies that offer software as a service (SaaS). There is a growing number of U.S. and European investors that have identified a similar trend and are seeking to use **RBF** to access fast-growing start-ups through **debt** versus **equity**. This type of **RBF** is now a "booming industry" in the U.S. with large investment groups such as Clearbanc and Lighter Capital adopting the model.

RBF funders in the U.S. are also using this type of financing to have an impact on the current wealth disparity among underserved founders. Funders like Founders First, see the possibility for founders to avoid or delay the **dilution** of **equity** funding as one of the advantages of the instrument. If underserved founders are able to own more of their companies, and thus more of the profits, as opposed to well capitalized venture capital firms and financial institutions, they believe this can be an important tool in fighting wealth disparity.

Both GetVantage and VIWALA represent a growing trend of **RBF** in emerging markets for smaller companies. In addition to creating additional accessibility, tech-enabled **RBF** may prove to be a valuable development tool as the world recovers from the COVID pandemic. The flexibility of **RBF** has meant that even though the COVID crisis has reduced payments in 2020, all of the companies in GetVantage and VIWALA's portfolios are still making payments based on their sales. Upaya Social Ventures (who we'll meet in Chapter 15) also built their Resilience Fund to disburse **RBF agreements** during the 2020 COVID pandemic to be able to make the payments affordable for the entrepreneurs and not place the pressure of traditional **debt** on them during a time of crisis.[5]

---

[5]We'll learn more about Upaya's fund in the Recoverable Grants chapter.

12

Redesigning Risk Capital

In this section, we've discussed a whole set of alternatives for you to redesign how you think about your **risk capital** options. In this chapter, we'll recap our **structured exit** discussion and talk about the key factors that you need to consider when evaluating your options. If you want to dive into the details of contracting a structured exit agreement, you'll find a large set of resources on the online companion.

For **Aner** from **Candide Group** (Chapter 6), designing **structured exits** was about creating funding that actually worked for the entrepreneurs he wanted to support as a funder, i.e., entrepreneurs who were forcing themselves into the VC mold in order to get **risk capital** to grow their businesses.

For **Luni** from **Fledge** (Chapter 7), designing his **redeemable equity** agreement was about creating a funding option for very early-stage social entrepreneurs that allowed the entrepreneurs to own their businesses in the long run. For **Gene** from **myTurn** (Chapter 7), the **redeemable equity** funding gave him access to very early-stage proof of concept funding to allow him to build his business on his own terms and not on a VC investor's terms.

For **Jonathan, Michael and Rink** from **Equal Exchange** (Chapter 8), a **preferred stock** instrument allowed them to invite aligned investors into their company but ensure that the company was able to pursue its social mission by creating specific limits on shareholders (including a **"no exit"** **clause**).

For **Erik and Rodrigo** from **Adobe** (Chapter 9), designing **convertible RBF** agreements were about designing a funding approach that allowed

A. Patton Power, *Adventure Finance*,
https://doi.org/10.1007/978-3-030-72428-3_12

them to create a portfolio of scalable social businesses with a clearer path to **liquidity**. For **Antonio** from Provive (Chapter 9), **convertible RBF** funding was about having access to growth capital that sat alongside his VC funding and provided him with a partner to build the business without requiring the ownership stake.

For **John and Jim** from **Eleos** (Chapter 10), building the **demand dividend**, a type of **convertible RBF** agreement, was about finding a funding option that could be used to support **social entrepreneurs** to grow in a way that was aligned with their social missions. For **Emily** from **Maya Mountain Cacao** (Chapter 9), the **demand dividend** was about having flexible **risk capital** that was designed with the early-stage nature and seasonality of her business in mind.

For **Bhavik** from **GetVantage** (Chapter 11), **RBF** was an opportunity to cater to fast growing, asset-lite ventures, who generally boot-strapped or have limited **equity** based and VC funding options and hence ideal candidates for alternative, **non-dilutive** options for growth capital. For **Karla** from **VIWALA** (Chapter 11), **RBF** was about offering quick, affordable working capital for small businesses that were not being well served by formal financial institutions.

Founders

As we discussed throughout this section, there are three key factors you need to consider before negotiating a **structured exit** agreement: *cost, affordability* and *future financing plans*.

Starting off with cost, it is important to note that **structured exit** agreements are generally more expensive than bank loans. Depending on the terms and what you are looking for from a funder with regard to involvement, if you qualify for attractive-rate financing from a bank or commercial lender, a **structured exit** may not be the right deal for you. In the online companion, we walk through the structures in an example to compare the different costs.

From an **affordability** perspective, structured exits work best for high margin businesses. This is particularly true of **RBF** agreements with payments calculated on revenue. Although **RBF** payments are variable, if you are running a low margin business, paying 5% of your revenue can become unaffordable. **Redeemable equity** agreements that rely on **dividends** or **RBF** agreements that rely on a free cash flow calculation will be affordable as they are based on the excess cash that the company generates, but will require projections of enough free cash flow that funders will see the investment as viable and will come with the complications we discussed around calculating free cash flow.

Thus, in order to create a realistic **structured exit** agreement, you'll need to have a firm understanding of your revenue and/or cash flow projections. This will be different from presenting a rosy set of projections to a potential **equity** funder. It will need to be pragmatic about what you can achieve to make sure that the loan is actually affordable. You'll need to play around with your revenue and cash flow model to understand what type of payment would be feasible for you.

Finally, you'll need to consider what your *future funding needs* will be. **Structured exits** can complicate future rounds of **equity** as funders may not appreciate you having an obligation to pay out a percentage of revenue or cash flow to previous investors. In the online companion, we will discuss the different options that you have to mitigate this risk through repayment and redemption options. If you plan to finance your business through **debt** in the future, you can use your repayments to establish a **credit history**. In that case, you will want to make sure that you are able to redeem all of your outstanding shares in a redeemable equity agreement. You will want to be sure that you are aligned with your funder in your future growth and funding plans. All **RBF** and most **convertible RBF** funders expect their returns to come from repayments, but many **redeemable equity** funders have some expectation of upside in the future. You'll need to make sure that this upside, whether through an **exit** in the form of a sale, an **IPO** or merger, or a redemption funded by debt capital or internal cash flows, matches your future plans.

Funders

Although **RBF** can be used for **working capital** alongside VC investment and redeemable equity rounds can increase founder ownership by delaying VC **dilution**, **structured exits** were not created to cater to the needs of unicorns. **Structured exit** agreements were created to make **risk capital** more accessible for the 99% of companies that do not fit the VC model. Fundamentally, **structured exits** present an opportunity to create funding that is better tailored to the underlying needs of entrepreneurs as well as your own **liquidity** needs as funders.

If you decide that a **structured exit** is appropriate for the types of companies you are funding, it is important not be too overwhelmed by the complexity of creating a deal structure. As we discussed in Chapter 7, **SAFEs, convertible notes** and **priced equity** agreements are considered standard because they've been done so many times and because they were designed for a very specific subset of companies—the 1% of companies that fit the VC mold, i.e., tech start-ups that are growth-oriented, asset light and that plan to be repeatedly financed by third parties. **Structured exit** agreements, on the other hand, can and should be considered for funding broad categories of businesses due to your ability to adapt them for different contexts and funding needs.[1]

Creating templates for new approaches to investing is, unfortunately, not an easy or simple process, so the transaction costs for funders attempting these types of investments for the first time in a jurisdiction can be high. It can be common to find lawyers and accountants who are not familiar with these structures and who thus try to talk you out of it. Hopefully, you can use the contracting tips in this book and the resources in the online companion to help reduce that complexity and cost by creating templates for a few different categories of investments that you might make, but it is important to remember that you may still have to adjust the terms based on underlying companies. This is part of the process of making capital actually work for founders.

A lack of understanding of the structure from the founder side can be another obstacle to closing a deal. It is important that each party starts with an understanding of **structured exits** or a commitment to climb a steep learning curve quickly. If one party is trying to convince the other skeptical party about the merits and the technical details of the deal, it can get contentious quickly and potentially cause the deal to fail. For instance, the Acumen Fund has worked with **co-ops** in Colombia using a **redeemable equity** model and the amount of time that it has taken to explain the model to potential partners has been considerable. The team is currently evaluating using a combination of a **recoverable grant**[2] and a **revenue-based structure**.

Another reason **structured exits** are more complex is that in traditional early-stage investing, investors almost always acquire some kind of perpetual **equity** stake. Without defined **liquidity**, equity investors are dependent on someone else to determine the investment return: typically, either a large, strategic buyer (who purchases the company) or an investment bank (who facilitates the company's IPO). By contrast, **structured exit** investors must work with the company to determine a repayment schedule that dovetails with the unique features of the company and its business. This requires a high level of investor-investee trust and mutual respect for each side's goals, as the parties must reach a more final agreement on what the investors' return

---

[1] Brian Mikulencak, Revenue-Based Financing for Impact Investing (draft available upon request).
[2] We'll learn about recoverable grants in the next section.

should be. Even seasoned investors may have a need to do some rethinking or recalibration if they're used to negotiating their return in an indirect sense (i.e., estimating future valuations based on future sales of equity). Once finished, however, structured exits don't require another party or transaction to dictate the investors' return—they only require the investee's generation of revenue or cash flow. In a sense, this means that structured exits, while more complicated to negotiate on paper, can result in overall lower financing work for the investee (once accounting for work avoided, and not merely work deferred).[3]

From a returns perspective, it is important to remember that while structured exit agreements generally schedule repayment terms, they oftendon't fix the investors' actual **IRR**, due to the repayment flexibility and variability.[4] So, this will need to be explained to **investment committees, boards** or potential **asset owners** investing in a fund. Nevertheless, most **structured exit** investors target a comfortable range of **IRRs** based on reasonable expectations of the company's performance, and safeguard against the possibility of zero-return by providing for payments shortly after funding, though often after an **initial grace period**.[5] In all cases, you can calculate an estimated cost of capital to the company and a **return on investment** to the investor, which will be the same except for taxes. If the company grows faster than expected, the repayments will be made sooner and the return on investment will be higher. Thus, all **structured exits** have upside potential. All also have downside potential as most have no more than a **personal guarantee** to underwrite the risk.

Most founders will not be familiar with the concept of a **structured exit** and might not have a robust enough financial model to do the projections required. For some funders, this means that they have to help entrepreneurs build out a financial model to understand what is affordable for them. For any **scheduled repayment** this means asking questions like how recurrent are the revenues? Does the company sell once-off goods or services, do they sell subscriptions, or do they enter into long-term purchasing contracts? Does the company have impending capital needs?

As a funder, if you are worried about extracting cash from a founder when they need it most, i.e., when they are growing their company, it is important to stress this affordability factor. For companies that have a very low margin, it might be very difficult to make this type of deal affordable. For those with a healthy enough margin to make the model work, it still might be prudent

---

[3]Brian Mikulencak, Revenue-Based Financing for Impact Investing (draft available upon request).
[4]Brian Mikulencak, Revenue-Based Financing for Impact Investing (draft available upon request).
[5]Brian Mikulencak, Revenue-Based Financing for Impact Investing (draft available upon request).

to make sure there are covenants or triggers around profitability designed to make sure that the plan makes sense for both of you. Some options include triggering repayments through specific levels of EBITDA or net profitability or using a ratcheted **interest rate**, i.e., one that increases over time, to put less pressure on founders up front.

Comparing Your Options

See Table 12.1.

Table 12.1 Comparison of structured exits options

Title	More Debt Like			More Equity Like
	Revenue-based Financing (RBF)	Mezzanine Debt	Convertible RBF	Redeemable Equity
Description	Loan that is repaid as a percentage of future revenue or cash flows	Loan that is paid back with a fixed interest and has upside through kickers such as warrants or profit share	Loan that is repaid as a percentage of future revenues or cash flows with an option to convert to equity	Purchase of shares that can be redeemed at a pre-agreed multiple or mutually agreed price
AKA	Cash flow financing, royalty financing[a]	SME risk capital, venture debt	Revenue-based debt, demand dividends, variable dividend, revenue-based investing, subordinated variable payment debt, revenue-based mezzanine debt, shared earnings agreement, royalty financing[b]	Redeemable preferred stock, performance aligned redeemable convertible preferred stock, equity redemption, Indie.VC, variable VC, preference shares

(continued)

Table 12.1 (continued)

	More Debt Like			More Equity Like
Title	Revenue-based Financing (RBF)	Mezzanine Debt	Convertible RBF	Redeemable Equity
Your profile				
Business registration	Non-profit, for-profit, co-op, social enterprise	For-profit, co-op, social enterprise	For-profit, co-op, social enterprise	For-profit, co-op, social enterprise
Revenue Model	Can be seasonal and variable, must have revenues and high margins	May have some seasonality	Can have some seasonality or variability, must have existing revenue and high margins	Pre or post-revenue
Company Stage	Early-stage, growth, scaling or established	Early-stage, growth or scaling	Early-stage, growth or scaling	Concept, early-stage or growth
Business Growth Projections	Category pioneer, niche enterprise, dynamic enterprise, livelihood enterprise	High growth venture, category pioneer, niche enterprise	Category pioneer, niche enterprise, dynamic enterprise	High growth venture, category pioneer, niche enterprise
Your mission				
Embeddedness	Not especially relevant	If you have high mission embeddedness, you may want to seek out funders that are mission driven	If medium to high embeddedness, you should look for a mission aligned funder	
Track Record		Impact investors may look for an impact track record for later stage companies	Mission aligned funders will likely require an impact track record	

(continued)

Table 12.1 (continued)

Title	More Debt Like			More Equity Like
	Revenue-based Financing (RBF)	Mezzanine Debt	Convertible RBF	Redeemable Equity
Your funding needs				
Spend funding on	Working capital or growth capital over the short term	Working capital or growth capital over the medium term	Working capital or growth capital over the medium term	Proof of concept or growth capital over the medium to long term
Assets for Collateral	Historic revenues and may require personal surety	Some mix of physical assets and alternative types of collateral. Some funders may be willing to be completely unsecured	May require personal surety	None
Planned Payback	Internal cash flow generation	Internal cash flows for interest rate and cash kicker, if warrants are included then also a third party exit	Internal cash flow or future funding	
Ownership	No impact on ownership	If payback is interest plus a cash kicker, then it is not necessary to be willing to dilute ownership. Warrants will require willingness to dilute ownership	No effect on ownership unless convertibility is triggered	Willingness to give up ownership in short term, but potential for long term continued ownership of company or transition to employee ownership

(continued)

Table 12.1 (continued)

Title	More Debt Like			More Equity Like
	Revenue-based Financing (RBF)	Mezzanine Debt	Convertible RBF	Redeemable Equity
Funding in Future	Equity can be raised in future, but generally designed for companies planning to use debt and internal cash flow generation for future funding	Can work with both equity and debt funding in future	Equity can be raised in future, but generally designed for companies planning to use debt and internal cash flow generation for future funding	Equity can be raised in future, but generally designed for companies planning to use debt and internal cash flow generation for future funding
Funder Involvement	Generally financial downside focused, although may be interested in growth, which could result in quicker repayment. Low ongoing involvement based on covenants in the debt agreement	Both upside and downside focused. Will have ongoing involvement. Covenants will act as downside protection and voting rights and information rights may be used as upside involvement	Both upside and downside focused. Will have ongoing involvement. Covenants will act as downside protection and voting rights and information rights may be used as upside involvement	High involvement while shares outstanding including board seats, voting rights and information rights
Most likely funders	Non-Bank Financial Institution, Specialized Fund, Debt Fund, Mezzanine Fund	Non-bank Financial Institution, Debt Fund, Mezzanine Fund, Bank	Mezzanine Fund, Debt Fund, VC Fund, Specialized Fund, Non-Bank Financial Institution, Family Office	Angel Investor, Incubator, Accelerator, Family Office, Specialized Fund, VC Fund

[a]The term **royalty financing** is used quite often to describe revenue-based financing, even though it is technically its own type of financing. A royalty agreement acts like a scheduled percentage of revenue calculation, but only applies to a specific revenue stream such as an identified product or service. Examples of this are revenues derived from specific intellectual property (IP) assets, oil wells, and mines. It is particularly common in IP heavy industries such as movies, tv, music and healthcare. Although many types of structured exits have been called royalty financing in the past as shorthand, a true royalty agreement uses the associated IP as security for the agreement and would take ownership of that IP in the case of default
[b]See above

Part III

What If: You Want to Be Innovative with Grant Funding?

Acts of sharing and giving are human nature. Gifts of food, resources, shelter and support have existed from our earliest history and represent early forms of donations from one person to another. The ancient Greeks required tithing (giving 10% of your income) to the poor at times of religious importance like the Olympic Games. Despite this long history of the act of giving, it was only in the late twentieth century that we started to re-examine *how* individuals and institutions made donations as a force for change or good.

In this part of the book, we will hear from founders and funders using innovative types of **catalytic philanthropic capital** that blend the properties of **grants, debt** and **equity** to support founders' purpose-driven start-ups, small businesses and non-profit organizations.[1] Such structures are an important, but often underutilized part of the non-profit finance toolkit.

We'll start with **program related investments (PRIs)**, a tax-code based term for US foundations' non-traditional funding activities. In Chapter 13, we see how foundations can use a **PRI** in the form of a loan to support organizations aligned to their programmatic missions. Non-U.S.-based readers should know that while **PRIs** are a unique concept in the U.S., the strategic use of charitable capital is not limited to U.S. foundations. Any institution in the world with capital that does not require a "market rate" return can choose to use its assets strategically.

Also, in this part, we'll explore the concept of **guarantees** (Chapter 14), which help organizations access lower-cost **debt**; **recoverable grants** (Chapter 15), which are grants that can be converted into loans; **forgivable**

---

[1]For funders interested in blending capital at the fund level, there are some resources on the online companion.

loans (Chapter 16), which are loans that can be converted into grants; and finally, we'll look at **convertible grants** (Chapter 17) which are grants that can be converted into **equity**.

13

The Studio Museum in Harlem: Our Program Related Investments Journey

In this chapter, we will join Mary Schmidt Campbell on her **program related investment (PRI)** funding journey for The Studio Museum in Harlem, New York. Through The Studio Museum's story, we'll explore some of the common questions and misconceptions that persist about **PRIs**, in spite of their growing use in the U.S. For funders outside of the U.S., this chapter will hopefully serve as an introduction to how grantmaking institutions can think strategically about using their capital.

Just off Martin Luther Boulevard

The Studio Museum in Harlem site faces the dynamic and historic 125th street, just off of Martin Luther King Boulevard in New York City. It is the U.S.'s first accredited fine arts museum dedicated to artists of African descent. The historic site will soon be replaced by a new building designed by the architect of the Smithsonian National Museum of African American History and Culture in Washington, D.C., Sir David Adjaye. But this is the story of the site that has been the museum's home since 1977 and the funding that made it possible.[1]

The Studio Museum was founded in 1968 to recognize and honor artists of African descent and display their work. For its first

---

[1] Adapted from: *Investing for Social Gain: Reflections on Two Decades of Program-Related Investments (1991)* Ford Foundation.

© The Author(s), under exclusive license to Springer Nature Switzerland AG 2021
A. Patton Power, *Adventure Finance*,
https://doi.org/10.1007/978-3-030-72428-3_13

10 years, the museum rented loft space at 2033 Fifth Avenue in Harlem as its collection began to take shape.

When Mary Schimdt Campbell became director of the museum in 1977, one of her first priorities was to look for a new building. She believed having a permanent space was a key element to the establishment's quest to become an accredited fine arts museum. After a long search, the museum found a building nearby on West 125th Street. It was a five-story office structure, owned by a bank, that had plenty of space for the museum as well as commercial space for tenants. When the museum approached the bank, they signaled their willingness to donate the available space to a non-profit organization. Mary was overjoyed, "The location was excellent, it had earned-income potential, and it was going to be *ours.*"

Despite the advantages, the building had many issues. It was in poor condition and required over $1 million worth of renovations.

Charging Ahead

Mary was undeterred. She helped lead the museum's staff and board through a complex maze of federal regulations, tax law, budgeting, fundraising, construction and building management, which she termed "an intensive course in various aspects of non-profit management." Eventually, the museum was awarded an $800,000 federal Urban Development Action Grant (UDAG) that would provide long-term financing for the necessary capital improvements. The museum developed their first-ever capital raising campaign to cover the remaining $250,000 in construction costs.

The problem was, the UDAG funding would only be available once construction was completed, and The Studio Museum team knew fundraising would take time, so the organization faced an imminent financing gap for its building renovation project. Mary decided to approach the Ford Foundation for help. The foundation had been supportive of the project, providing a **grant** for Studio Museum to hire a property consultant to help in the search for the building. One of the principals at Ford recommended that Mary apply for a loan for the renovation project through the foundation's **PRI** office. Mary wasn't familiar with **PRIs**, so employees from the Ford Foundation's **PRI** office explained what they were and how they worked.

A PR What?

In the US, private foundations are required to disburse 5% of their **endowment** annually. They can do this either through traditional grantmaking, or through PRIs, which is the tax-code based term for any type of non-grant financial commitment made to advance a foundation's mission. The concept of PRIs in the U.S. tax code allows foundations to disburse capital in a wide variety of forms, including **debt, equity** and **guarantees**, to organizations that are furthering the foundation's programmatic goals. (In fact, U.S. foundations could use their PRI strategies to implement many of the financing structures discussed in this book.) Any returns on these investments are then recycled to make additional **grants** and **PRIs.**

The Ford Foundation has a special relationship with the **PRI**: The foundation effectively invented it. Ford pioneered the concept in 1968, and the following year, it was written into the U.S. tax code as an exception to the Tax Reform Act of 1969, which stipulates that private foundations must avoid investments that might jeopardize their ability to carry out their mission. According to the code, private foundations are allowed to make investments with higher than normal risk levels if the investments meet three criteria:

1. The primary purpose is to accomplish one or more of the foundation's exempt purposes.

2. Production of income or appreciation of property is not a significant purpose.

3. And, influencing legislation or taking part in political campaigns on behalf of candidates is not a purpose.[2,3]

For Mary and The Studio Museum, the funding that they needed was bridge financing to allow them to get the construction started, qualify for the government subsidies and begin a larger fundraising program to build a base of benefactors for the foundation. While the Ford Foundation planned to continue to be involved with the Museum as a patron going forward, this specific capital need, in size and in use, best fit into Ford's PRI program.

---

[2]IRS Website: https://www.irs.gov/charities-non-profits/private-foundations/program-related-invest ments.

[3]These rules do not apply to community foundations, which the IRS classifies as public charities, not private foundations.

A Collecting Museum

Mary spent several weeks with foundation employees preparing the necessary paperwork. The Studio Museum was eventually approved for $1.05 million, which would be loaned to the museum against the future UDAG and fundraising campaign capital. It also provided a $25,000 grant so the museum could hire a development director and a professional project manager to oversee the renovations.

The museum also received support from the City of New York, which stepped in to **guarantee** part of the PRI in case the museum's independent fundraising campaign failed.

The capital in hand, The Studio Museum, was able to move forward with renovations at 144 West 125th Street. Meanwhile, it successfully achieved its $250,000 fundraising campaign goal. Studio Museum was able to fully repay the Ford Foundation's PRI after successfully completing its renovations and securing the UDAG funds.

Mary looks back at The Studio Museum's journey in securing the 144 West 125th Street Building and says it was a "profound" moment for the organization, allowing the museum to evolve from being "a small center to a collecting museum with an archival function."

Today, The Studio Museum in Harlem is considered the world's leading visual and fine arts institution for artists of African descent. It is now headed by Thelma Golden who began her career as a Studio Museum intern in 1987. Under her leadership, the museum has become renowned as a global leader in the exhibition of contemporary art, as a center for innovative education and as a cultural anchor in the Harlem community.[4]

The Ford Foundation, meanwhile, has continued to expand its PRI program, investing over $700 million since its first PRI in 1968. It has also continued its support for the arts through **grants** and PRIs, becoming one of the largest funders of arts and creative expression in the U.S., with a projected spend of over $205 million in 2021.[5]

[4]The Studio Museum Harlem. (2019) Gagosian Quarterly, Spring 2019 Issue. Available at: https://gagosian.com/quarterly/2019/07/14/interview-thelma-golden-david-adjaye-studio-museum-harlem.
[5]Sixteen Major Donors and Foundations Commit Unprecedented $156 Million to Support Black, Latinx, Asian and Indigenous Arts Organizations. 24 September 2020: Available at: https://www.fordfoundation.org/the-latest/news/sixteen-major-donors-and-foundations-commit-unprecedented-156-million-to-support-black-latinx-asian-and-indigenous-arts-organizations/.

Is a PRI Right for You?

Funders

The concept of PRIs only appears in the U.S. tax code, where they count toward the requirement that U.S. foundations pay out 5% of their net assets each year to mission aligned causes. PRIs are not a **grant** and they are not a traditional investment; they are a legally distinct third option. PRIs can be used in virtually any type of financial vehicle as long as the underlying investment is aligned to the foundation's mission. In addition, financial return is not deemed a "significant purpose." They can be made directly into organizations or through intermediaries and can be made to both for-profit and non-profit entities. Common intermediaries include community development financing institutions (CDFIs), banks and impact investing funds.

PRIs have grown considerably in the past 20 years thanks to pioneering work done by early adopters such as the Ford, MacArthur, Annie E. Casey foundations and others.[6] Although **low interest loans** to non-profits for real estate development is still a common form of **PRI**, foundations have made PRIs by purchasing **equity** in early-stage equity investment funds and **social enterprises**, as well as **recoverable grants** (Chapter 15) and **forgivable loans** (Chapter 16). They have also been used as **guarantees** (Chapter 14).

To evaluate whether it is possible to make a **PRI**, you have to determine whether a prudent investor would make the same investment decision. You'll need to break this down in terms of the riskiness of the investment itself, the risk you are taking as an investor and the return that you are expecting. If the investment is too risky for a prudent investor, then you can justify using a PRI. If a prudent investor would invest, if you structure your own investment to take on more risk by sitting subordinated or junior and/or by requiring a lower return, then you may still be able to justify using a PRI.

Determining questions that you can ask include:

Is the social impact inherent in the business model such that impact will grow in line with the enterprise's growth? The impact needs to be sufficiently clear to align to the foundation's stated purpose.

Is it a first-time fund or is it a team working together for the first time? First time fund managers and inexperienced entrepreneurs are considered riskier

---

[6]This group plus the George Gund, Heron, David and Lucile Packard, Prudential and Rasmuson Foundations and the Meyer Memorial trust founded the Mission Investors Exchange in 2005, which is credited with expanding the understanding and use of PRIs and other innovative forms of grant making.

by most investors and thus, may not pass the prudent investor test, meaning that a **PRI** could be suitable.

Is there enough data to give us confidence that we can get a risk-adjusted market-rate return? If so, it may be hard to argue for the use of a **PRI**—a traditional investment out of the endowment may be more suitable.

Legal guidance in the form of a **PRI** opinion from your internal or external council is incredibly important for funders making their first **PRIs** or making **PRIs** into non-standard structures or enterprises, like **equity**, but contrary to popular belief, a letter ruling from the IRS is rare and generally not needed. Foundations can manage their **PRIs** from inside their **grant** portfolio or from their **endowment**. If managed in the **endowment**, the **PRI** can be managed as an **asset class** with a **return on capital hurdle** that is not a **market-rate** return.

Another consideration is expectations around **impact measurement and management (IMM)**. Generally, donors have more complex **IMM** requirements than investors. Also, established, large non-profits that foundations are used to engaging with will have more robust **IMM** systems in place. Funders will need to recognize that there might be differences in impact reporting when they are working with smaller ventures and in an investee-investor relationship.

PRIs are a very specific tool that has been used in very specific instances. As Tracy Karty from the Annie E. Casey Foundation observes, "It is the flexibility of the tool that really creates endless possibilities. What it does for philanthropy is it allows us to think creatively about how we do risk, how we catalyze capital to flow into communities, to support people of color, to address some of these gaps that we see in the financial system. And I think that flexibility is kind of the thing that is most exciting about PRIs as a construct. It is also often the thing that is the hardest to grasp."

Finally, how do PRIs differ from Mission Related Investments (MRIs)? **MRI** is not a legal term but describes an investment that integrates mission alignment into the investment decision-making process. **Impact Investment** is often used interchangeably with MRI. MRIs are a component of the foundation's overall endowment and investment strategy and must comply with the state and federal prudence requirements applicable to a foundation's investing activities generally. They are unique in that the degree of mission alignment becomes an essential factor in the prudence analysis, allowing for, in some cases, a lower financial return objective than for a non-mission aligned endowment investment. In many cases, **MRIs** in a foundation portfolio will look exactly like investments you would find in any portfolio;

however, the diligence in selecting those investments will have an additional impact lens.[7]

Tax Considerations

PRIs are required to be reported on the 990-PF IRS form filed annually by public charities and private foundations. The U.S. Internal Revenues Service (IRS) uses this form to assess compliance with the Internal Revenue Code. Both forms list organization assets, receipts, expenditures, **grants, PRIs** and compensation of officers.[8]

If a private foundation claimsan investment as a **PRI** on its annual IRS Form 990-PF, it can include the amount in its annual 5% required charitable distribution in the year. However, the foundation's payout requirement for the year in which the investment is repaid is increased by the amount of the principal recovered.[9] This means that PRI principal repayments (not including capital gains, **dividends**, or interest) count as a "negative distribution" against payout requirements to be applied to the tax year in which the repayment is received.[10] **PRIs** are also excluded from the foundation's assets on which the 5% required distribution is calculated. Interest, dividends and capital appreciation count as regular income to be included in the calculation of Excise Tax on Net Investment Income, and **PRIs** generally are not subject to the Unrelated Business Income Tax (UBIT) by being "substantially related" to a foundation's exempt purposes. For details on how to report PRI income, appreciation and asset value on the annually required tax form 990-PF, refer to the IRS's Instructions for Form 990-PF68 and search "program-related investment."[11]

Technically, **PRIs** could "incidentally" make **market-rate** returns as the legal requirements do not explicitly stipulate below-market returns. In fact, the tax code states that a significant return does not in itself disqualify an investment as a **PRI**. "If an investment incidentally produces significant

---

[7]Briand, P. & Godeke, S. (2020) *Impact Investing Handbook: An Implementation Guide for Practitioners*. Rockefeller Philanthropy Advisors.

[8]Emerson, J. (2003) Where Money Meets Mission: Breaking Down the Firewall Between Foundation Investments and Programming. *Stanford Social Innovation Review* (Summer 2003).

[9]Emerson, J. (2003) Where Money Meets Mission: Breaking Down the Firewall Between Foundation Investments and Programming. *Stanford Social Innovation Review* (Summer 2003).

[10]The amount of a loan guarantee is not an eligible distribution and therefore does not count in a private foundation's 5% payout requirement.

[11]Mintz, J. & Ziegler, C. (2013) *Mission-Related Investing: Legal and Policy Issues to Consider Before Investing*. MacArthur Foundation.

income or capital appreciation, this is not, in the absence of other factors, conclusive evidence that a significant purpose is the production of income or the appreciation of property.[12]" However, many foundations have interpreted the IRS rules to mean that they are not permitted to achieve market or near-market returns with their **PRIs**, and they therefore only classify below market-rate mission investments as **PRIs**.[13]

[12]IRS   Website: https://www.irs.gov/charities-non-profits/private-foundations/program-related-investments.

[13]Cooch, S. & Kramer, M. (2007) *Compounding Impact: Mission Investing by U.S. Foundations*. FSG Social Impact Advisors.

14

Riders for Health: Our Debt Guarantee Journey

In this chapter, we are going to jump between San Francisco, The Gambia and the UK to learn from Riders for Health's journey to a debt **guarantee**. In the last chapter, we looked at innovative ways **grant** funders can think about using **grant capital** strategically, and back in Chapter 4, we discussed the importance of **collateral** and how to use **customer orders** and **invoices** as **collateral** to access **debt financing**. In this case, Andrea and Barry Coleman from Riders for Health use a debt **guarantee** from a foundation to access debt and reduce their **cost of capital**.

Abandoned Vehicles and Long Walks to Clinics

In many parts of Africa, health interventions such as vaccines, disease treatment and public health services are out of reach for millions of people. This results in lower life expectancy and millions of preventable deaths. For rural populations, one of the key barriers to accessing healthcare is lack of transportation: Without reliable means to transport, medicine, vaccines and equipment, lifesaving treatments and interventions can't get to where they're needed most. It's a crucial missing link in the delivery supply chain.

Social entrepreneurs Andrea and Barry Coleman saw this issue first-hand as they traveled around Africa as motorcycle adventurers. In many of the African countries the British couple visited, Andrea and Barry were shocked by what they encountered: healthcare workers walking 20 km or more each

© The Author(s), under exclusive license to Springer Nature
Switzerland AG 2021
A. Patton Power, *Adventure Finance*,
https://doi.org/10.1007/978-3-030-72428-3_14

day in order to reach the communities they served, broken vehicles donated by charities and aid programs, abandoned on the side of the road when they could have easily been put back into service with minor repairs and maintenance. So, in 1996, the Colemans harnessed their knowledge of motorcycles to address the lack of reliable, affordable transportation for healthcare workers and goods and founded Riders for Health.

The Colemans took a bold step to get their idea off the ground: They took out a new mortgage on their home. This gave them the capital to build a Transport Resource Management (TRM) system that would underpin Riders' solution for low-resource healthcare systems. The TRM places vehicles on preventative maintenance schedules to eliminate breakdowns, reduce costs and improve vehicle efficiency, keeping the overall fleet in good working condition for the duration of its intended mechanical lifetime.

Over time, Riders would grow to manage healthcare delivery fleets in seven African countries and go on to win numerous social enterprise awards and accolades.

But first, we go back to the start of Riders' journey in The Gambia.

Managing Motorcycles and Ambulances in the Gambia

Riders for Health's first market was The Gambia, where it partnered with the Ministry of Health and Social Welfare to manage their vehicle fleet in 2002. The non-profit organization's early work was funded with **grants** from the Skoll Foundation and other foundations.

After seven years managing The Gambian fleet, Riders saw an opportunity for a new approach to fleet management—one that would potentially improve its own financial sustainability while helping its government customers save on costs. Instead of just managing the maintenance schedules of the vehicles, Riders would manage the fleets themselves. They called this Transport Asset Management (TAM), and in 2008, they pitched the idea of a national TAM vehicle-leasing program to The Gambia's Ministry of Health. Riders for Health would replace the government's aging healthcare fleet with entirely new vehicles, including ambulances, trekking vehicles and motorcycles, and the government would lease the vehicles directly from Riders, saving the state the outright expense of buying the fleet with taxpayers' money.

The Gambian government was intrigued by the idea. After all, it would give the government access to an entire fleet of reliable, well-maintained vehicles that would be able to deliver complete healthcare services to the entire nation, including those who lived in the most remote communities—all at a reasonable cost. With a verbal agreement from the government, Riders for Health set out to raise the $3.5 million it needed to buy the fleet.

As a **non-profit**, Riders knew that getting access to this amount of cash for a capital investment would be difficult and doing it in a small country like The Gambia would create additional complexity. The Skoll Foundation, which had given Riders a **grant** to create a business plan and financial modeling for its new asset ownership approach, supported the organization's new strategy. Andrea asked Skoll's Edward Diener, then the General Counsel for the foundation, if Skoll would loan Riders the money for the fleet.

Edward had a different idea. Why not approach one of The Gambian banks for the loan and have the foundation act as a **guarantor**? This way, in the future, Riders would be able to use local capital to fund the acquisition of assets.

West Coast Guarantee for West African Cash

Edward traveled to The Gambia to get a better sense of how feasible that approach would be. Edward had joined the Riders' team in their initial conversations with lenders, including local Gambian banks, an Islamic Bank and a social enterprise bank. None were able to extend the financing due to internal or external constraints. Some didn't understand a non-profit having a business model that could support **debt financing**. Several of The Gambian banks were keen to participate, but the Central Bank in The Gambia wouldn't allow them to lend that much capital because their asset base wasn't big enough. In essence, the size of the loan Riders needed was just too large.

Despite not yet finding a lending partner on the trip, when Edward returned to the U.S., he proposed to the board that Skoll provide the **guarantee** as a **"program-related investment (PRI)"**.[1] He also advocated that the deal be structured in a way that eliminated the need for the guarantee over time. "The financial model showed that after five years, which is the normal fleet life, Riders' would have enough cash for a 20% down payment on the next fleet," explained Edward. "So when they needed to access the **debt** to purchase the second fleet, then we would offer a smaller guarantee. The idea was that by the time they got to the third fleet, they'd be able to pay for nearly half of it themselves, so they wouldn't need a guarantee to access the **debt financing** at all."

---

[1]Program related investments were discussed in Chapter 17.

While this was happening, the Riders' team approached the Guaranty Trust Bank (GTBank), a Nigerian bank with an extensive network across West Africa and with which Riders had a relationship. GTBank offered Riders the loan... at a 27% annual **interest rate**. Andrea laughingly recalls how ludicrous the offer sounded to both her and Edward. Nevertheless, they continued conversations with GTBank to see if they could reduce the cost of the loan.

Andrea says they made two key arguments: that the loan would benefit the bank's image because the entire population of The Gambia would know that the bank was supporting a social initiative, and that the transaction would enable the bank to learn about vehicle leasing and build that capacity.

GTBank agreed to reconsider the terms, but it would first require a signed contract from The Gambian Health Ministry to prove Riders' revenue stream.

Ink on the Paper

It took considerable work on behalf of the Riders team to finalize the contract, as the TAM vehicle-leasing system was a new and untested concept for the Ministry. Up to that point, the Ministry had covered its upfront fleet and transportation costs through donated vehicles, only contracting Riders for the management of those donated vehicles. So actually securing the agreement for the total cost of the system in a long-term contract took a considerable number of discussions at a high level.

Even with The Gambia's signed contract, six months passed and the loan from GTBank was still unresolved. Edward couldn't understand what was causing the delay, so he boarded a plane and headed back to The Gambia where he worked with GTBank's finance director to rewrite the loan's term sheet and met with The Gambia's health ministry officials. He even appeared on local television with the Minister of Health explaining that because of this deal, every citizen of The Gambia would have access to healthcare. Still, it wasn't until Edward's final day, when a senior manager from GTBank flew into town from Nigeria, that they officially closed the deal.

In the end, GTBank offered a 3% **interest rate** on condition that Skoll would "fund" the **guarantee** upfront by depositing the money into GTBank's account in The Gambia. That way, if Riders for Health **defaulted** on its loan, the bank could count on the money Skoll deposited. This arrangement mitigated the bank's risk that The Gambian government might not honor its commitment to pay for the transportation services and leave Riders unable to service the loan. Riders and Skoll agreed to the terms. Riders also agreed to pay an additional 5% to Skoll to cover the **foreign exchange losses** on the original loan. Finally, in 2009, Riders for Health purchased the vehicles for The Gambian healthcare fleet.

Rolling Forward

Riders' roll-out of the fleet didn't immediately go as planned. The Gambia's Ministry of Health didn't have the money in the first year to lease the entire fleet. Historically, the government had relied on donated vehicles, so building the cost of leasing the vehicles into the annual budget was a systemic shift. But after Riders' first year in operation, that changed. The Ministry of Health's statistics department started reporting significant improvements in the number of women giving birth in health centers, the national immunization rate, and other vital health statistics. It was a turning point, because the health impact data proved the utility and value of the program at scale and created a sense of political urgency for the government to sustain it. The Gambian government thus rearranged its finances to fund the program from general tax revenue instead of relying on money from donors.

Andrea is quick to acknowledge how significant GTBank's **loan** and Skoll's **guarantee** were for Riders' operations. When Riders began looking for new fleet financing several years later, banks engaged in a bidding war to extend the organization a new loan. It was a stark contrast from navigating rejection after rejection or exorbitantly priced offers. "They could see that it worked," remarked Andrea. And it was "a really good PR exercise for healthcare reaching rural communities."

By the time the first Gambian fleet needed to be replaced in 2016, Riders was able to secure the financing at a 1.7% **interest rate** without a **guarantee**.

The other benefit of the original round of financing was that it gave Riders an asset lease financing model that could be replicated in other countries.

Today, Riders operates over 1,400 vehicles that provide ambulance services and transport medicines, vaccines and healthcare workers throughout seven African countries. The organization has yet to replicate its TAM model, but it is working to roll it out to several other countries, including Nigeria and Lesotho. In early 2020, the government of The Gambia even hosted the Lesotho Deputy Health Minister in The Gambia for conversations about the program.

Andrea laments that in spite of "the amount of evidence that we're able to give, people still won't put that emphasis on transport" in their health-care system investments. But, she adds, "We have a model, and we'll keep persisting and trying to get Ministries of Health to accept it."

The Skoll Foundation, meanwhile, recovered most of the money it had put up for the guarantee by repatriating the money kept at GTBank and the 5% payments from Riders, although significant **depreciation** of The Gambian Dalasi resulted in some losses. From the foundation's perspective, the real value of the investment was the systemic change at The Gambia's Ministry of Health in how it funded its healthcare transportation infrastructure and proved Riders' asset leasing model for replication.

When asked if they would change anything about the deal, Andrea says that she would have asked for more money upfront to create a more robust monitoring and evaluation system. Edward says he wishes he recognized earlier the limitations of GTBank in structuring the deal because he would have played a more active role in pushing it through.

Is a Guarantee Right for You?

Founder

Using a **guarantee** is very similar to, say, relying on a friend or relative to co-sign an apartment rental agreement. If you're a young person without a history of paying rent, a landlord might not be willing to rent to you because they don't know whether you'll be able to pay. But when someone with a longer **credit history** steps forward and promises that you'll pay your rent if you can't, that reduces the landlord's risk. Getting a guarantor for your **debt** basically has the same risk mitigating effect on lenders and can help you to access debt capital and/or borrow at a much lower **interest rate**. The catch is that you need to have a **guarantor** that has a strong enough reputation or a dedicated amount of cash to set aside on your behalf.

There are two ways **guarantees** can be set up: **"funded,"** which means the guarantor places some or all of the amount into an account that can be accessed by the lender, (as Skoll did on Riders for Health's behalf); and **"unfunded,"** which is really more of a pledge that the loan is guaranteed.

With **funded guarantees**, there are sometimes additional fees and costs to consider. For example, Skoll Foundation ended up taking on some **currency risk** with its **funded guarantee** to Riders for Health, as well as the risk that Riders would not repay the loan. This resulted in a small financial loss, despite the 5% payments that Riders for Health made to the foundation to cover the **foreign exchange losses**.

With an **unfunded guarantee**, its success depends on the lenders' trust in the guarantor. If the lender doesn't believe the guarantor will pay if you **default**, they're unlikely to accept the guarantee. As a founder, looking for large funders with significant balance sheets will give you the best odds of securing a usable **unfunded guarantee**.

The cost of a **guarantee** will vary depending on the provider. Some foundations use guarantees as part of their philanthropic strategy and might offer them at no cost or relatively inexpensively. **Development Finance Institutions** might offer subsidized guarantees as part of their development programs, as the U.S. International Development Finance Corporation (DFC) does. Banks also offer commercial guarantees, but they are usually based on market rates. As a founder, you'll need to evaluate whether the cost of the guarantee and the amount of **due diligence** required by the **guarantor** is worth the effort.

Funder

Years ago, I was on a panel at an impact investing conference and one of my fellow panelists made the statement that **guarantees** were the *"single most under-utilized tool"* in a foundation's financing toolkit. That comment has stayed with me as I work with early-stage organizations as they struggle to access **debt** funding in local currencies.

There are several legitimate reasons that **guarantees** are under-utilized at the individual deal level. Firstly, they add cost, stakeholders and complexity to a transaction. We can see this in the Riders' case where Edward spent considerable time negotiating the **loan**. Additionally, Skoll was willing to bear the **currency risk** depositing the entire amount of the loan into a Gambian account. This level of involvement and capital at risk is not possible for most funders. Complexity and cost are two of the reasons that many funders prefer to offer fund level guarantees, which allow fund managers to use a guarantee to their risk appetite or decrease the fund's cost of capital.

Secondly, there is a concern that they create perverse incentives for borrowers i.e., knowing that the loan is guaranteed, the borrowers are less incentivized to pay it back. One way to mitigate this is to ensure that the **guarantee** is designed with an eye to future funding. In Riders' case, the guarantee was designed to build their **credit history** and allow them to access local capital in the future, so they were incentivized to be a responsible borrower and make timely payments.

Thirdly, there is confusion about whether **guarantees** are addressing **real** or **perceived risk**. **Real risks**, such as **currency risk, political risk, early-stage risk**, are risks that we can build into our financial models and can use to price capital accordingly. **Perceived risks** are risks that are based on a lack of data. Skoll saw their **guarantee** for Riders' as addressing the **perceived risk** of the banks around lending to a **non-profit**. Once the banks saw that Riders' **revenue model** was stable and sustainable, the belief was that they would adjust their risk models to accommodate them. **Guarantees** themselves do not address real, underlying risks of a company. Funders using **guarantees** to lower the cost of capital for companies that have a high real risk profile, as opposed to perceived, must be willing to bear the cost of **default**.

As a funder, you'll need to evaluate what type of **guarantee** works for your organization's balance sheet and risk profile. If you are a smaller organization, you may need to consider creating a guarantee fund that is leveraged to provide guarantees. If you are a large funder who is keen to increase access and reduce the cost of **debt** for early-stage and small businesses, you may also have the option of creating an **unfunded guarantee** program that leverages your balance sheet. Just like with any investment, you'll need to evaluate what kind of guarantees you want to make, what the cost of the guarantee will be to the borrower, and how you will source deals and perform **due diligence** to assess the risk.

Tracey Karty explains the Annie E. Casey Foundation's approach to **guarantees**: "All of our guarantees are unfunded. They are contingent liabilities on the balance sheet. We maintain a kind of loss, a paper reserve, so that we will mark down our assets as a result. There are two ways we have structured these guarantees. One way is that if it is called, it goes out as a charitable distribution and then it is done. Another way is to make it recoverable. So if we guarantee a loan for an affordable housing developer, there is an asset there. If they **default** on the payments to the bank, the foundation can step in, make the bank whole and then have a recoverability clause with the bank. If there are additional payments down the line from the developer then the foundation can recover them. The agreement then shows up on the foundation's balance sheet as a PRI loan that we are tracking and expecting repayment on."

From a U.S. tax perspective, it is important to note that if a foundation is using a guarantee as a **PRI**, it does not count as distribution until it is actually disbursed to cover defaults.

15

Upaya Social Ventures: Our Recoverable Grant Journey

Next, we are going to look at a versatile tool called a **recoverable grant**, through the journey of Upaya Social Ventures. A **recoverable grant** is a grant that is repaid to funders depending on the success of the project. **Recoverable grants** can be used globally by foundations, governments and other grantmaking organizations to support non-profit organizations with flexible, low-cost capital.

The Power of Stable Jobs and Dependable Wages

Sachi Shenoy, Sriram Gutta and Steve Schwartz founded Upaya Social Ventures to create dignified and meaningful jobs for India's poorest of the poor. The founders built the Seattle and Bangalore-based non-profit around the idea that stable jobs offering fair and dependable wages are key to breaking the cycle of poverty. The name Upaya, Sanskrit for "skillful means or method that helps someone to realize a goal," underscores the organization's mission, which it fulfills by investing seed capital to help India's small businesses grow.

Since launching in 2010, Upaya has made mostly **equity** investments in 23 businesses in India, which have in turn created more than 17,000 permanent, dignified jobs. Upaya's seed funding has facilitated this growth in part by enabling its portfolio businesses to attract **follow-on investment** to the

A. Patton Power, *Adventure Finance*, https://doi.org/10.1007/978-3-030-72428-3_15

tune of 4 × Upaya's own invested capital. Upaya has successfully exited three of its investments to date.

But Upaya itself was caught in a bit of a growth capital conundrum of its own for years. The organization had a rich **pipeline** of viable, early-stage companies needing seed capital, but it lacked the capital to invest in many of these promising businesses. As a non-profit, Upaya had to secure **grants** that it could then invest as **patient capital**. Raising **grants** for its own funding—and hence, not needing to generate **market-rate returns** for its funders—ensured that Upaya could make risky bets on early-stage businesses, and also extend the technical advisory that these businesses often need. The organization had successfully raised $600,000 in **grants**, but they knew that the demand in their **pipeline** far outstripped their supply of capital.

A Recoverable Experiment

In 2015, Upaya came across a private philanthropic initiative called Open Road Alliance that was experimentingwith **recoverable grants**,[1] which are **grants** that are repaid to the funder if the grantee achieves certain pre-agreed financial outcomes.[2] Repayment terms are customizable, depending on the funder and grantee's needs.

Sachi reached out to one of Upaya's founding board members, Kate Cochran, to brainstorm how to use this type of capital to support Upaya's own growth. In their discussions, both women agreed that raising **recoverable grants** might give them access to a greater pool of flexible capital that they could use to increase the number of investments they could make to promising entrepreneurs. So they applied and were accepted for a $25,000 **recoverable grant** from Open Road Alliance. This was followed by two more **recoverable grants** from funders in 2017.

While **recoverable grants** were game-changing for how Upaya financed its investment activities, its early **recoverable grants** were each tied to specific investments, meaning that for each **grant** Upaya secured, it invested in one new business. Kate wondered whether Upaya could instead pool a group of **recoverable grants** into a kind of fund?

---

[1]These agreements can also be called **reimbursable grants** and confusingly, some funders call these **convertible grants** (which are covered in Chapter 17). Ideally, the language around these agreements will standardize as they become more commonplace.

[2]Social milestones can also be used with recoverable grants. We'll discuss how to do this in Chapter 22.

From Experiment to Fund

Over a period of 11 months, Upaya began reaching out to foundations interested in **impact investing**, but which hadn't yet made any investments. Sachi, Kate and the Upaya team pitched them a **recoverable grant** fund as a way for foundations to get their feet wet without getting too far outside of their traditional grantmaking comfort zone. The organization managed to raise $1 million for its pooled **recoverable grant** fund by the end of 2018. Investors in the fund include the 3rd Creek Foundation, Chintu Gudiya Foundation, Galloway Family Foundation, Vibrant Village Foundation, the Norwegian Interhands Foundation and the Delta Fund.

The fund is structured so that Upaya can draw down $50,000 at a time, as it approves investments. It expects to make 20 investments through the fund over five years. By pooling foundations' capital, Upaya is spreading **repayment risk** across the entire group of investors and also increasing the chance of a **portfolio-level return**. **Grant** capital will be repaid as Upaya **exits** its investments; additional returns will be paid out once all of the capital has been repaid by Upaya's portfolio companies in year 10. How much donors get back will of course depend on how much Upaya recoups. Upaya has committed to repaying donors proportionately, based on how much each donor committed to the fund, up to a maximum annual return of 5%. Until the 10-year mark, however, Upaya can reinvest any upside it makes into its portfolio companies, helping them to achieve greater job growth and impact.

During the fundraising process, Kate and Sachi fielded a number of questions from foundations interested in Upaya's social thesis, but curious to know why traditional **equity** or **debt** capital was not appropriate for its fund. They explained that Upaya purposefully makes below **market-rate investments in** enterprises that are creating jobs for the poorest of the poor in India; **recoverable grants** enable Upaya to be flexible and patient with their **equity** investments, which in turn enable companies to prioritize the creation of good jobs. To ensure that Upaya could have maximum impact with its fund, they raised an additional $1 million to defray operating expenses related to sourcing, selecting and supporting its portfolio companies.

The first two investments from Upaya's **recoverable grant** fund were in FreshR, a tech-enabled platform for meat farmers, and Laymen Agro, a dairy and produce distribution platform. Upaya was introduced to the two companies through its 2018 **accelerator** program for Indian agri businesses. They were impressed by the companies' mission to create dignified jobs and drastically improve incomes and livelihoods for people living in extreme poverty. Going forward, Upaya also intends to target businesses in industries like waste management, skill-building and rural manufacturing. In all, the organization believes the $1 million it will invest through its fund will translate to 50,000 jobs created.

"What is exciting about this **recoverable grant** pool," says Sachi, "is that we are building on traditional philanthropy, creating additional innovative tools to help plug gaps in market-based economies, and benefit those who may otherwise be left behind."

Venturing Below 0%

For Upaya, accessing **recoverable grants** allows them to make investments in promising entrepreneurs who are creating dignified jobs in India. Their donors expect to be repaid their capital plus a small return only if Upaya is able to successfully **exit** these investments. In order to offset the costs of distributing and managing these investments, Upaya raised a traditional **grant** alongside the **recoverable grant**. But what if you want to combine these and use a **recoverable grant** to make risky **loans** to impactful enterprises and cover the cost of making and managing those loans? In other words, what if you want to design a **recoverable grant** where funders are promised less than their **principal** back? Ted Levinson from Beneficial Returns has done just that with his latest fund called the Reciprocity Fund.

At Beneficial Returns, Ted has used **recoverable grants** similarly to Upaya, as a way to access low cost, flexible capital. He uses the **recoverable grant** capital that he raises to lend to social **enterprises** at **below market rates**. He targets a 2% **return** for his donors. This strategy allows him to work with **social enterprises** that would not be able to support **market-rate returns** and also to cover the costs of managing the fund.

In 2019, Ted was approached by a funder asking why he didn't fund **social enterprises** that support indigenous communities in the US. Ted told him that their current model wouldn't work for these enterprises due to their remoteness, language barriers, the very small size of these enterprises and their willingness and ability to absorb **debt**. Even though Beneficial Returns' 2% return target allowed them to provide below **market-rate loans**, Ted knew that effectively reaching **social enterprises** in indigenous communities would require even more flexible capital.

So together with the donor, Ted designed a new fund that would be appropriate. The funder made a $500,000 commitment over seven years and Beneficial Returns promised to pay back all principal payments that were received during that time. The **interest payments** go to Beneficial Returns to cover the cost of distributing and managing the loans. This allows Beneficial Returns to do much smaller, riskier loans to projects that require significantly more time and effort to reach.

Are Recoverable Grants Right for You?

A **recoverable grant** should be done from a non-profit entity to a non-profit entity and the repayment should be at the discretion of the recipient, based on mutually agreed financial milestones. **Grant** making funders may choose to make **recoverable grants** to for-profit **social enterprises** when the odds of repayment are low or there is a need for subsidized capital, but they must be cognizant of the accounting and tax considerations discussed in Chapter 18.

Before coming to an agreement on a **recoverable grant**, it is critical that both funders and founders are on the same page with regard to what is expected in terms of repayment. The terms of the repayment can be agreed in a **side letter** to the contract or in the contract itself.

Just as importantly, a **recoverable grant** should be a cultural fit for the funder and the founder. Funders should be in a position to assume that this is a very risky investment that may or may not be returned. Funders should also not be expecting **market-rate returns** for this type of investment if it is repaid.

Founders

Recoverable grants can be a great option for founders who need timely **bridging capital**, low risk **proof-of-concept** capital, the opportunity to build a **credit history** or **flexible capital** to on-lend or invest.

As **non-profit** founders, you can often face funding gaps in between large projects or prior to the start of large projects or the fulfillment of donor commitments. This is similar to for-profit founders' need for **working capital**. Timely capital to help bridge these gaps can be critical for the continuity of your organization and the achievement of social objectives. Structuring this funding as a **recoverable grant** gives you breathing room and only requires repayment if the additional funding is secured. It can also be structured as a **forgivable loan**, as we discuss in the next chapter.

As an organization trying to establish your **creditworthiness** in the market, a track record of repaying a **recoverable grant** can build trust in your ability to take on more traditional **debt**. In addition to a public track record, it can help to build the internal systems necessary to interact with traditional lenders.

Recoverable grants are also well suited to enterprises that are still in a **proof-of-concept** stage or are testing an early-stage product or building out a new market. In these situations, **risk capital** will inevitably be scarce even though the potential social or environmental benefits may be so great that they merit high levels of **subsidies** before there is **market traction**. These circumstances are often very high risk, where booking a loan would likely result in a loss, yet where there is a possibility that the enterprise may become financially sustainable.[3] Similarly, companies that are operating in a market that just doesn't lend itself to market-rate returns may see **recoverable grants** as a necessary part of their **capital structure**.

Recoverable grants may be most relevant to non-profit organizations that wish to on-lend to non-profits and **social enterprises**, like Beneficial Returns, or to invest **equity** in early-stage social enterprises, like Upaya.

Just as with any external capital that you take on, you'll need to make sure that it aligns with your mission as an organization. Even **recoverable grants** require a balancing of financial returns and impact priorities. For instance, Upaya has been seen, until now, as a charitable organization that prioritizes job creation over financial returns. Yet, for these new funders, they'll have to keep managing that balance of impact and financial returns.

Funders

For philanthropic funders who are interested in recycling their capital, this mechanism provides an opportunity to do so. In jurisdictions where **recoverable grants** are established, this can be a relatively simple way to step into the **impact investing** field. It can be less complicated than **equity** investing and can be done with current non-profit partners. As discussed in this chapter, this funding should be treated as high-risk and the terms of repayment should be clearly articulated in the agreements or side letters signed with founders.

Additionally, **recoverable grants** allow funders to broaden their financial returns spectrum. Historically, the conversations around financial returns for impact were split between the assumption of negative 100% return for a traditional **grant** to 0% + return for any impact investment. This leaves the entire 0%–100% return spectrum without meaningful strategic options. Although many **recoverable grants** stipulate a 0% + return (i.e., **principal**

[3] Armeni, A. & Ferreyra De Bone, M. (2017) Innovations in Financing Structures for Impact Enterprises: Spotlight on Latin America. Transform Finance. Available at: https://transformfinance.org/briefings/2017/9/1/innovations-in-financing-structures.

paid back plus a return), there is significant scope for funders to explore the possibility of structuring contracts that specifically fall into this 0%–100% return spectrum. As we saw with Beneficial Returns, it is possible to design a **recoverable grant** where only a portion of the principal will be recovered.

A lack of legal templates and accounting guidance has been an issue for some funders and founders as some legal counsel has been unsure of how to draft **recoverable grant** agreements and companies have been unsure of how to account for the capital raised. The team at Prime Coalition found this out when they were fundraising for their Prime Impact Fund, which was created to fund early-stage, climate-focused technology companies that would not otherwise be funded by traditional markets. In 2020, Prime Impact Fund raised $50 million in **catalytic capital**. This capital includes traditional **grants, recoverable grants, program related investments (PRIs)** and **mission related investments (MRIs)**. Prime Impact Fund uses the flexibility of **recoverable grant** agreements from its investors to support companies that would be considered too risky by conventional investors.

Prime accepts **recoverable grants** in one of two ways. The first is through a **recoverable grant** agreement, signed by Prime and the **donor advised fund (DAF)** sponsor. The second is done using a **side letter**[4] directly between Prime and the donor after they issue a traditional **grant**. Both the agreement and the side letter specify that, in the event that Prime earns a **return on investment** in the fund, they will return capital to the funders on a **pro rata** basis at a rate equivalent to 1–15% per annum return. The return rate is flexible in order to allow participation from foundations or other philanthropic entities with internally set limitations on the amount of return they can earn on their **impact investing** portfolio. The most likely scenario is that returns will be much lower than 15%, but they were capped at that level to reflect the high-risk, high-reward nature of the underlying investments that Prime is making. As we've discussed in other parts of the book, with early-stage **equity** investments, there is the possibility that they will create exceptionally high returns for investors and an equal possibility that they will fail completely.

Finally, when you are evaluating **recoverable grants**, you'll also need to weigh up the costs and benefits in relation to a **loan**. We'll discuss this more in Chapter 18.

---

[4]A letter that sits outside of the main contract that contains additional terms of the agreement.

16

IkamvaYouth: Our Forgivable Loan Journey

In the last chapter, Upaya used **recoverable grants** (grants that convert to loans), to drive affordable capital to Indian entrepreneurs. In this chapter, we head to South Africa to see how funders can use **forgivable loans** (loans that convert to grants), to support non-profits and **social enterprises**.

Two Different Worlds

Joy Olivier and Makhosi Gogwana founded the education non-profit Ikam-vaYouth after discovering their mutual passion for equitable education as researchers at the Human Sciences Research Council (HSRC) in Cape Town. While working together on an education research project, the two shared with one another their own experiences with South Africa's education system. They realized that the divergence of their own schooling experiences epitomized the painful legacy of South Africa's decades-long era of racist segregation, apartheid[1]: Joy went to a privileged school in Pietermaritzburg, in the province of KwaZulu-Natal; Makhosi went to a poor school in the black township of Khayelitsha in the Western Cape. Joy had access to all of the resources and information that she needed to excel in her studies and to go

---

[1]Apartheid is an Afrikaans word meaning "separateness," or "the state of being apart." It refers to the legal system of racial segregation put in place by the National Party in South Africa from 1948 to 1994.

© The Author(s), under exclusive license to Springer Nature
Switzerland AG 2021
A. Patton Power, *Adventure Finance*,
https://doi.org/10.1007/978-3-030-72428-3_16

on to access tertiary education; Makhosi lacked access to basic school materials, outside help, and even the consistent presence of teachers, as they didn't always show up for work. His experience enrolling at University was tough; although he had managed to access a bursary (scholarship), he didn't have any information or support in figuring out what to study.

The statistics Joy and Makhosi were researching painted a depressing picture of the impact that racial segregation and oppression had on education in the country: Only half of South African children enrolled in Grade 1 make it to their final year of high school and, of those, only a third gain admission to tertiary education institutions. Essentially, more than half a million children fall out of South Africa's education system every year. Almost all of the tiny fraction of matriculants (the final year of high school in South Africa) with grades ensuring eligibility for Science and Mathematics at tertiary level come from privileged, well-resourced schools.

Joy and Makhosi decided they needed to do something to change the fate of South Africa's poor, black and mixed-race students. What started as a weekend gig as high school tutors hanging out in public libraries quickly grew as the learners enrolled made significant academic gains and went on to access tertiary education. These students transformed from beneficiaries into benefactors, as they joined the vibrant community of volunteers like Joy and Makhosi who were passionate about helping South Africa's underserved young people succeed. The two formalized this work into a non-profit organization in 2004. IkamvaYouth's mission: to equip learners from disadvantaged communities with the knowledge, skills, networks and resources to access tertiary education or employment opportunities once they matriculate from high school.

Room to Grow

IkamvaYouth took off quickly, a testament to the model's impact, and the need for academic support in South Africa. Thanks to supportive foundations and corporates, the organization was able to expand its reach to five provinces across the country, realized by an ever-growing team of young professionals ensuring the back-end functions—from financial management to monitoring and evaluation—were executed effectively to enable scale. IkamvaYouth's acceleration was twinned with ever-growing needs for more space for this growing team.

"Every time we moved into an office, we were like, 'wow, this is so big' and then four months later we'd have to pack up and find another one," recalls Joy. It took 13 years and countless moves for the team to start thinking seriously about buying a property to house them for the long term. Once the team got the idea, however, they realized how beneficial it would be to find a building with enough space for them to grow into. It would also be a great asset for the organization, because IkamvaYouth could rent out any space it wasn't using to help pay off its mortgage.

Joy began spending her evenings and weekends scouring property websites, and then one day, spotted the perfect location in an area easily accessible by public transport. Right away, she knew it was *their building*. It was in an up-and-coming neighborhood, so its value would likely increase; it was close to public transport; and ticked every one of the non-profits spatial needs. Joy called IkamvaYouth's Business Development Manager, Alex Smith, and asked her if she thought the organization could afford to buy it with the proper financing. Alex said she did: the organization had been diligently saving and it had gotten a large, but delayed, check from one of its funders, which meant that the organization had only a few months left in the year to spend a year's worth of grant support from that funder. IkamvaYouth was in good shape for making a sizable down-payment. With rental income potential, it could more than cover its mortgage payments.

An Offer, Rejected

IkamvaYouth confidently put in an offer on the building and took its financial calculations to the bank to apply for a mortgage. When the first bank said no, the team thought it was unlucky. By the eighth or ninth rejection, they realized that it wasn't.

Because IkamvaYouth was a non-profit, every bank the team approached said "no" to their mortgage request. "We were told that we just weren't eligible for a bond even though we were probably in a stronger position than many businesses," Alex recalls. It was "because we had grant agreements for the subsequent year and weren't relying on sales or income to make our bond repayments."

Joy and the team shifted gears and tried to secure a different type capital: mezzanine funding. That process proved too lengthy; they realized they'd never be able to finalize a deal in time to secure the property. Without funding, IkamvaYouth's offer fell through and that seemed to be the end of that.

Months later, Joy relayed the experience of trying to get a mortgage, to friends, over lunch. One of her friends thought she knew of a foundation that might be interested in helping IkamvaYouth with their financing problem.

This is where Michael Byron at the collaborative philanthropic trust, Mapula Trust entered the story. Michael remembered getting an email from Joy's friend asking him to take a look at IkamvaYouth as an organization and see if he could help them acquire a new site for their headquarters.

> "IkamvaYouth needed funding to buy the building and at the time had a 13-year history of doing great things," he recalls. "Since Mapula had been put in contact with IkamvaYouth through a trusted connection, we decided to meet the IkamvaYouth team, check out the building and see what we could do."

An Offer, Accepted

After speaking with Joy, Michael was incredibly impressed by IkamvaYouth's story and by what the team had achieved. He was also impressed with the building the organization wanted to buy and saw it as a great investment for IkamvaYouth, so he approached Mapula's board to get permission to extend a 2 million Rand ($130,000) two-year **interest-free loan** to the **non-profit**. It was the first time Mapula had considered making a **loan** instead of a **grant**, and the board members were intrigued. They approved the loan in record time.

Joy got back in touch with the building's property agent and was thrilled to discover that the building was still available. IkamvaYouth put in another offer for the building, this time at a lower price, since the building had not sold at the previous asking price. After a quick consultation with the owner, the agent gave Joy good news: The building was IkamvaYouth's to own–at the lower price. The team was elated, and before they even moved in, they started hustling to raise enough money to repay Mapula.

"We did everything we could to ensure we raised enough and allocated funding appropriately, and to ensure that we got enough rental income and even registered with South African Revenues Service (SARS) in order to get historical value-added tax refunds for the previous six years," recalls Joy.

A Loan, Forgiven

Members of Mapula's team checked in on the IkamvaYouth team occasionally at their new site, to witness firsthand the impact of the trust's loan. Mapula's executives were so impressed with what they saw that at the end of the payment period, the foundation forgave the entire loan amount, converting the loan into a grant.

Today, IkamvaYouth provides after-school tutoring to more than 5,000 underserved high school learners in five South African provinces.

Looking back on the deal, Joy says she never anticipated it to turn out as it did. "It's really hard to find these opportunities, and it would be great to see more foundations help out non-profit organizations by buying assets that can generate revenue, the way Mapula did for us. It's a really smart way to spend **grant** money."

Michael says he believes firmly that lending should be part of philanthropic funders' arsenal because "not everything has to be a **grant**. And an **interest-free loan** is actually quite valuable. It might not be ideal for every organization, but it could be a lifeline for some."

He adds, "Also, you can't always set commercial standards in terms of seniority for a non-profit organization, so you need to be flexible and generous."

Is a Forgivable Loan Right for You?

Founders

For founders who need capital that is flexible and aligned to their social mission, **forgivable loans** are an excellent option. As we'll discuss in the next section, these loans can be linked to social milestones, which can allow social enterprises to access cheaper capital by achieving social and environmental goals.

You will need to be conscious of the signaling effect. By taking a **forgivable loan**, you may be signaling to the market that you qualify for below market financing that may not be repaid. For all the reasons that this kind of flexible financing will be beneficial to you, if at a later period, you are looking for more traditional **debt**, you'll need to be able to communicate that your company can afford it and is able to take on more expensive and potentially less flexible financing.

For for-profit founders looking for forgivable loans for their organization, you will need to demonstrate a similarly strong impact thesis and justification for why traditional **debt** funding is not appropriate.

Funders

Regardless of whether it is forgiven, low-cost **debt** from mission aligned funders can be a powerful tool for both **non-profit** and for-profit organizations. Funders interested in supporting social impact organizations should not overlook its value.

In IkamvaYouth's case, there were no explicit milestones that triggered the repayment or the forgiveness. Michael used the **loan** mechanism to ensure that as a new grantee, IkamvaYouth was creating the impact that they promised they would with the money they had borrowed from Mapula. Due to the nature of the agreement, Alex and her team prepared financially as if they were going to pay the loan back, which resulted in a surplus when the loan was forgiven. So, as funders, you can choose the lending strategy that you feel best serves the needs of the borrower to achieve the targeted social and environmental impact.

During the response to the COVID crisis, we have seen large swaths of capital being allocated as **forgivable loans** with **social metrics** embedded in the conversion that incentivize companies to maintain workforce levels and there is discussion around embedding climate change metrics into loans of large polluters. Having clearly defined metrics agreed upfront with SMEs can help ensure that the capital allocated will help create the social and environmental impact necessary, which we will discuss in Chapter 18.

17

Trackosaurus: Our Convertible Grant Journey

Now that we've explored recoverable grants (**grants** that convert to **debt**), and forgivable loans (**loans** that convert into **grants**), we'll walk with Luke Crowley at Trackosaurus to explore how a **grant** can convert to **equity**. These types of agreements are called **convertible grants** and are applicable only in very specific circumstances, where early-stage for-profit start-ups wish to access **grant** funding for uses like **research and development (R&D)** that may or may not have a commercial upside. While this structure is not broadly applicable, it is an interesting innovation that was worth exploring in our study of how **grant** capital can be used **catalytically**.

Preschool 2.0

In 2017, Luke Crowley launched the Earlybird Educare Network, an early childhood development (ECD) organization, with his wife Meg Blair after spending more than a decade overseeing randomized control trials of large-scale development projects in South Africa. Luke had worked for a number of different organizations, including Innovations for Poverty Action, the Abdul Latif Jameel Poverty Action Lab (J-PAL) and the University of Cape Town evaluating the efficacy of projects covering mobile health, natural resource management, finance and education. In the field of education, he knew there were a number of effective and potentially scalable interventions designed to foster development in children's earliest years. So, he and Meg, a teacher who had recently completed a master's degree in education policy, launched an organization they believed would offer young learners the best of those interventions.

Luke and Meg describe Earlybird Educare Network as "Preschool 2.0." As they were building out the concept, Megan took on the development of the curriculum, nutrition guidance and the teacher training side, while Luke investigated tools and resources that would help educators evaluate learners and their progress.

Tablets for Toddlers?

Luke quickly saw that there was a significant gap in ECD evaluation. On the one side, there were high quality, well-vetted, scientifically backed assessment tools that were completely unaffordable and impractical for most preschools. On the other side, there were relatively low-cost observational tools that were simple to use, but there was also growing evidence that they did a poor job at differentiating between individual kids—which is exactly what a formative assessment tool needs to do. Earlybird Educare Network needed something that was effective, simple and affordable.

Although skeptical of a technology-based approach at first, Luke felt what that was needed was a child-facing tool that asked very little of teachers and wouldn't require administrators to hire a third-party assessor. He knew that using emerging technologies like artificial intelligence could optimize kids' attention, and that machine learning capabilities could help assessments improve over time. Luke thought something that was tablet-based probably made the most sense.

He quickly realized that such a tool could have applications outside of Earlybird Educare Network's own curriculum, and so he began speaking to others in the ECD space about his idea. One of the people that he spoke to was Dhun Davar from the UBS Optimus Foundation (UBS-OF). Luke met Duhn at the Think Future conference in November 2017. Think Future, hosted in South Africa by ECD funder Innovation Edge, is designed to stimulate innovation around ECD by inviting practitioners, innovators and funders from a wide variety of fields to interact with ECD specialists. Duhn, who was attending from Switzerland, spoke with Luke about EarlyBird and the company's difficulty identifying affordable, practical and rigorous evaluation options. As someone with a long history of funding ECD interventions, Dhun immediately understood the problem and recognized the validity of

Luke's tablet-based idea. She asked him to keep her informed of his progress as he continued building out the idea.

A Prototype, an Accelerator and a Workshop

Luke made progress fairly quickly. Just prior to Think Future, his assessment tool idea had been accepted into the first cohort of Injini, an edtech accelerator in Cape Town. Luke used cash and other resources from the program to build an early prototype, which he called "Bird Tracks."

By April 2018, Luke went back to Dhun with an early prototype for the tool. Duhn was impressed. She believed the tool could be valuable to UBS as ECD funders and pressed Luke on how he intended to build and market it commercially. Luke said he believed Bird Tracks could be spun-off as its own for-profit **social enterprise**, but he was adamant that he didn't want to continue down the development path without adequate funding. He estimated that he would need about five million South African Rand ($400,000).

For Dhun, the amount of money required was feasible, but she had questions about whether spinning the idea off was the best approach. Luke pointed out the long history of academic and non-profit developed assessment tools that did not have the type of distribution to allow them to scale nor the effective maintenance to allow users to continue to use them years down the line. His plan for Bird Tracks was to cross subsidize the company by selling the product at market rates in places like the U.S., where there was a large established market, and closer to cost price in places like the South African market.

Grant funding didn't strike Dhun as the right option for what was effectively start-up capital. As a funder, Luke's proposed start-up enterprise for Bird Tracks presented challenges for UBS-OF. The foundation didn't feel comfortable giving **grants** to for-profit entities, but it was also unable to make **equity** investments due to its current charter. Duhn was keen for UBS-OF to get involved in Luke's idea, so without an immediate funding solution, she agreed to stay in touch and continue exploring options.

A few weeks after that conversation, Luke attended a workshop hosted by Innovation Edge on innovative financing instruments. The person facilitating that workshop was... myself, Aunnie Patton Power. It wasn't the first time I had met Luke or heard of his work in ECD. I had also attended the Think Future conference and had conducted a couple of workshops with the Injini cohort around innovative revenue streams and negotiating early-stage investment. I'd even asked Megan to pitch Earlybird to one of my **impact investing** classes. For the Innovation Edge workshop, I was focusing on how early-stage funders and entrepreneurs could embed impact into investment contracts. One of the funding options I presented was the convertible grant.

Grants That Convert?

Convertible grants are similar to **SAFEs** and have been used in early-stage R&D investing for decades. Historically, funders used **convertible grants** to allow companies to develop a product or service before raising investment capital. Then, if a company raised **equity** in the future, the **grant** would convert to **equity** ownership. This arrangement gives funders the possibility of recycling grant capital for new innovations, though of course doing that depends on getting an exit from earlier equity conversions. **Convertible grants** differ from **SAFEs** and **convertible debt** agreements in that they remain as **grants** if a founder does not raise investment capital later on; no repayment is required then. This means that funders using the instrument provide the funding as a **grant**, with the expectation that they will not be repaid.

The reason that I featured the **convertible grant** at the workshop was because I knew several of the attendees were foundations interested in exploring how they could fund early-stage for-profit companies. My goal was to present them with an option to use their grantmaking capabilities to do so while capturing upside, if the business became profitable.

In preparation for the workshop, I had asked all of the participants to send me some cases, deals or potential funding opportunities that we could use to evaluate some of the different options. Luke, who was one of the few social entrepreneurs attending, instead sent me a short note that read:

> I think UBS-OF might be interested in being a co-investor in Bird Tracks, our game-based formative assessment technology that Injini seeded. We need about five million Rand over 2.5 years to reach market launch.

During the workshop, I could see the wheels turning in Luke's head based on the questions he asked about the sample **convertible grant** term sheet I had handed out. He knew that while UBS-OF was interested in **equity** investing, it would be at least another year before they could. So he effectively needed a way to allow them to delay their equity investment, while still securing the cash needed to build out his technology.

A Decent Proposal

Luke went back to Dhun and UBS-OF with a proposal for a **convertible grant**, using the term sheet template from the workshop. Dhun, intrigued, presented the proposal to her team. Other members of the team had seen interesting for-profit ECD social enterprises that they wanted to support, so Dhun decided to present the Bird Tracks convertible grant idea to the foundation's board as a test case. Her argument was that having an eventual **equity** stake in Bird Tracks would give UBS-OF some influence in ensuring that the company retained its social mission as it grew, while also giving the foundation the possibility of recycling its capital.

Dhun took a few preemptive steps in anticipation of questions from the board. She worked to get approval from UBS-OF's regulator and tax authority in Zurich and continued negotiating with Luke on the particulars of the agreement. The terms Dhun eventually agreed to put in front of the foundation's board were for a $440,000 **grant** that would be disbursed in installments. If Bird Tracks went on to raise an **equity** round of at least $225,000 (200,000 Swiss francs, per the terms), the **grant** could convert to ordinary shares in the company at UBS-OF's discretion, for up to five years. To incentivize Bird Tracks to raise money, the shares would be bought at a 0% **discount** if the **equity round** happened within six months of the grant's disbursement, at a 15% discount within 18 months and at a 25% discount anytime thereafter. If Bird Tracks secured no qualified financing during the three-year grant period, UBS-OF could still exercise its option by instructing Bird Tracks to seek an independent **valuation** of the company.

When approval came in from the Swiss regulator, Dhun took the agreement to the board. And although the foundation still did not have clearance from the corporate side of the organization, UBS bank, to make **equity** investments, the board was sufficiently swayed by the deal's delayed option to give its approval. In January 2019, Bird Tracks secured the **convertible grant** from UBS-OF.

Today, Bird Tracks, now Trackosaurus, is finalizing its first product. Luke has been negotiating with funders about the company's financing needs for its next stage of business. One of the risks he considered while negotiating the **convertible grant** deal was that the agreement could deter future investors, particularly if UBS-OF became a sizable **equity** owner through the conversion. So far, however, this has not been raised as a significant issue. Funders have tended to regard the convertible grant as just another type of early-stage investment, similar to a traditional **convertible note**.

For UBS-OF, this deal added to the organization's financing toolkit. This has proven useful already in several ways, primarily in that it allowed the foundation to test drive **equity** deal making even before having formal approval to do so. This has helped the foundation think through questions that will be critical when it does get full approval. For example, UBS-OF has found that there are companies they have funded with **grants**, that are able to spin off an idea to become a for-profit **social enterprise**. Previously, they only had the opportunity to fund these spin-offs through debt, which was not applicable in all cases. With the **convertible grant** options, it allowed them to take a very early-stage equity-like risk with these companies, with the potential that some of that capital will be returned. Other questions that UBS-OF was prompted to think through include: How much **impact measurement** should portfolio companies be required to do? What level of measurement is actually feasible? And how can UBS-OF ensure that the company maintains its social mission?

UBS-OF continues to test variations of its **convertible grant** contract to better understand what terms make the most sense for the organization as a funder, and which terms make sense for entrepreneurs at different stages of development and growth.

Is a Convertible Grant Right for You?

Founders

As you saw in Luke's case, this type of instrument works well for a company that has an **impact thesis** that is very strong and highly embedded in the company's governance documents. This is great for founders who are looking for larger amounts of grant like capital for R&D that may, or may not, have a commercial upside.

It is important to think long term about what a **convertible grant** agreement means. If the agreement converts, the **convertible grant** funder could be an investor in the company for a significant period of time. Founders need to be willing to work with this funder going forward and need to be confident that the funders will add value to the company as it grows. Additionally, for a for-profit entity, grant income is taxable income, so you will likely need to treat this similarly to a **forgivable loan** from an accounting perspective. Tax treatment is highly localized and this is a potential gray area as it has been used so infrequently, so I highly recommend you consult with a tax expert regarding your specific circumstances.

Funders

As I said at the beginning of this chapter, this structure is only applicable in very particular circumstances where a non-profit funder wishes to support the R&D of an early-stage for-profit start-up. Historically, other funders of early R&D, such as universities, have used **convertible grants** as a way to encourage start-ups to develop new technologies. For instance, the Oxford University Challenge Seed Fund was launched in 1999 with capital from the UK Government, the Wellcome Trust and the Gatsby Foundation to make **grants** to technology projects that needed support to reach the market. The fund can award up to £250,000 and must be the first cash that the company has received. Awards are made on the basis of a simple one-page Offer Letter with six provisions covering: use of funds, ownership of **intellectual property (IP)**, conversion to **equity** at the same price as external cash investors, a share of **licensing income** if licensed to an existing company rather than a new spin-out, reporting obligations and duration of offer. For a copy of this letter, please see the online companion.

For **grant** funders who are keen to get into investing, but do not feel comfortable leading a deal, it does provide an opportunity for upside in a **social enterprise**. The agreement can utilize your current ability to allocate **grants**, but can include the option for those grants to convert to equity at a later stage. That being said, similar to **recoverable grants** and **forgivable loans**, there may be tax implications for this structure that should be explored prior to structuring.

18

Innovative Grant Funding

In this section, we have looked at a variety of options for mission aligned funders and founders to come together to tackle social and environmental issues. Although much of the book so far has focused on for-profit founders and investors, philanthropic funders and non-profit founders have an important role to play in the early-stage funding ecosystem. The structures that we have explored in this section form a part of the non-profit finance toolkit.

Traditionally **grants** are non-repayable funds, assets or services that **grant makers** (usually the government, a foundation or a trust) offer recipients (usually a non-profit entity, educational institution, business or an individual) based on a stringent set of criteria and strict restrictions on how the **grant** can be used. Each of the chapters of this section introduced a slight tweak on this traditional view of grant capital and many of the options work for social enterprises structured as for-profits.

It's also worth noting that while **grant** funding can be very valuable in the prototyping and start-up phases of social innovation for **social enterprises**, it isn't a reliable source of long-term funding for most for-profit businesses. That's why most businesses that start with any form of grant money should have a strategy to transition away from grant dependence toward diverse revenue and funding streams, including more commercial finance, if they want to thrive.

© The Author(s), under exclusive license to Springer Nature
Switzerland AG 2021
A. Patton Power, *Adventure Finance*,
https://doi.org/10.1007/978-3-030-72428-3_18

Mary (Chapter 13) knew that she needed to raise funding to get The Studio Museum's building project off the ground. As a non-profit, she struggled to access funding from a bank. Accessing that funding in the form of a program related investment (PRI) loan allowed her to work with a funder who believed in the vision and the potential impact of the museum. For the Ford Foundation, using debt, equity and guarantees alongside their grant capital allows them to support both non-profit and for-profit organizations with the type of capital that these organizations need in order to grow.

Andrea and Barry (Chapter 14) knew that Riders for Health needed sustainable capital to make their healthcare vehicle management system a success, so they used a guarantee to access local bank funding at a reasonable cost. By repaying their loan to the bank, they were able to prove their creditworthiness and access cheaper debt in the future. The Skoll Foundation wanted to help Riders build a sustainable business model in The Gambia that they could expand to other African countries. Being able to access local debt at a reasonable cost was paramount to that goal. A guarantee was used to address the perceived risk of default by the local banks that were not comfortable with the non-profit's credit history.

Sachi and Kate (Chapter 15) knew that Upaya's model of providing low-cost loans to small businesses in India was creating impact, but they felt that raising grant capital to fund these loans was limiting their growth. Raising recoverable grants for their fund allowed them access to flexible, low-cost capital from a larger pool of donors (including Donor Advised Funds) who were interested in the opportunity to recycle their philanthropic contributions.

Joy and Alex (Chapter 16) had a similar experience to Mary from The Studio Museum in Harlem. They were struggling to access capital that they needed to fund the purchase of their building for IkamvaYouth's headquarters. Accessing a loan from Mapula Trust helped them to purchase the building and the loan being forgiven gave them a significant surplus to spend on their youth development programs. For Mapula Trust, using a forgivable loan that had a building as collateral allowed them to support IkamvaYouth with more capital than they would normally provide a new grantee.

As the founder of a for-profit social enterprise needing research and development (R&D) funding to develop his first product, Luke (this chapter) was able to work with UBS-OF to create a convertible grant structure to access funding. For UBS-OF, they were able to extend grant funding to a very early-stage enterprise and still maintain the potential for upside if the product was successful.

Recoverable Grants Versus Forgivable Loans

Often the term **recoverable grant** is used to refer to a **recoverable grant** and a **forgivable loan** interchangeably. As you can see from the two chapters in this section, there are differences in application that can be important. From a tax and accounting perspective, these differences are paramount, so let's talk through some suggestions for choosing between the two structures.

Recoverable grants are easiest when they are done from a non-profit entity to a non-profit entity and the repayment is at the discretion of the recipient or based on mutually agreed financial or social milestones. This repayment agreement can be done in the form of a **side letter** to the contract or in the contract itself. In this case, **recoverable grants** can be booked as a **grant** for both parties. If a repayment is made to the funder in the future, it can be counted as a donation.[1]

In cases where funders wish to make a **recoverable grant** to a for-profit entity, the for-profit entity will need to record this like a **forgivable loan** (see below). Funders may want to examine whether they should treat this as a **forgivable loan** on their end as well, to be consistent in the accounting.

For U.S. foundations, as long as all other **PRI** considerations are met, a **recoverable grant** can count as a **PRI**. Any repayments will be subject to the negative disbursement clause. Also, when you do any kind of grant to a for-profit entity, you need to do **expenditure responsibility**. This means that you have to track all of the expenditures that the funding covers and be able to prove that they are being spent in the name of a specific charitable purpose, so that in the event of an audit, you can produce the supporting paperwork. Some funders have developed processes to make this more efficient, but many are deterred from granting to for-profits based on the additional paperwork required. For other jurisdictions, you should seek advice from tax experts regarding your specific circumstances.

A **forgivable loan** can be made by a non-profit or for-profit entity into a non-profit or for-profit entity. The repayment can be at the discretion of the funder or based on mutually agreed financial or **social milestones**.

For the founder, the **forgivable loan** should be booked as a liability on the **balance sheet**. For the funder, they should be booked as a **receivable** on

---

[1]This is how it is being done in the U.S. and UK, but this should be confirmed with the tax authorities if trying this in a new jurisdiction.

their **balance sheet**. If the loan is forgiven, a non-profit borrower will need to book the amount forgiven as a **grant** and a for-profit borrower will need to book the amount forgiven as **ordinary income**. The funder will need to write-off the obligation as a loss.

Depending on the jurisdiction, if a loan is forgiven, a for-profit borrower will likely need to pay tax on the amount that is forgiven. For funders, unless the loan is to a non-profit, it may not qualify as a tax write-off, but tax treatment is highly localized and this is a potential gray area, so I highly recommend you consult with a tax expert regarding your specific circumstances (Fig. 18.1).

So how do you decide on a recoverable grant versus a forgivable loan? Open Road Alliance, a private philanthropic initiative, which first introduced Upaya to the idea of **recoverable grants**, was one of the first in the industry to make **recoverable grants**. They started using them in 2014 to make one-time financial support to organizations that ran into an unexpected roadblock or cash crunch such as a delay in a large grant or project funding that took longer to negotiate than expected.

They found there was a significant demand for this type of philanthropic bridging capital and ended up making over 40 **recoverable grants in** three years. But the paperwork to get the **recoverable grants** through required one to two months for the team to close the funding, which wasn't aligned with the concept of quick bridging capital that they were wanting to provide. Part of the issue was that some of these organizations were for-profit, which required **expenditure responsibility** for a **grant**, and part of it was the internal requirements of the **donor advised fund (DAF)** to complete the transaction. So, the team decided that they would try making loans to the organizations directly out of the family office, instead of recoverable grants through the **DAF**.

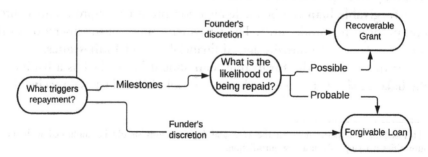

Fig. 18.1 Recoverable grant and forgivable loan decision tree

Although the **loans** made to for-profit entities can't be written off against taxes in the same way that **grants** to non-profits can, Open Road was comfortable with the switch as they were already consistently maxing out on charitable deductions allowed under U.S. tax law. With that change, they went from 4 to 6 weeks for getting **recoverable grants** disbursed out of their **DAF** to 48 hours for disbursement of the loans. Their default choice is now loans unless the non-profit board isn't comfortable taking on a **loan** or its their first repayable structure of any kind and they feel more comfortable with a **grant** structure.

Convertible Grants

One last tool that can be powerful for **mission aligned** investing is **technical assistance (TA)**. TA facilities are pots of money that are reserved for skills building, capacity development and for the specific consulting needs of a company. These are often used by development funders to accompany **debt** or **equity** investment funds. With this **grant** funding, founders can access the technical expertise necessary for their growth without using their debt or equity funding.

Comparing Your Options

See Table 18.1.

18.1 Comparison of innovative grant funding options

	Guarantees	Traditional grant	Recoverable grant	Forgivable loan	Convertible grant
Description	Security provided by a third party	Capital that has no expectation of financial repayment	Grant that converts into debt	Debt that converts into a grant	Grant that converts into equity
Business registration	For-profit, non-profit, co-op, social enterprise	Non-profit[a]	Non-profit[b]	For-profit, non-profit, co-op, social enterprise	Social enterprise
Revenue model	Any				May not yet be established

(continued)

18.1 (continued)

	Guarantees	Traditional grant	Recoverable grant	Forgivable loan	Convertible grant
Company stage	Any				Concept stage
Business growth projections	Any				High growth venture or category pioneer
Embeddedness	For a guarantee from a mission-driven funder, high mission embeddedness will be necessary	High mission embeddedness required			
Track record	Significant impact track record may be required for a concessional guarantee from a mission-driven funder	Impact track record likely to be required		Impact track record will be important if impact milestones are used for forgiveness or interest rate rebates	No track record required, but commitment to measure impact is necessary
Spend funding on	Assets, working capital	Proof of concept, growth capital, working capital, assets			Proof of concept
Assets for collateral	Guarantee acts as collateral for another transaction	None required		Dependent on funder, but generally low	None
Planned payback source	If payment required, internal cash flows	None	None or internal cash flow	None, internal cash flow, or future funding	None or third-party exit through sale, IPO, merger or secondary
Ownership	No effect on ownership				Willingness to dilute ownership of company in the future

(continued)

18.1 (continued)

	Guarantees	Traditional grant	Recoverable grant Forgivable loan	Convertible grant
Funding in future	Can help create credit history for future debt funding	No significant impact on future funding	Can help create credit history for future debt funding	Supports equity funding in the future
Funder involvement	If mission driven, funder will be both impact and downside focused with covenants relating to both. Otherwise, just downside focused	Will be focused on impact and financial spend reporting	Likely to be impact focused with covenants used to embed mission in contract (such as convertibility or cost of capital linked to impact achievement)	Impact and upside focused. Likely to be ongoing involvement with potential for board seats, voting rights and information rights, if converted
Most likely funders	Development Finance Institution, Foundation, Family Office, Non-Profit Funder	University, Foundation, Government	Foundation, Family Office, Development Finance Institution, Government, Non-Profit Funder	University, Foundation

[a]Can be for-profit, but see the online companions for notes on tax considerations
[b]See above

Part IV

What If: You Want to Link Financing to Impact?

In the last part, we explored a number of creative options for repurposing philanthropic funding as catalytic investment capital. In this part, we will explore how philanthropic institutions and mission aligned investors can influence social and environmental impact performance by linking the cost and distribution of capital directly to **impact milestones**. In other words, allowing social and environmental impact performance to directly influence *when capital is allocated and how much it costs*. Sometimes such **impact-linked financing** is grant-based, but it doesn't have to be.

In Chapter 19, we'll see how the Michael and Susan Dell Foundation have structured contracts with **interest rate rebates**, which link the impact performance of borrowers with cost of their **debt**. In Chapter 20, we'll learn from Clinicas del Azurcar about **social impact incentives (SIINC)**, a structure that uses outcomes payments to encourage social enterprises to achieve deeper impact. In Chapter 21, I'll use the story of my own experience with **Impact Bonds**, another outcomes-based payment structure, to introduce you to the concept and discuss some of the opportunities and challenges of the model.

As you'll note in these journeys, the essential ingredient to linking impact to financing is that the funding is linked to a **theory of change** framework. A **theory of change** is the rationale and plan for achieving social and environmental outcomes. It articulates the intended changes for people, issues and systems to realize the impact you want. It makes explicit the connections and logic between activities (what you will do), outputs (the short-term, direct results), and outcomes and impacts (the longer-term shifts that occur, either directly or indirectly, from your activities).

A **theory of change** can be developed at the enterprise, investment or port-folio level. Whether you're an entrepreneur or a funder, you build a theory of change by first identifying your desired long-term goals and then reverse engineering the steps and activities and intermediary outcomes required to achieve them. You have to consider the context you'll be working in and scru-tinize the assumptions and evidence you rely on to make your case. This is crucial for **impact-linked finance**, because without solid assumptions, rele-vant metrics or reliable data, the terms of the financing are unlikely to succeed in achieving the desired impact.[1]

Obviously, the difficulty comes in setting appropriate **milestones** and actu-ally achieving these goals. If you are a more established business, you might have a good idea about the level of **impact performance** that would be achievable based on your products and end users. If you are a start-up, you will still be designing what you are bringing to market and will need the flexi-bility to adapt your **business model** and products as you build your company. Regardless of stage, all founders need to be able to pivot. So, any **milestones** embedded in agreements, should allow you this flexibility or you'll need to have a pre-agreed process for how you renegotiate milestones.

In the next three chapters, we are going to look at options for you to link your financing to impact milestones. We'll get a chance to learn from initial pioneers in this newly emerging space. There can be a lot of complexity in adding **impact milestones** into funding agreements, so hopefully, these chap-ters can help you think through your options and as well as the opportunities and challenges.

---

[1]I've yet to come across a standard format for how to build a theory of change; however, a good place to start, is the *Impact Investing Handbook*, by Steve Goedke, Patrick Briand and Karim Harji.

19

Michael and Susan Dell Foundation: Our Interest Rate Rebate Journey

In Chapter 16, we saw Mapula Trust convert their entire **loan** to IkamvaYouth into a **grant** through a **forgivable loan**, but this is not a viable strategy for most funders. In this next journey, we join Rahil Rangwala from the **Michael and Susan Dell Foundation** as he develops a contract that aims to incentivize school operators in India to achieve better educational outcomes by linking the cost of the loan to impact outcomes. In other words, the contract he designs allows the school operators to qualify for **interest rate rebates** through achieving pre-defined impact goals. This is an example of **impact-linked financing**: the linking of financial incentives to the achievement of social and/or environmental performance targets.

Impacting Education in India

The Michael and Susan Dell Foundation (MSDF) is a global philanthropic foundation dedicated to catalyzing system level changes in education. A key focus market for the foundation's programmatic work in education is India, where an underfunded government school system and expensive private school system has spawned an intermediary network of low-fee private schools aiming to fill the education gap for low- and middle-income Indian school children. There are approximately 300,000 affordable private schools

A. Patton Power, *Adventure Finance*, https://doi.org/10.1007/978-3-030-72428-3_19

in India serving more than 92 million children.[1] The growth of this education sector has, in turn, given rise to a booming ecosystem of lenders, education service vendors and infrastructure businesses eager. Yet despite such investment, low-fee private schools, like their government school peers, struggle to deliver. Indeed, roughly 75% of their students perform below grade level.[2]

MSDF has been working for the past 15 years to bolster the quality of both public and private primary and secondary education in India and has partnered with a range of organizations to improve teaching processes and develop effective standardized assessments that measure students' learning outcomes. The foundation has increasingly turned its attention to low-fee private schools as a growing number of poor families enrolled their children in these institutions in hopes of giving them a better education than the government school system could.

One of the areas in which the foundation believed it could have an impact on the affordable private school sector and the quality of education it provides was by improving the financial resources available to such schools. Indian laws stipulate that no school can be managed by a for-profit private entity,[3] so school operators cannot access **equity financing** and must instead rely on **debt** to satisfy any capital needs they have beyond earned income from tuition. Thus, as the number of low-fee private schools grew, so did a network of non-bank financial lenders to satisfy the needs of these educators' needs.

The Indian School Finance Company (ISFC) is one such non-bank financial institution serving low-cost private schools. The organization provides loans to school operators for the purpose of improving infrastructure and acquiring resources to improve the quality of education they deliver. Founded in 2008 by Steve Hardgrave, the ISFC began lending after going through an incubation program with the impact venture capital firm Gray Matters Capital. By 2015, ISFC itself needed an **equity** infusion to scale up its main product: a three- to six-year loan designed for private schools to make infrastructure upgrades and other capacity improvements.

Rahil Rangwala, the director of MSDF's India programs, and his team evaluated ISFC for the **equity** investment. But, as with other deals the foundation explored in the affordable private school sector, MSDF team did not feel that ISFC sufficiently prioritized learning outcomes at its borrower institutions. The foundation declined to go forward with the investment. The

[1] Faces of Budget Private School in India. (2018). Center for Civil Society. Available at: https://ccs.in/sites/default/files/attachments/faces-of-bps-in-india-report2018.pdf.

[2] Rangwala, R. 17 January 2018. A New Impact Investing Model for Education. Available at: https://ssir.org/articles/entry/a_new_impact_investing_model_for_education#.

[3] Chattopadhay, T. & Roy, M. 18 May 2017. Low-Fee Private Schools in India: The Emerging Fault Lines. Columbia University.

example nevertheless tugged at Rahil. He knew there must be some way for the foundation to incentivize funders and school operators to prioritize learning outcomes, so he turned to his past career experience in other sectors of finance to puzzle it out.

The Road to a Rebate

Before joining MSDF in 2011, Rahil had worked for hedge funds, small business lenders and microfinance institutions. In more mainstream finance, traditional lenders link **interest rates** to borrowers' financial performance so he wondered why couldn't a lender do the same from an impact performance perspective? Many of non-bank financial institutions like ISFC needed **debt** to grow their operations and Rahil wanted to see if it was possible for MSDF to help such organizations meet their funding needs while incentivizing better learning outcomes. In short, he decided he would tie the interest rate on the foundation's loan directly to learning outcomes. As Rahil developed his idea, he quickly realized that the school principals, as well as the lenders, needed to be incentivized on improving schools' learning outcomes. So, Rahil and his team began designing a loan product whose interest rate could be adjusted as desired learning outcomes were achieved. This would mean that both the lending institutions and their borrower school operators would benefit from a lower cost of capital if learners' performance increased over time.

Selling the **impact-linked debt** idea internally to the foundation was fairly easy, though some colleagues raised concern that school principals could be incentivized to game the system by excluding poor performing students or trying to doctor assessment tests, for example. So the team designed a rating system—Gold, Silver and Bronze—to categorize schools' baseline performance. With the basics of an impact-linked funding product in place, MSDF approached ISFC with a loan offer.

MSDF agreed to lend ISFC $2 million in the form of a three-year, **non-convertible loan** with a **variable-interest rate** tied to learning outcome achievements in its portfolio. Schools could apply for **loans** from ISFC and voluntarily participate in the assessment program. Participating institutions that met certain learning-level targets would get an interest payment rebate (equal to roughly 10% of the total loan) as a reward. Learning achievement targets would be set upfront, and based on an assessment by an independent agency, paid for by MSDF. A second assessment would be conducted after two years to measure success, at which point the rebate could be disbursed.

Where schools succeeded in achieving their improved learning targets, MSDF would absorb the cost of the rebate by adjusting ISFC's interest payments.

Getting Good Marks

Practically speaking, here's how this would play out: Let's say a school, Sri Vidya Bharathi, was serving students to grade 10 and wanted to be able to expand instruction to grades 11 and 12. In order to get government approval to do this, they would need to build four additional classrooms and a science lab. Sri Vidya Bharathi couldn't finance those additions through student tuition payments alone; it would need a loan to cover the costs. ISFC offers the school a $29,000, five-year **loan**, explaining that it can lower the rate, provided the school achieves certain learning targets. An independent evaluator would test a sample of Sri Vidya Bharathi students in grades 3, 5 and 7 in English and math, at no cost to the school. If in two years, students' test scores improved by 5–10 points, the school could get up to a 10% **interest rate rebate**. MSDF would then compensate ISFC for every dollar it paid out in the rebate through an adjustment on ISFC's own interest repayments to the foundation.

ISFC was receptive to the idea, but hesitant about how to sell the product so as not to confuse its borrowers or the market more broadly. As the two organizations continued their discussions, the ISFC team realized that the product could be a good hook for their sales team, if messaged correctly. That's because invariably, school principals approaching ISFC for a loan always asked for a lower interest rate. With this product, ISFC had a ready answer for how they could secure one.

For MSDF, the next step was to work out the legal and regulatory implications of the new product. Indian law is exceptionally strict for foreign investors and grantmakers. MSDF, being an American institution that provides both investment and philanthropic capital, needed to take extra care to ensure its **loan** structure conformed to the local laws and regulations. One requirement: MSDF needed to make clear that the **principal** on their loan was expected to be repaid in full, so it would not be confused with a **grant**. The foundation also needed to clear the product with the Reserve Bank of India (RBI). Finally, MSDF needed to make sure that IFSC and its school borrowers received clear accounting advice on how to record the loan on their books.

There were hurdles to getting the product cleared, as it was the first time lawyers and regulators were assessing a loan product linked to social impact.

Rahil and his team relied on other examples of **variable-rate loans** interest interventions to get the lawyers and auditors comfortable with the structure. In the end, IFSC treated the rebate paid to the school as an interest rebate. For the adjustment to IFSC's rate, instead of making every interest payment variable, MSDF made the rebate cumulative. This meant that the final payment from IFSC, which included the loan principal, would be adjusted by the total amount of rebates earned.

With regulatory clearance granted, MSDF approved the $2 million, three-year loan to ISFC, offering a 12.5% interest rate. ISFC signed up 96 schools for loans under the impact-linked terms. MSDF calculated that even if all of the participating schools hit their learning targets and successfully repaid their debt, the foundation's loan to ISFC would still generate 8.3% interest. With that calculation, Rahil says, "our $2 million can touch many more schools and students than if we spent those philanthropic dollars on a more traditional one-time grant."

MSDF did, in fact, generate a positive return once the loan term had ended, even with the incentive payouts. For MSDF, which typically accounts for the impact of its education funding internally on a "cost per child" basis, that meant its costs for the initiative were negative. Rahil recalls that penciling in negative costs was a strange bit of accounting for an organization that typically gives away its money or makes steep concessions on its investment terms.

Tweaking the Model

Since its first **impact-linked debt** agreement with ISFC, MSDF has replicated the product for another low-cost private school lender, Varthana. It has made a few tweaks to the design, however. For one, the product's rewards are now a lot simpler. The Gold, Silver, Bronze rating system ended up being too complicated for ISFC's sales team to explain and just created confusion among school principals. It also turned out that this hedge against potential fraud was unnecessary; ISCF saw no evidence that schools tried to fake or pad their performance numbers.

Second, MSDF shortened the school assessment timeline from two years to one, at principals' request.

Finally, they added supportive services for teachers in the Varthana loan agreement to help with learning improvements. Many teachers, when told their baseline performance measures, were very eager to fix problems and boost learning achievements in their classrooms but lacked the tools to do so. The addition of these support services increased the cost of the intervention for MSDF but was nevertheless included because it aligned with the foundation's mission.

In all, Rahil and his team had succeeded in designing a tool for **impact investing** in which the desired social results were clearly defined, incentivized, measured and paid for by the instrument itself, with minimal overhead. He says that looking back at both transactions, the foundation will likely use **impact-linked debt** agreements again in the future.

Is an Interest Rate Rebate Right for You?

Founder

For social enterprises and non-profits, linking your interest rate to impact targets is one option to embed impact into your deal contract and create a financial incentive to achieve your social or environmental mission. In order to sign a contract like this, you'll need to have a clear understanding of the metrics that would be appropriate for your company and context. You'll also need a mission aligned funder that is willing to pay for the achievement of social or environmental impact. Foundations or family offices that have flexibility over how they allocate their capital would be likely to be the best type of funders to begin to have this conversation. We'll discuss the mechanics of this in more depth in Chapter 22.

Funder

If you are a mission aligned funder, linking impact to the **cost of capital** of the **debt** that you issue can be a concrete way to incentivize the achievement of social or environmental impact of your borrowers. In the long term, the achievement of social and environmental outcomes may end up benefiting the borrower financially. But as the lender in an **interest rate rebate** deal, you must be willing and able to give up some of your financial return if the borrower hits the targets. So, you must be mission aligned and have flexibility around your return requirements to your own stakeholders.

Rahil believes that these contracts can be replicated beyond the education sector, by following these three criteria:

- Clearly defined, simple, objective, measurable **impact metrics**.
- **Impact measurement** costs that don't exceed the reward amount paid out.

- An on-the-ground partner with a last-mile network and reach, who shares the investor's objectives.

As Rahil observes, you have to be aware of the cost of measurement, so that it doesn't exceed the amount of the reward. This means that you'll have to weigh up the difference between **outputs** that are easily captured rather than **outcomes** that might be more fulsome, but more expensive and complex to track. Working with companies that already have a strong impact measurement and management program, and choosing metrics that align with that program, can reduce these costs.

The size of the reward is also important. It can't be too big that it will encourage borrowers to game the system, but it can't be too small that it isn't significant to incentivize change.

It is of vital importance that borrowers are aligned with the outcomes that you are incentivizing. Incentivizing borrowers to perform in a way inconsistent with the mission of their organization, financial or social, will be difficult and likely end in frustration for both parties. Put another way, the best use case for this is incentivization for goals that are part of the company's mission, not bribing companies to become social or trying to punish companies for underperformance.

Finally, another way to increase your impact for these types of contracts is to crowd in other funders that are aligned with the mission. MSDF was able to do this with Triodos during their loans to Varthana, where their interest was being used to incentivize schools that were receiving loans from Triodos. Although that caused a reduction in the financial return to MSDF, it provided significant more coverage of their program without having to extend additional loan funding.

20

Clinicas del Azucar: Our Social Impact Incentives Journey

In our next journey, we head to Mexico to join Javier Lozano and Miguel Garza on their **Social Impact Incentive (SIINC)** funding journey for their **social enterprise** Clínicas del Azúcar. Like the Dell Foundation's **impact-linked debt** contract in the previous chapter, **SIINCs** are a type of **impact-linked finance**, though a bit more complex in that it pulls together multiple stakeholders to incentivize social and/or environmental impact.

A One-Stop Shop

Javier Lozano started a low-cost health services company, Clínicas del Azúcar, after watching his mother struggle for years to manage her diabetes. In Mexico, diabetes is one of the leading causes of death. Javier's mother, despite having all the benefits of private insurance and ample resources, faced a continual battle with the disease. Javier knew that if his mother was struggling, many other poorer or rural Mexicans must be having a much harder time. Javier had worked on a number of education and nutrition projects in Mexico's native communities and witnessed firsthand how difficult it was for them to access basic services. Indeed, nearly 80% of Mexican's living below the poverty line cannot afford private healthcare treatment. He could

© The Author(s), under exclusive license to Springer Nature
Switzerland AG 2021
A. Patton Power, *Adventure Finance*,
https://doi.org/10.1007/978-3-030-72428-3_20

only imagine how hard diabetes management was for low-income Mexicans without access to specialized care.[1]

In 2010, Javier teamed up with Fernanda Zorrilla to tackle unequal access to quality diabetes care in Mexico through **social enterprise**, which he had discovered doing his MBA at MIT's Sloan School of Business. The partners scoped out an idea for a "one-stop shop" for diabetes treatment and management. Their goal in launching Clínicas was to offer high-quality, comprehensive diabetes care to all Mexicans, regardless of socioeconomic status, through a chain of retail clinics where patients could simply walk in, find what they need and pay an affordable price.

Javier and Fernanda toiled away on Clinicas for six years, opening nine clinics throughout Mexico. By 2016, Clinicas had grown into the largest provider of private diabetes care in Mexico, serving more than 50,000 patients through an innovative business model built around a flexible subscription payment structure, and machine learning technologies to enhance treatment efficacy and efficiency. The company was successfully delivering services for 40% less than what other private care options were charging. Still, the founders were unsatisfied by the number of very low-income patients they were reaching.[2] The team was concerned that with the company's ambitious plans to open 200 more clinics by 2021, Clinicas would have difficulty also prioritizing care for Mexico's most vulnerable communities.

Miguel Garza, Clinicas' CFO, felt frustrated by the trade-off Clinicas faced between pursuing deep social impact and financial sustainability as he strived to raise growth capital for the company's expansion. Clinicas' social mission was one of the reasons he joined the company in 2014. But the funders he spoke to seemed more interested in the commercial success of the business. He wasn't feeling optimistic that Clinicas could balance the goal of increasing access for the neediest patients, while still continuing to scale its footprint.

SIINC-ing Incentives

An ocean away, in Europe, Roots of Impact and the Swiss Agency for Development and Cooperation (SDC) were working on a way to address the very conundrum Clinicas faced in raising social venture capital. Bjoern Struewer,

---

[1]This case was adapted from the Roots of Impact SIINC Clinicas Case and a Clinicas case by O'Mara Taylor and supplemented by interviews with Roots of Impact and the Clinicas team.

[2]Base of the pyramid refers to individuals at the bottom of the economic pyramid of earning, i.e., those making less than $2–5 per day (depending on the context).

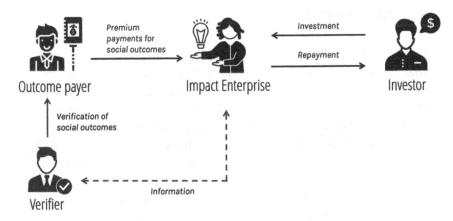

Fig. 20.1 SIINC illustration

the founder of Roots of Impact, and Peter Beez from SDC wanted to ensure that financing for high-impact social enterprises didn't compromise their impact missions by prioritizing financial returns to investors. Together they worked to design a financial product that ensured alignment on impact objectives. What they devised was an instrument that they called **"Social Impact Incentives"** or **SIINC**.

SIINCs are meant to get social enterprises the impact capital they need, while also providing financial incentives for them to stay "on mission." To design a SIINC, two funding entities are required: an investor, who provides the upfront operating or growth capital that the social enterprise needs, and a public or philanthropic "outcomes payor," who agrees to kick in some grant capital as "bonus funding" for the social enterprise if it achieves certain impact milestones. These impact-linked payments effectively function as a new revenue stream for the business and are meant to help the enterprise attract investors in spite of its less commercially viable (but high-impact) business streams[3] (Fig. 20.1).

Bjoern and Peter were eager to see if their **SIINC** instrument would work and approached the Inter-American Development Bank (IDB), New Ventures and Ashoka as pilot partners for their first deals. All they needed was a willing social enterprise to test the idea.

---

[3] Roots of Impact Web site.

Meet Me at FLII?

Bjoern knew Javier and his work with Clinicas from Javier's turn as an Ashoka Fellow. In 2016, he reached out to check in with the team at the upcoming Foro Latinoamericano de Inversión de Impacto (FLII), an **impact investing** conference held in Mexico every year. Miguel was keen to speak with Bjoern about Clinicas' fundraising efforts. For the discussion, Bjoern brought Peter with him, as well as his program manager Rory Tews, and the four chatted about Clinicas's strategic plan and growth aspirations. Bjoern, Peter and Rory probed on the question of how aligned Clinicas' growth ambitions were with the company's social mission. Miguel laid out the dilemma Clinicas' was facing, and Bjoern, Peter and Rory thus took the opportunity to present the **SIINC** concept. For Miguel and Javier, it was a no-brainer: They were more than willing to make Clinicas a test case for the instrument if it offered the company a way to reach more people in need, and helped other social enterprises avoid potential impact-financial returns trade-offs in the future. For Roots of Impact and the SDC, Clinicas seemed like an ideal pilot case, given its proven, highly scalable and financially solid business model, combined with its huge potential for impact by reaching more lower-income patients.

With all participants aligned, the critical next step in making the first **SIINC** a reality was agreeing on the metrics on which to base the impact-linked payments. Javier and Miguel wanted to make sure that the targets both matched the company's short-term objectives and supported its mission of serving more vulnerable customers. For the funders, it was imperative that the targets drive Clinicas to create additional impact. It took several months of negotiating, but the parties eventually arrived at two target metrics:

(1) The ratio of low-income patients served to Clinicas' overall patients served.
(2) The level of mid-term blood sugar level improvement realized—a crucial indicator of diabetes management—within its low-income patient segment.

The agreement established a baseline for each impact metric and defined relative performance targets that would trigger the impact-linked payments. It is important to note that the targets were not "all or nothing" milestones that Clinicas had to achieve in order to benefit from the impact payments; Clinicas would get paid as it made progress, albeit with certain timeline milestones in place. So, if Clinicas reached targets sooner than expected, they would get paid sooner; if they missed a milestone, they lost out on the impact-linked funding only for that target.

For the **SIINC** agreement to go into effect, Clinicas had to first close its **equity** funding round. Then, the SIINC payor would come in alongside the **equity** investor, giving Clinicas an extra funding boost as it achieved its impact goals alongside its business growth goals. In late 2016, Clinicas successfully closed a $1.5 million equity round.

A Rousing Success

Clinicas' SIINC was a rousing success. The company achieved well above their social outcome's targets over the agreed 2.5 years and received their maximum of $275,000 in impact-linked payments ahead of schedule. In all, both the **equity financing** and **impact-linked payments** have enabled Clinicas to expand its services to more than 100,000 patients, while growing the percentage of low-income patients from 32 to 37%. It also managed to raise an additional $6 million in funding from the International Finance Corporation (IFC), the Inter-American Development Bank (IADB) and other investors,[4] which will help the company scale to 100 clinics in the next few years.[5]

An interesting outcome of Clinicas' early discussions about the **SIINC** is that those conversations alone gave the company's impact outcomes a boost. See, the mere task of identifying relevant impact performance targets and ways to achieve these helped the team mobilize energy and resources to better serve Clinicas' most vulnerable patients. Its impact performance therefore started to improve even before the SIINC agreement was signed—so much so, in fact, that Javier had to update the baseline low-income-patient ratio before signing the final SIINC contract.

Unfortunately, the Clinicas team has also seen the inverse effect unfold, now that the **SIINC** is finished. They continue to measure the impact KPI, but measurement alone is not as powerful as being rewarded for it. Both Javier and Miguel say that if they were to do the contract again, they would prefer smaller impact milestones or lower payments over a longer period of

[4]IFC. (2019). Case Study: A Retail Approach to Diabetes Care. [online] www.ifc.org. Available at: https://www.ifc.org/wps/wcm/connect/industry_ext_content/ifc_external_corporate_site/health/publications/a-retail-approach-to-diabetes-care [Accessed 27 May 2020].

[5]IFC. (2019). Case Study: A Retail Approach to Diabetes Care. [online] www.ifc.org. Available at: https://www.ifc.org/wps/wcm/connect/industry_ext_content/ifc_external_corporate_site/health/publications/a-retail-approach-to-diabetes-care [Accessed 27 May 2020].

time, because having targets to which they were held accountable was itself a sufficient motivator.

Nevertheless, Javier and Miguel agree that the **SIINC** has shifted the company in a positive direction. The team has gained valuable insight into how to engage and retain low-income customers through the experience. The company now also has solid data on how its services are impacting Mexico's most vulnerable diabetes patients, which has given the team the confidence to expand into more low-income communities.

Roots of Impact too has learned a lot from its first **SIINC** deals. The organization has evolved the concept so that impact-linked payments can be built into any financial instrument, from **equity** to **debt** to **guarantees**, so long as there are three essential ingredients in place:

1. A clearly defined set of impact objectives and/or key performance indicators by which to measure the organizations impact performance
2. Terms on how and when data must be collected to assess the performance indicators
3. Terms of how performance correlates to the impact-linked payments, including how much and how often, and whether and how impact target adjustments can be made, if necessary.

"**Impact-linked finance** can be powerful in correcting market failures in underserved markets," says Bjoern. In fact, **impact-linked financing** is increasingly used in blended-finance agreements, where public or philanthropic funders and development agencies provide incentives in order to mobilize private investment and close commercial viability gaps while also guaranteeing impact.

Impact-linked finance also does not necessarily have to focus on enterprises that are commercially less attractive to traditional investors; rather, notes Bjoern, "it can be used to enable and incentivize market-based enterprises to accelerate and deepen their positive impact by generating additional outcomes, such as serving lower-income customers, women, or focusing on more rural areas."

Are SIINCs Right for You?

Founders

In order to qualify for **Impact-Linked Financing**, you need to have a strong **impact thesis** embedded in your strategy and you need to have a data set that can illustrate your **impact track record**. This means that you need to be collecting impact data that is relevant to your business performance and can be independently verified. You also need to be able to show how this impact data can be used to make strategic decisions.

You also need evidence of market failure. You'll need to be able to show that deepening impact and/or targeting highest impact areas will lead to higher risk and lower profitability, even if just in the short term. This means that you'll need to prove that making your product more affordable or better quality and/or serving very low-income groups or reaching more rural areas will create a short-term financial trade-off for your business.

Finally, you'll need to show high scalability and medium-term potential for commercial self-sustainability or public contracting, i.e., contracts with governments for service delivery. In addition to proving that you need to address a market failure in the short term, you'll need to be able to prove that after the funding contract ends, that you'll continue to be sustainable as an organization and continue to create impact. These contracts are intended to incentivize additional impact, not build in permanent levels of subsidies for organizations that are not commercially viable.

Funders

Mission aligned funders regardless of their financial constraints can be involved in **Impact-Linked Financing**. For funders that have LPs looking for market-rate returns, a partnership with a private or public funder that is willing to pay for additional impact can provide the necessary pieces to develop a contract. For private or public funders, impact-linked finance can be an effective way of "scaling what works" at the intersection of **blended finance, impact investing** and **results-based finance** (discussed in the next chapter).

For funders that are interested in developing **Impact-Linked Financing**, questions to ask include:

What is the right level of incentive to produce the desired results?
How can market distortions be avoided?
How to create maximum transparency about your impact?

To answer these questions and deliver on its promise, Roots of Impact in partnership with the Boston Consulting Group (BCG) has created the Design Principles for **Impact-Linked Finance**. These were formulated to promote the most effective use of this new practice. They represent a springboard for a broader involvement of practitioners, experts, academics and other stakeholders.

Due to the bespoke nature of many of these transactions, Impact-Linked Finance continues to suffer from high transaction costs and complexity, so harnessing technology to roll out these contracts will be imperative.

21

My Outcomes-Based Financing Journey

For this chapter, I'm going to walk with you on my own journey with **outcomes-based financing**. It begins in England and ends in South Africa, where I now live. This journey recounts my experience building a **social impact bond**. It was an incredible learning experience and proved the true impact potential of creative financing. I will preface this story, however, by saying that **social impact bonds (SIBs)** and **development impact bonds (DIBs)** are never the easiest and rarely the most useful structure for most founders and funders.[1] They are difficult for a founder to implement, as **impact bonds** require multiple stakeholders and complex contracting. Nevertheless, they're an important innovation in the world of **impact investing** and they are relevant to the broader narrative of this book, which focuses on making venture finance work better for a larger group of stakeholders.

A Social Impact Bond Primer

Before we go further, let's step back for a second and talk about what a **impact bond** is.

The first thing to note is that it isn't a bond. When Toby Eccles coined the term in 2010, he meant bond in the sense of a *promise*, not a listed debt

---

[1] A SIB refers to an agreement where government acts as the outcomes payor and a DIB refers to an agreement where private funders act as the outcomes payor. In this chapter, we'll refer to them as impact bonds to encompass both.

© The Author(s), under exclusive license to Springer Nature
Switzerland AG 2021
A. Patton Power, *Adventure Finance*,
https://doi.org/10.1007/978-3-030-72428-3_21

structure in the financial markets. A **impact bond** is a type of **outcomes-based contract** that operates like an equity agreement but instead of linking investors' returns to a company or organization's financial performance, returns are linked to impact achievements. This makes the calculations for returns more complex, and in turn, requires a number of different stakeholders to succeed.

How it works is essentially like this: A **social enterprise** or non-profit needs capital to implement a new program or business line, or expand their existing operations, in the service of their impact missions. Governments or donors interested in those missions may ultimately be willing to finance those enterprises or nonprofits, but first, they want to see that they can achieve the impact they say they will—they're not going to put up the capital upfront. Other funders or investors may be willing to risk some capital in the immediate term to give enterprises and non-profits a chance to prove themselves, but they're not going to take that risk without the chance of some upside— they'll want their money back, with a return, if those impact outcomes are achieved.

Impact bonds can take a painfully long time to structure and close, given that there are multiple stakeholders involved, all with slightly different objectives. A typical **impact bond** structuring process looks, in practice, like this:

1. A government, foundation or other funder commission's a contract from a nonprofit, social enterprise or other service provider, with a specific social or environmental objective in mind. This actor is known as an **outcomes payor** because they are ultimately responsible for paying for the initiative. Traditionally, Social Impact Bonds (SIBs) refer to contracts where public funders (i.e. government) are outcomes payors and Development Impact Bonds (DIBs) refer to contracts where private funders are outcomes payors. I'll use impact bonds going forward to include both types of contracts and those where there is a mix of public and private outcomes payors.
2. An **intermediary** organization is recruited to tap private investors for the working capital needed to achieve those objectives.
3. The capital is funneled to the **service provider** implementing the program or intervention that (hopefully) will achieve the outcomes payor's desired impact.
4. The **intermediary** keeps track of data and milestones on the initiatives' targeted social and environmental outcomes and helps the service provider make real-time adjustments to its program or intervention as needed.

5. At certain milestones, an independent **third-party assessor** reviews whether the pre-agreed outcomes are being met. Successful social achievements then trigger payments to the private investors that supported the initiative. Returns to investors (and service providers) are often funded on a tiered basis in **impact bonds**, meaning the more successful the intervention, the greater the return.

From Dreaming Spires to Endless Sunshine

My relationship with **impact bonds** started in November 2012 at the University of Oxford. I was working then with my colleague, Dr. Alex Nicholls, on a symposium on **social impact bonds** co-hosted by the university and the U.K. Cabinet Office. **Social impact bonds** were only officially two years old at the time. A total of seven had launched worldwide: five in the U.K., one in the U.S. and one in Australia. And each one has substantially different stakeholders, issue areas, structures and desired outcomes. Our goal for the symposium was to convene as many experienced people from the very small **social impact bond** world as possible to establish some consensus around best practices, trends and future direction of the instrument. We ended up with 38 people from five countries in a lecture hall.

At the time of writing, there were 138 **impact bonds** worth $440 million dollars launched globally, but that's getting ahead of the story. Back to Oxford.

The conversation at the symposium was lively and interesting and yielded a few points of consensus around social impact bond best practices. Following the convening, I authored a short paper to capture reflections and learnings about the state of the market.

A few months later, Francois Bonicci and Tamsin Jones at the University of Cape Town's (UCT) Graduate School of Business, got in touch with me. They were doing impact investing and public policy work for the Rockefeller Foundation while at UCT's Bertha Centre for Social Innovation and Entrepreneurship, and they invited me to Cape Town to engage with them on the project and present some of my own impact investing work to stakeholders. The opportunity to present my work and get a break from the U.K. drizzle was very appealing, so I flew down in April of 2013.

I focused my presentations to Francois, Tamsin and their colleagues on insights from the impact bond symposium and other social finance policy work that I had been involved in the U.K. I could tell there was an appetite from both public and private stakeholders to test out the impact bond concept in South Africa.

Scoping Out the Possibilities

Fast forward to March 2014. I had been living in Cape Town since June the previous year, had raised funding for a scoping study on **impact bonds** from the Government of Flanders, and hired my first full-time team member, Susan de Witt, at the Bertha Center's newly formed Innovative Finance Initiative. Sue and I were gearing up to present a policy paper to the Western Cape provincial government's public policy unit. The paper recommended opportunities for developing **impact bonds** in South Africa, and one area that the Western Cape government was particularly interested in was early childhood development (ECD).

The government of the Western Cape, where Cape Town is based, was at the time grappling with the issue of how to deliver ECD instruction for all of the province's children. Such an effort would require coordination between two departments, the Department of Health (DOH) and the Department of Social Development (DSD). It would also be costly. The government was interested in social impact bonds as a way to bridge their budgetary gap while delivering the educational and social services the province's young children needed and deserved. At that time, however, social impact bonds hadn't been tested in any emerging markets.

Sue and I saw three key advantages of **impact bonds** for South Africa. First, they could bring in new capital, primarily from the private sector, to fund public services. Second, they could improve cost-efficiency and services delivery, by focusing on outcomes. Third, introducing "market-like" mechanisms could drive innovation in public services and enable the private sector to share in the risks and returns.

Several key players within the Western Cape government likewise saw the potential. But **impact bonds**, as I noted, are complex and often time-consuming to structure. To succeed, several crucial ingredients were needed:

- First, significant political support and agreement among stakeholders about what constituted a successful outcome;
- Second, capable service providers with strong evidence backing the efficacy of their programs and interventions;

- Finally, robust data to determine the appropriate pricing for social outcomes, so that investors and payers could be certain they would receive value for their money.

A Lego Building Block

A month after our presentation to the Western Cape government, Sue and I secured a grant from the Lego Foundation to engage U.K.-based consultancy, Social Finance, in the design of an ECD-centered bond for the province. Social Finance had orchestrated the "Peterborough" **impact bond**, the first social impact bond in the world, focusing on criminal recidivism in the U.K. The team made recommendations that would help us galvanize interest from national, provincial and private stakeholders and design a **impact bond fund** that would make it possible to target multiple aspects of ECD.

By October 2014, with the PPU firmly behind our efforts, Sue and I secured a **grant** from the ECD-focused philanthropic organization Innovation Edge and continued working on the design of the ECD bond fund, which we named the Impact Bond Innovation Fund (IBIF). We convened a group of 14 individuals, including national and provincial government officials, investors, ECD practitioners, academics and monitoring and evaluation specialists to sit on the IBIF Advisory Board and to determine:

- Who will be the beneficiaries of the fund?
- What results should the fund target?
- What type of interventions can achieve these outcomes?
- How much are these outcomes worth?
- And how will the innovation fund operate?

These questions formed the basis of *three years* of design work that followed. At the IBIF Advisory Board meeting I had cautioned that it would likely take six to 12 months to complete the landscape research needed to inform the design of the impact bond. One of the new board members shot their hand up and asked "Why will it take that long? Surely, it could be done more quickly." Little did Sue and I know, our forecast would prove to be a massive underestimation.

Remember how I mentioned that a **social impact bond** had never been implemented in an emerging market, much less South Africa specifically? There was simply no local frame of reference for it, and the models that had been implemented in the U.K., U.S., Australia and elsewhere were only so applicable in such a different context. We were building the concept effectively from scratch, and that involved numerous complexities we couldn't have realistically anticipated in advance. Such as:

- Establishing a policy framework for outcomes-based contracting at *all* levels of government, local, provincial and national;
- Navigating stakeholders' needs for this particular contract, based on the aforementioned framing questions. (Do not be deceived by how short and simple they seem. They were anything but short and simple to answer.);
- Troubleshooting around the lack of available ECD data to reliably set baselines and determine the true cost of outcomes.

And then there were stakeholder disputes to address. The IBIF was set up to fund two different bonds: one with DoH and one with DSD. But a last-minute disagreement with the selected service provider for the DoH bond in mid-2017 derailed the entire project. Unwinding that portion of the ECD **impact bond** initiative caused significant delays to the DSD bond, the contract for which was only finally signed a year later, in mid-2018.

Costly and Complex

The **impact bond** for the Western Cape's Department of Social Development aimed to improve cognitive, language and motor skills for 3,000 children. The kids would receive regular home visits from Western Cape Foundation for Community Work (FCW), the contract's service provider, over a period of three years, and their progress would be measured using the Early Learning Outcomes Measurement (ELOM) tool. The outcomes payors included both the Western Cape DSD and a private donor, corporate foundation ApexHi. The private investors who committed the upfront capital needed to implement FCW's intervention included LGT Venture Philanthropy, the Standard Bank Tutuwa Community Foundation and Futuregrowth. Mothers2mothers, an international NGO providing health services to mothers and children throughout Africa, was brought in as a technical intermediary, providing program, budgeting, and monitoring and valuation capacity to the fund, while Volta Capital, a consulting firm, joined the effort as the financial intermediary.

Now, just over two years into the South Africa's first impact bond initiative, multiple other government-backed outcomes-based contracts and innovative financing instruments are in the works.

Reflecting back on this process, there is clear value in the policy work Sue and I conducted with various government agencies on structuring outcomes-based contracts. But the complexity, cost and staggering amount of time required to design these contracts have not improved at the rate we had hoped in South Africa or globally. Outside of the U.K., and to a lesser extent, the U.S., where an ecosystem of government-backed outcome funds had emerged, **impact bonds** remain highly bespoke transactions that require significant investment in contracting infrastructure, stakeholder education and policy advocacy.

Work continues to decrease the costs and reduce the complexity of impact bonds and other outcomes-based contracts, pioneered by Social Finance and the Global Steering Group, led by Sir Ronald Cohen. Technology is also being harnessed to streamline and automate aspects. That said, as we saw with Clínicas del Azúcar (Chapter 20) and the Dell Foundation (Chapter 19), impact-linked and outcomes-based financing doesn't have to be so complex. Impact incentives can be achieved more efficiently and expediently through simpler financing models and when fewer stakeholders are engaged.

Is an Impact Bond Right for Me?

Founder

If the **impact bond** infrastructure has already been created and you are evaluating whether or not to participate, you'll need to consider whether you have sufficient evidence linking your intervention to the outcomes identified by the **outcomes funders**. This evidence will be analyzed by the **impact bond investors** to build a financial model, so it will need to be verifiable and linked to program costs. You will also need to decide if you have the internal capacity to be able to not only deliver the services but undertake the required real-time **impact measurement** and engage with that data to make adjustments to your model as required. Finally, you will need to be comfortable partnering with the **investor** and/or **intermediary** involved in managing you and potentially other service providers.

If you are a founder evaluating creating an **impact bond** when there is not currently a willing **outcome funder** and the **contracting infrastructure**, this will likely not be a good use of your time and resources. I suggest you look at other financing options on the innovative financing spectrum.

Funder

As you've seen throughout the book, there are a myriad of ways for mission aligned funders to innovatively fund founders that are creating positive social impact. If you are a large private or public funder that has resources that do not require a financial return, participating in an **outcomes fund** may be an interesting option to explore. Additionally, providing philanthropic funding for the development of the infrastructure of the industry such as seeding technology providers, policy advocates and other intermediaries can be **catalytic.**

As a mission aligned funder with a required financial return, seeking out **impact bonds** and **impact bond funds** could present investment opportunities that allow you to fund particularly innovative and effective non-profit entities.

When evaluating these opportunities, it is important to understand if the **impact bond model** is truly the appropriate mechanism to address the outcomes sought. Using the evaluation framework at the end of this book may be helpful in this regard, additionally there are many resources available on the online companion to this book.

22

Linking Financing to Impact

After reading Chapters 19–21, you may be asking yourself *why? Why would you want to link the cost and distribution of capital to the achievement of social or environmental goals? Doesn't that just make things more complicated?*

You aren't wrong. It can make things very complicated (sometimes unnecessarily so). But realistically, incentives are everything and if you are a **social enterprise, a non-profit** or a mission focused funder, you need to be closely examining the incentives in every contract that you sign. We've discussed this concept throughout the book, beginning with the misalignment of incentives around equity.

It is important to remember that you don't need to jump all the way to an impact bond if you want to add incentives for impact, there are much simpler ways to integrate impact milestones into your funding contract.

Let's go through these options one by one to better understand how we can start to think about putting them into contracts. Just a warning that this chapter can get quite technical quite quickly, so you may want to skim over it for now and then come back and use it as a reference when you are designing a funding contract. You'll find additional resources around linking impact to financing on the online companion (Table 22.1).

A. Patton Power, *Adventure Finance*,
https://doi.org/10.1007/978-3-030-72428-3_22

Table 22.1 Impact linked financing options by category

Category	Relevant terms	Impact linking options
Cost of capital	*Interest, dividend/profit share, repayment, redemption*	Interest rate rebate, margin step down, outcomes-based payments
Funding disbursement	*Disbursement schedule*	Impact milestone tranched disbursements
Ownership	*Vesting, employee ownership*	Impact-linked vesting, Equity Earn Back
Convertibility	*Convertibility*	Impact milestone linked convertibility

Cost of Capital

In Chapter 19, we met **MSDF**, who is an impact-first investor that can be flexible with reduced returns. Thus, they were able to use an **interest rate rebate** to incentivize deeper impact. This type of rebate encourages entrepreneurs and businesses to prioritize impact in the short term or focus on lowering costs for their customers and end users. As an impact-first debt provider, **MSDF** was willing to reduce its financial return on investment to drive education quality in the short term.

A similar example of an **interest rate rebate** is UBS-OF's six-year impact loan to the Jacaranda Maternity Clinic chain in Kenya, which has three sets of **outputs** they use to adjust the **interest rate**:

- Level of clinical care: This is measured by how much time it takes to perform an emergency C section after they have identified the need for the procedure.
- Population served: This is calculated as the share of the patient population that is on public health insurance.
- Customer satisfaction survey.

UBS-OF chose these **outputs** by aligning their own **impact goals** as a foundation with those of the business, being careful not to restrict the sustainability of the business. Being able to do the transaction themselves, as opposed to working with an external **outcomes funder**, has reduced the time and effort that it takes for them to close these transactions, compared with the

impact bonds they have been involved with. It has also allowed them to be flexible in dealing with Jacaranda as they are the lender as well as the **outcomes payor**, so they are incentivized to ensure the company succeeds financially as well as achieving the impact **milestones**.

A margin step-down is a similar option for equity investors. In this case, an equity investor would agree to reduce their return if the company achieved specific milestones.

Realistically, the achievement of many social or environmental outcomes requires *a trade-off* to create deep impact. Nonetheless, there are some outcomes which are *aligned to financial performance* that do not require a trade-off. For instance, if a microfinance lender developed a risk scorecard that showed that specific actions like lending to women and conducting financial literacy training led to a lower **default** rate, they could show that outputs such as higher percentages of loans to women and the number of financial literacy trainings conducted were aligned to a reduction of risk and increased financial performance. For finance first funders who are not able to be flexible with their return, they are only able to take an **interest rate rebate** in cases where the milestones are *aligned* to short-term financial performance or the direct reduction in risk.[1]

Financial first investors structuring deep impact milestones that involve a potential *trade-off* require an external **outcome payer** who is willing to pay for the trade-off (i.e., the delta) in order to enable the venture to create the envisioned impact. **Social Impact Incentives (SIINC)** (Chapter 20) and **Impact Bonds** (Chapter 21) are examples of outcome payers engaging with investors in contracts.

In **Clinicas del Azucar's** case (Chapter 20), focusing on poorer customers caused the company to face a trade-off between creating deep impact and servicing the more profitable customers. Thus, these social milestones required *a trade-off to achieve deeper impact*. While **Impact Bonds** (Chapter 21) may seem similar, there are important differences: **SIINC's** pay premiums to businesses as revenue top-ups while **Impact Bonds** are generally used for non-profit interventions and pay for the whole cost of the intervention including investor returns.

---

[1]On the equity side, it would be possible to use a margin step-down similarly to an interest rate rebate, although I have not seen this in practice.

Funding Disbursement

Funders can choose to **tranche** an investment or a grant based on financial, social and/or environmental **milestones**. This means that you decide to break the disbursement of cash into smaller amounts. **Tranching** can help funders reduce their financial and social/environmental risk and ensure that the company is achieving its projections before disbursing additional funding. For an impact focused funder, mixing impact and financial milestones in tranching requirements can signal to founders that they care about both the financial and impact performance of the company.

Here is an example of impact milestones that needed to be achieved before the Global Innovation Fund (GIF) would distribute the second tranche of an investment:

1. Sourcing from more than, or equal to, 7 target groups and 20% of total sourcing from target groups for the 6 months immediately preceding the second tranche;
2. No more than 20% of the total sales volume to non-target groups for the 6 months immediately preceding the second tranche;
3. A minimum of 4,000 target beneficiaries to be onboarded on to the Company's proprietary platform.

These impact milestones stood alongside financial milestones such as levels of revenue and profit to be achieved. When Ginny from the GIF reflects on their use of impact **tranching**, she notes that it is a powerful tool for them as funders. The key, of course, is getting the milestones right. GIF includes an economist on all of their deal teams, who gets to know the company and can help create the appropriate, achievable milestones that will align the founder and funders' interests. Whenever they include these in a contract, they are a key topic in the contract negotiation with founders.

Ownership

In an **equity** investment, a funder might require the founder to agree to a **vesting** schedule[2] for their shares, so that if the founder was to leave the company, the shares that had not yet vested would be used to recruit a new operator. Traditionally, vesting schedules are time based or financial milestone

---

[2]For more on vesting and vesting schedules, please see the online companion.

based. There is also an option to base them on **impact milestones**, similar to **tranching**.

Another option around ownership is to create an incentive for founders to earn back ownership that the funder has purchased through the achievement of impact milestones. This is called an equity earnback. In this case, the contract would spell out the percentage ownership that could be redeemed by the founders and the specific milestones that must be achieved for them to do so.

If these **impact milestones** were *aligned* to financial performance, this option could make sense for both impact first and finance first investors. It would depend on the modeling, of course, but incentivizing founders to achieve additional aligned impact should also grow the company and increase its value, so even though the funder would be sacrificing ownership, they would be making their shares more valuable.

If the milestones created a *trade-off*, they would require an impact first investor willing to reduce their return in exchange for the achievement of additional social impact or a public/philanthropic funder compensating the investor for any concessions such as loss of earnings. Transactions where public or philanthropic funders collaborate with investors in order to catalyze (additional) impact are referred to as blended finance.

Convertibility

For types of funding that have a **convertibility** clause, you can choose to have that conversion be triggered by financial or **impact milestones**. This could be a **recoverable grant** that is linked to **impact milestones**, such as the number of women employed as a percentage of your workforce or the percentage of customers who were categorized as **base of the pyramid (BOP)**. In this case, funders might be looking for you to hit these milestones to keep the funding a **grant**, otherwise it would trigger the conversion and become repayable. This approach can be applied to relative impact performance instead of meeting absolute impact **milestones** (all or nothing) so that the entrepreneurs continue to be incentivized for each additional "unit" of impact. In some cases, staggered impact milestones can be agreed upon

Impact milestones are prevalent in **forgivable loans. Funders** can specify milestones by which the **founder** can reduce the **principal** owed on the loan, sometimes causing the entire **loan** to be **written off**.

Impact milestones are less likely to be used for **structured exits** or **convertible grants** as they could add significant complexity. **Funders** who

Table 22.2 Convertible instruments by type

Convertible Instruments			
Converts	Into		
From	Debt	Equity	Grant
Debt		Convertible Debt; Convertible Revenue-based Financing (Convertible RBF)	Forgivable Loan
Equity	Redeemable Equity		Equity Earn Back
Grant	Recoverable Grant	Convertible Grant	

are concerned about the achievement of impact in those contracts are more likely to have **mission-related default clauses** (see Chapter 27) in place.

Below are all of the different types of convertible agreements that we have discussed throughout the book (Table 22.2).

Linking financing to impact is not the right answer for every founder or funder, but as I said at the beginning of this chapter, it is worth examining the incentives in any funding contract that you sign as they will be extremely important in guiding how your company grows or your capital is used.

Part V

What If: You Want to Redesign the Entire Funding Process?

In Part II, we explored how to redesign **risk capital** to better suit the needs of founders that are not aspiring **Unicorns**. But what if investment structures aren't the only issue that makes appropriate **risk capital** inaccessible for most founders, particularly those that don't fit the traditional criteria of a "tech entrepreneur"?

Within the small percentage of founders that are aspiring **Unicorns**, there are significant disparities in which types of founders succeed in venture fundraising. In the U.S., the largest venture capital market in the world, all-women founder teams raised less than 3% of total VC funding in 2020[1]; companies founded by Black Americans received less than 1%.[2]

And this disparity doesn't get any better in the rest of the world. Companies founded solely by women garnered just 1.1% of the total capital invested in venture-backed start-ups in Europe.[3] In a 2017 study, Village Capital found that only 10% of VC funding raised in East Africa went to East African founders, with the remaining 90% raised by expat founders.[4]

A big reason for this inequality has to do with who makes the investment decisions. In the U.S., only 12.4% of investment decision-makers at

[1] Pitchbook.com data 2021.

[2] Citation: Nornam, J. (2020) A VC's Guide to Investing in Black Founders. Available at: https://hbr.org/2020/06/a-vcs-guide-to-investing-in-black-founder.

[3] Pitchbook.com data 2021.

[4] Baird, R., Fram, V., Tashima, R. & Matranga, H.S. *Capital Evolving: Alternative Investment Strategies to Drive Inclusive Innovation.* John D. and Catherine T. MacArthur Foundation. Available at: https://adobecapital.org/wp-content/uploads/2019/01/Capital-Evolving-Village-Capital-1.pdf.

Table 1 Redesigning the funding process

Sourcing	Due Diligence	Exit
In Chapter 23, we'll explore the world of crowdfunding through **Code for All's** experience	In Chapter 24, we'll join **Ross Baird** on his journey toward more democratic decision making during the due diligence process	In Chapter 25, we'll look at employee ownership as an exit opportunity for an investor through **Cal Solar** and **Project Equity's** journey

VC firms are female[5] and 81% of VC firms have no Black investors.[6] A recent study found that men were 60% more likely to raise funding than women when pitching the same business.[7] These gender and racial disparities in both venture capital and institutional investing have been present for decades and will persist unless the system is radically changed.

In this part, we'll explore ways that founders and funders can level the playing field for funding accessibility and equity, i.e., access to capital and obtaining capital on equitable terms, by taking a mission aligned approach to **sourcing, due diligence** and **exiting** investments (Table 1).

---

[5] Heller, J. (2020) The Hazards of Raising Venture Capital While Black. Available at: https://www.barrons.com/articles/the-hazards-of-raising-venture-capital-while-black-51593103012.

[6] Heller, J. (2020) The Hazards of Raising Venture Capital While Black. Available at: https://www.barrons.com/articles/the-hazards-of-raising-venture-capital-while-black-51593103012.

[7] Wood Brooks, A., Huang, L., Wood Kearney, S. & Murray, F.E. (2014) Investors prefer entrepreneurial ventures pitched by attractive men." PNAS. Available at: http://www.pnas.org/content/111/12/4427.

23

Code for All: Our Crowdfunding Journey

This chapter follows coding bootcamp Code for All, exploring the role that individuals can play in funding early-stage companies through **crowdfunding**. **Crowdfunding** allows your community of supporters, end users and everyday individuals to participate in your fundraising journey and business evolution. It can take many forms, but the most common are: **donation-based**, **rewards-based**, and **debt** and **equity crowdfunding**. In this chapter, we will also look at how participatory government budgets and "direct public offerings" fit into the **crowdfunding** picture. All of these are options to involve your community of supporters and end users in your fundraising journey.

Calling All Coders

Despite how integral technology is to our daily lives, there is a world-wide shortage of technical skills, particularly software developers. The skills shortage is so large, in fact, that there could be a global shortage of more than 85 million tech workers by 2030. Meanwhile, one in seven young people globally is unable to find work. Youth unemployment is a massive problem in many parts of the world. Even in parts of Europe, a wealthy region, the level of youth unemployment can range between 25 and 40%.[1]

---

[1] Youth unemployment rate in EU countries June 2020. 26 August 2020. Published by H. Pletcher. Available at: https://www.statista.com/statistics/266228/youth-unemployment-rate-in-eu-countries/.

© The Author(s), under exclusive license to Springer Nature Switzerland AG 2021
A. Patton Power, *Adventure Finance*,
https://doi.org/10.1007/978-3-030-72428-3_23

João Magalhães, Domingos Guimarães and Rui Ferrão saw this problem firsthand in their home country of Portugal, where all three were flummoxed by how there could be such a large unmet need for skilled software developers alongside high levels of unemployment. For them, the workforce skills mismatch presented a business opportunity to address an evident need and create social impact. Together they decided to build a computer programming bootcamp based on the intensive courses that were being used successfully in the U.S. and called it Code for All.

In 2015, the team needed funding to develop and run their first bootcamp. They decided to apply to what could be described as the original crowdfunding: public grants from the city of Lisbon's **participatory budget**. A participatory budget is a pool of public **grant** capital that citizens decide how to allocate. Portugal is a world leader in municipal participatory budgets, having established them in the early 2000s. Specific structures and processes guide the applicants through the proposal, deliberation and decision-making phases. The Code for All team submitted their application for €150,000 to Lisbon's participatory budgeting committee and received one of the highest number of votes on record, successfully securing the cash.

Reporting to Bootcamp

João, Domingos and Rui marketed their first bootcamp through their friends, networks and free PR from Start-up Lisboa and they received 600 applications from unemployed persons for just 15 places. Applicants didn't need to have any experience in programming or software development; rather the team's assessment focused on individuals' motivation and drive to get through the program.

Code for All's first bootcamp was a success, but when they were trying to place the graduates in jobs, the team encountered a lot of skepticism that software development could be taught in just 14 weeks to people who didn't have any experience. João, Domingos and Rui had to personally call their friends and acquaintances at start-ups and tech companies to convince them to give the graduates internships to get started in the field.

Over the course of its first year, Code for All successfully trained 102 people through its bootcamps and began teaching programming to young kids in public and private schools. The founders were keen to accelerate the growth, but they needed more capital, and the team was finding it increasingly difficult to secure funding. Despite having a proven track record of success and being cash-flow positive, funders were hesitant to get involved.

Few knew what an impact start-up was, and since Code for All's mission was based around unemployment, traditional VC and PE investors assumed the organization's model was closer to a **non-profit** and steered clear. The only source of external funding available that they were aware of was a **bank loan**. But being inaccurately perceived as a **non-profit**, meant that even the banks wouldn't loan Code for All the amount of money it needed to expand.

Code for All decided to look into raising money via **crowdfunding**. These were their options:

Donation-based crowdfunding: individuals donating money toward a social or environmental project.

Rewards-based crowdfunding: individuals donating to a project or business with the expectation of receiving a non-financial reward in return, such as goods or services, at a later time.

Equity crowdfunding: individuals investing into a company in return for ownership in the company.

Debt crowdfunding: individuals lending money to a company over a set period of time.

Code for All's unique needs helped them assess the different options. The team decided against **donation-based crowdfunding** as they knew they would need to raise a significant amount of capital in the coming years, and getting individuals to donate to the company wouldn't help convince investors of their financial viability. **Rewards-based crowdfunding** seemed more applicable to companies designing a physical or digital product that they could pre-sell—a training program didn't fit that description. The team didn't want to dilute their ownership at such an early stage by selling shares of the company through **equity crowdfunding**.[2] That left them with the option of **debt crowdfunding**, which is also known as **peer-to-peer lending (P2P)** or **loan-based crowdfunding**. This type of financing would allow them to borrow money from individual investors through a **crowdfunding** platform. The team figured it would be a quick way to launch a funding round, raise the money it needed, create brand awareness in the market and build a financial track record for investors.

---

[2]The legal framework of **crowdfunding** in Portugal was created in 2015 but only enforced much later by the securities regulator. Despite this gray legal environment a few crowdfunding platforms were operating in Portugal way before (e.g., Raize for P2P lending and Seedrs for **equity crowdfunding**).

Tapping the Crowd

João, Domingos and Rui settled on using Raize, the most popular **P2P** platform in Portugal. They were amazed by just how quickly the process went. It took just two weeks to go from Raize's onboarding process to putting their deal live on the platform in June 2016. As this was their first round, they offered an annual **interest rate** of 9.21% for an 18-month loan. The raise worked beautifully with the company raising the €25,000 it needed in less than 24 hours, with 138 investors participating in their campaign.

Code for All was hooked on crowdfunding. So were their investors—a group that kept on growing. In March 2017, Code for All launched another successful campaign for €75,000 for an 18-month term, this time at 7.82% **interest**. This raise attracted 380 investors. The company successfully paid off both **loans** and launched two more successful raises: €200,000 for a four-year loan at 4.25%, supported by 3,769 investors in December 2018, and €400,000 on the same terms, supported by 5,784 investors in July 2019.

The funding was necessary, but Code for All also benefited from a major unexpected side-effect of choosing **crowdfunding** to finance its early-stage growth: their track record on Raize helped with the company's other investment talks. "Investors were happy to see that we were very disciplined about cash and that we could repay our loans," said Bernardo Afonso, an angel investor who has been an integral part of the Code for All journey.

In 2018, Code for All leveraged its early **crowdfunding** track record to raise a round of **redeemable equity** funding from a socially responsible investment firm in Portugal called Fundo Bem Comum. The investor secured an **exit** in July 2019 after Code for All redeemed the shares. One month later, Explorer Investments, one of the biggest equity funds in Portugal, invested €1.5 million in **equity** in Code for All.

Pushing Beyond Portugal

Code for All's business success is underpinned by its social impact success. The company has a 90% placement rate for the candidates who complete its training; more than 80 companies have hired its bootcamp graduates. Their bootcamp admission rate is just 7%, which compares with top universities, and the candidates are chosen using data science techniques to identify the most promising future programmers and developers. Code for All now has an alumni network of more than 1,000 students and has expanded to seven locations across Portugal, the Netherlands and Cape Verde, with additional expansion planned. The company also continues to teach computer programming skills to school children through its own software called Ubbu. Schools teachers do not need to have any previous computer science background to use the software.

Bernardo, who first invested in the company in 2016 and later joined as its CFO in January 2019, says he believes that **crowdfunding** really was the best funding option for the business. While it could have been helpful to investors at the table during Code for All's initial growth stages, it was clear from their early conversations with funders that they didn't fit the typical VC model. Had a VC investor's capital been at stake, a potential push to purse growth at all costs could have also threatened their social mission.

Instead, being able to borrow from the community helped Code for All's founders avoid ownership **dilution** and helped Code for All raise awareness of its program within Europe.

Bernardo's advice for other founders? "No investor should force you to follow a specific model for growth. You should find investors that fit your growth model, your mission, and your culture."

Is Crowdfunding Right for You?

Founders

Crowdfunding is about more than just money. Whether you are tapping the crowd via a **donation-based, rewards-based, debt or equity** raise—or even through participatory budgeting—financing from the crowd is about building and engaging a community around your business.

One of the most famous **equity crowdfunding** campaigns was launched by ice cream company Ben and Jerry's, which raised $750,000 in 1984 with a structure called a **direct public offering (DPO)**. **DPOs** were the starting point for modern equity crowdfunding, giving business founders the option to fundraise directly from investors of any kind (wealthy or not) without dealing with all of the traditional intermediaries required for an **IPO**, like investment banks, broker-dealers and underwriters. All founders had to do was register with their state regulators to receive a qualification to proceed. **DPOs** continue to be an option for founders interested in engaging directly with potential investors.

As a founder, you can use tech-enabled **crowdfunding** platforms to structure your raise using a variety of different instruments depending on your capital needs. **Donation-based** and **rewards-based** campaigns can be simple to set up and do not require funders to invest in your business. When you move into the realm of **securities-based** (i.e., **debt** and **equity**) **crowdfunding**, you can structure your campaign around many of the options we've discussed in this book. From a **debt** perspective, these may include "**mini-bonds**," **loans, revenue-based finance (RBF)** and **convertible notes**.[3] From an **equity** perspective, these may include: **common shares, preferred shares, redeemable equity** and **SAFEs**.

Outside of these categories, **crowdfunding** can be used for the acquisition or development of real estate, investment into livestock or the facilitation of leasing equipment. It can also be used in **invoice** and **receivables factoring**.

As we saw with Code for All, **crowdfunding** can be a more efficient and accessible process for raising early-stage growth capital and **working capital**. It can also offer access to networks, non-financial support and mentorship from your crowd of investors. From a brand and marketing perspective, it can help you build traction, prove your product or service, provide market validation and generate marketing leads through social media and news coverage.

There are a few potential drawbacks to consider. Founders with limited networks—often disproportionately lower-income people and those from marginalized backgrounds—and a limited social media and online presence may find it difficult to raise capital using **crowdfunding**. The same is true for companies that sell their product to businesses (B2B): you might find that your story is more difficult to tell in a crowdfunding campaign if you are not selling directly to customers (B2C).

It also might end up being quite costly to raise capital, as some platforms require significant marketing campaigns to launch a raise. If you are in an uncertain regulatory environment, this may create risks to both **crowdfunding** intermediaries and founders.

Finally, it is important to remember that this is a very public arena should a company fall behind even temporarily on repayments. Disgruntled investors may use social media channels to voice their complaints about the company, which can be public and potentially damaging to the brand. Even when making on time payments, founders may find it onerous to manage a large group of investors without appropriate tools and governance processes.[4]

---

[3]Howard, E. & Mbengue, M. (2020). *ACfA Label Framework*. African Crowdfunding Association.
[4]http://africancrowd.org/faq-for-project-sponsors/.

Funders

As an individual funder, it is easy to get involved with causes that you care about or in which you spot economic opportunity—or both. Nonetheless, an important consideration for debt and equity **crowdfunding** is the **investment risk** for non-accredited investors. Some countries may not have clear regulations limiting investment amounts based on income, net assets or other considerations, but a good equity or debt crowdfunding platform should have steps to mitigate the risk of over-investment. This might include self-declarations, investment limits if one cannot demonstrate they are an accredited investor or require proof of accredited investor status to invest above a certain amount.

If you're interested in investing in the **crowdfunding** intermediaries themselves or evaluating them as a tool through which to disburse capital, you'll need to evaluate the selectiveness of the platform. Do they accept any issuer or is there a process that screens or vets issuers for both impact and financial considerations? Some platforms do a fairly thorough job of this, which can reduce risk for investors.

It is also important to understand the regulatory status of the different platforms and the implications on their service offering economics and scale. Some jurisdictions may consider **crowdfunding** intermediaries as similar to **broker-dealers**, while others may view them as akin to **investment advisors**. Globally, there have been significant movements by governments to effectively regulate crowdfunding, and the most mature markets like the U.S. and the UK are experiencing industry consolidation through mergers and acquisitions.

Most emerging market **crowdfunding** industries are in their infancy, hampered primarily by a lack of regulatory visibility. But there are industry associations and groups working to unlock crowdfunding as a tool for bridging business financing gaps. The African Crowdfunding Association (ACfA), for example, sees crowdfunding as a new form of intermediation that bridges the funding gap between **microfinance** and venture capital/private equity because **crowdfunding** platforms often have lower transaction costs compared to traditional funds, particularly for small investments. Additional clarity around regulation and increased awareness may improve the viability or attractiveness of smaller investments through **crowdfunding**, particularly for **impact investors** seeking solutions to the chronic lack of funding for emerging market small businesses that form part of the "**missing middle**".

Formalizing **crowdfunding** as a fundraising tool ultimately improves the pass-through rate of small businesses from the private to the public markets, thereby supporting existing capital markets infrastructure such as SME segments of a national stock exchange. **Crowdfunding** may also provide a new channel through which diaspora communities can invest in productive projects and promising businesses back home.

24

Village Capital: Our Community Led Capital Journey

Our next journey follows Ross Baird, the founder of **social enterprise** accelerator and investment firm Village Capital, who has been focused on making early-stage business funding more accessible and equitable for the past decade. Similar to the funders whom we met in Section 2, Ross has embraced **structured exits** as one tool. But the real innovation that he and Village Capital's co-founder Victoria Fram have brought to the market is how founders' wisdom, experience and insights are leveraged during deal **due diligence** phase through **peer-based decision making**.

Ross Baird began thinking about how to solve access to early-stage business funding while working in the **microfinance** industry in India, supporting India's low-cost private schools. He had seen just how impactful access to capital was in giving Indian children better schooling and wanted to similarly support businesses and entrepreneurs in other high-impact sectors. Ross was particularly inspired by the "**village bank**" methodology in microfinance, a **peer-driven investment approach** with its roots in ancient cultures, whereby financial services are administered locally rather than centralized in a formal bank.

"The original village banking model was based on trust," Ross explains. "Billions of dollars of capital have been directed by women in small villages, who know each other and understand what the needs and challenges are, and it is these women who are making decisions over who gets a microloan."[1]

---

[1] Paxton, J. (1998). *Sustainable Banking with the Poor: Case Studies in Microfinance.* The World Bank.

© The Author(s), under exclusive license to Springer Nature Switzerland AG 2021
A. Patton Power, *Adventure Finance,*
https://doi.org/10.1007/978-3-030-72428-3_24

Small Capital, Big Change

His introduction to Bob Patillo, head of Gray Ghost Ventures, in 2009, marked a turning point for Ross. Bob was also rethinking **venture capital** and how to make it fairer and more accessible to entrepreneurs. He was particularly troubled by the power dynamic between the investors and entrepreneurs—the people with the money to solve social problems versus the people who understood what needed to be done. Together, Ross and Bob launched a new investing strategy within Gray Ghost called First Light Ventures. First Light's focus would be on speedily disbursing small amounts of capital to promising but early-stage enterprises. They also began incubating a new idea that would completely change how venture capital decision making is done. Their inspiration: **the village banking model**.

Here's how their idea worked: A group of early-stage impact ventures would be selected to participate in an acceleration program and given **an investment readiness framework** at the outset to assess one another. They would then periodically reassess and rank each other against the framework and against their peers as the program progressed. The two ventures that ranked highest at the end of the program would receive investment offers from First Light. Ross and Bob hypothesized that the entrepreneurs would be shrewd judges of who was the best placed to receive the investment. They also hoped that the multiple viewpoints would improve the accuracy of assessment and limit the influence of individual bias in decision making.

Ross and Bob piloted this **peer selection** investment idea within First Light's portfolio and in partnership with Indian incubator DASRA in September 2009. One pilot in Mumbai expanded to three, with new cohorts in San Francisco and New Orleans. "We originally were pushed to start in the Bay, like Y-Combinator, but there's more impact when you build a successful company in New Orleans or Mumbai than New York or San Francisco," said Ross.

A Company of Its Own

As the model began to show promise, Ross started to think about spinning out the idea into its own investment company. The seminal moment came in New Orleans, where Ross had spent time after the city was devastated by Hurricane Katrina in 2005. During that time, he had witnessed how a disaster had given birth to an entrepreneurial renaissance that was committed to rebuilding the city. And yet, New Orleans was still not a hotspot for venture capital. Ross wanted to change that. In November 2009, he teamed up with a local incubator, the Idea Village, to run a dedicated peer selection program in New Orleans, which ended up making investments in LKickboard, a local education technology company and Jack and Jake's, a local food market.

Ross recalls the buzz in the room on the very first night of the program. For him, that was the moment that encouraged the creation of a company that supported entrepreneurs through community and tangible empowerment rather than the traditional financing model. Thus, Village Capital was born.

Ross joined forces with Victoria Fram, an investor with both U.S. and emerging market experience, and built a team to spin-off Village Capital from First Light. Village Capital has since hosted more than 90 peer selection programs with 1,100 entrepreneurs. In research associated with their approach, its participants have reported a 3x increase in their ability to raise capital than the average start-up. Village Capital has itself invested in 110 of the participating enterprises, 80% of which are still operating. It has exited 16 investments with positive returns.

The **peer selection process** has also had unexpected positive impacts on Village Capital's portfolio diversity, relative to more traditional venture capital peers. Forty-four percent of the portfolio are female-led ventures, and 34% of the U.S. portfolio is composed of founders of color. Geographically, more than 80% of the portfolio is based outside of California, New York and Massachusetts—the three states that together account for roughly half of all venture capital activity worldwide.

Ross acknowledges that there are challenges with **peer selection**, not least the unique nature of the methodology. Investors must feel comfortable outsourcing a large piece of their traditional business **due diligence** process to other entrepreneurs. In the high-risk world of early-stage investing, that can be a hard sell to traditional investors, many of whom don't believe that entrepreneurs have the training, experience and expertise necessary to reliably identify promising, investment-ready companies, or know how to accurately assess a company's value.

Beyond that, **peer selection** is a resource intensive process. Structuring programs is time consuming and costly, and perhaps not feasible for investors who are already inundated with start-up pitches. Village Capital continues to work on reducing the unit economics of the peer selection model without sacrificing the quality of decision making.

Pushing Deeper

While **peer selection** was disruptive to traditional venture capital, the financing tools Village Capital uses were not. "Our program and our decision-making process was highly democratic, but the financing tools that we were using were not," he acknowledges. "Venture capital is a very specific kind of financing for a very specific kind of business, and it leaves most out." It's an issue that Ross felt he and the Village Capital team needed to address.

Village Capital has since begun integrating more flexible and founder-friendly **structured exit** agreements into their portfolios. As a Kauffman Foundation fellow, Ross also launched a new organization, the Capital Access Lab, which supports finance innovators working on new and creative investment structures. The Lab's first request for proposals yielded applications from more than 100 fund managers and other capital providers. Ross realized the **alternative financing** space was much bigger than he and his colleagues at the Lab realized. The Kaufmann Foundation ended up funding five firms in partnership with the Rockefeller Foundation.

Reflecting on his entire journey, Ross says his work is only the beginning of a long process to make the start-up investment world more democratic and inclusive. "When we think of the word 'innovation,' we think a lot about *what*... great tool or product or service will change the world," he notes. "We don't think much about *how*...how we decide who gets an opportunity, how we fund it, how we structure it for success."

He adds, "The Village Capital journey has shown that we need less *what* and more *how* in order to build a better world."

Is Community-Led Decision Making Right for You?

Founders

Very often, investors hold all the power and capital. The true innovation in Village Capital's **peer selection** model is that it devolves power in the decision-making process to founders. The Village Capital model should encourage founders to pursue investment paths that have transparency for founders on how the decision is made, and diversity within decision-makers.

Funders

Investors who care about getting results that exceed benchmarks need to be thoughtful about the process—*how* they make investments as well as *what* they invest in. The Village Capital model has significantly outperformed other impact investment firms in diversity and inclusion metrics—and financial returns—by changing the composition of the people who decide who gets investment capital. Whether or not a funder is interested in **peer selection** specifically, integrating participatory structures and decision making into investments can mitigate bias and make entrepreneurship more meritocratic.[2]

As Ross reflects on their learnings, he has specific advice for funders who are interested in applying **peer-based decision making**. Providing a detailed and concrete matrix for evaluation can help improve the assessment of a venture and facilitate the **due diligence** discussion. A clear, detailed framework used in **peer selection** for evaluating **investment readiness** not only allows founders to articulate the specific milestones they have achieved across different facets of their company—testing their customer discovery hypothesis or validating their market, for example—but it also allows their peers to provide very specific and nuanced assessments of a company's performance and potential.

Multiple viewpoints can help improve the accuracy of assessment and limit the influence of individual bias in decision making. A key aspect of the **peer selection** process is that the rankings are composed of an average of multiple scores: combined not just from a single peer-to-peer review, but from up to 11 separate scores for each company. The back-and-forth of the peer selection process and the ability of multiple peers to focus on a variety of different components of a business, in turn, allow for a more comprehensive understanding of an early-stage company.

Finally, moving beyond a fully peer led process, bringing entrepreneurs on to **investment committees** or **advisory boards** can mean another insightful voice that adds value to the **due diligence** process. Remember Morgan Simon (who we met in Chapter 6)? She has done this with her Olamina Fund, which lends to financial institutions serving Black, indigenous and low-income communities. As part of their investment vetting and voting process, she created a Community Advisory Board made up of individuals from the rural, native and southern communities that the fund planned to target. The Board makes recommendations on specific investments and overall strategy to the

---

[2]Baird, R., Fram, V., Tashima, R., & Matranga, H. S. *Capital Evolving: Alternative Investment Strategies to Drive Inclusive Innovation.* John D., & Catherine T. MacArthur Foundation. Available at: https://adobecapital.org/wp-content/uploads/2019/01/Capital-Evolving-Village-Capital-1.pdf.

fund's investment committee, where two of the Advisory Board members also serve—and hold veto power.[3]

Entrepreneurs bring valuable experience of the market, with a deep knowledge of market factors, competition and differentiation within a given industry. The ranks of angel and venture capital investors are filled with former entrepreneurs, but it is evident in Village Capital's research that their ability to assess the investability of their peers is present long before they begin investing.[4]

[3] https://beeckcenter.medium.com/deciding-together-flipping-the-power-dynamics-in-impact-investing-b4c3d086f818.

[4] Baird, R., Fram, V., Tashima, R., & Matranga, H. S. *Capital Evolving: Alternative Investment Strategies to Drive Inclusive Innovation.* John D., & Catherine T. MacArthur Foundation. Available at: https://adobecapital.org/wp-content/uploads/2019/01/Capital-Evolving-Village-Capital-1.pdf.

25

Cal Solar's Journey to Becoming a Worker-Owned Co-Operative

Our next journey takes us into the world of **employee ownership**, where we join Cal Solar on their journey to becoming a **worker-owned co-operative**.

Taking the Reins

In 2008, Lars Ortegren found himself at the helm of a California solar power company. Lars had joined California Solar Electric, or Cal Solar, as its second employee in 2002. Now, amid hardship during the global financial crisis, Cal Solar's owner had turned the company and its 3 employees over to Lars, making him the company's owner operator.

In his new role, Lars got an up-close look at how much the success of the company depended on the employees carrying out its work. "When you're talking about renewable energy systems, we're installing these systems that typically have 25-year warranties on the working components, and they involve putting a lot of holes in people's roofs," he explains. "Given the risks," he added, "the idea of everyone equally owning that responsibility really seemed to make a lot of sense."

And so, Lars began thinking about a **shared ownership** model for Cal Solar that would directly link the risks and responsibilities to everyone in the organization. Also, because the home solar market was still fairly nascent and unproven at the time, Lars believed **shared ownership** would also create stronger incentives for workers to think about the business's long-term growth and success. Like any start-up, the risks for failure were fairly high—if the company succeeded in such a challenging economic environment, Lars believed the employees who made that possible deserved to be rewarded.

Lars' hunch about the benefits of **shared ownership** structures was well-founded. Democracy at Work Institute's 2014 annual survey of **worker co-ops**, for instance, found **worker co-ops** in several industries to be 2–4% more productive than non-employee-owned peer companies. A report by Cass Business School in London found much larger productivity gains: **Employee-owned enterprises** reported being 9–19% more productive than traditionally-structured businesses.

That said, shared ownership is woefully under-utilized in entrepreneurship and in mission-driven companies. It is also almost entirely absent in economic development conversations.

Interrogating the Options

In 2009, Lars started investigating options for converting Cal Solar to a **broad-based employee** ownership model. There were several different models Cal Solar could consider, all of which required commitments in time and resources; it was up to Lars and his team to decide how they would proceed.

Employee Stock Ownership Plans or **ESOPs** are the most common **broad-based employee ownership model** in the U.S. They effectively function like a **401(k) employee benefit plan** in the U.S. that allows a company to transfer full or partial ownership to its employees. With an **ESOP**, there is no requirement for profit-sharing or democratic governance, wherein employees have strategic decision-making rights. That said, the most successful **ESOPs** have highly participatory cultures and often have formalized ways to engage employees in the strategic decisions.

Although the structure is accompanied by tax benefits that offset the cost over time, **ESOPs** have high upfront costs and higher ongoing costs. To make financial sense, a company should have 40 employees or more. With only 6 employees at the time, Cal Solar would have had a relatively large upfront bill to implement an **ESOP** and outsized regulatory costs going forward.

There was also the option of a **worker co-op transition**, which is similar to a **management buy-out**, but instead of just a few key managers purchasing the business, most or all employees are offered an equal ownership stake and have the opportunity to participate in profit sharing. To do this,

Cal Solar would have to formally convert the business entity into a **worker-owned structure**, and then sell the company's assets to that new entity. Each worker would then "buy into" the co-op and as a new owner, would receive a single voting equity share. The company would then appoint a democratically elected **board of directors**, with **worker-owners** holding the majority of those seats. Company profits would be shared among worker-owners based on their status as full- or part-time workers, known as "patronage." An advantage of the co-op model for small companies like Cal Solar is that the transaction and administrative costs are lower than an **ESOP**.

A third option, also suitable for a smaller company, is known as an **Employee Ownership Trust** (EOT) or a **Perpetual Employee Trust**. EOTs are designed to preserve the business over the long term for employees' benefit. Employees don't pay for their ownership benefits, and they receive a share of the company's annual profits. These, however, are more common in Europe than in the U.S.

Lars considered Cal Solar's choices. "The idea of **co-operative ownership** always seemed really enticing to me," he says of the decision to go with the second option. He reached out to Democracy at Work Network (DAWN), a group of certified peer advisors who provide technical assistance to **worker co-ops**, to look at Cal Solar's financials and outline the steps that transitioning to a **co-op** would entail.

The advisor at DAWN told Lars that Cal Solar's transition to a **worker-owned co-op** was certainly feasible. The first phase of the **co-op** conversion process calls for strong financial readiness, however, the company would also need to be prepared to invest significant time into facilitation and support for legal and governance work. The fees would amount to at least $30,000. It was more than Cal Solar could afford at the time.

Even though Cal Solar wasn't financially in a place to proceed with a **co-op** transition, Lars felt that the exploratory exercise with DAWN had been informative. There was a lot Cal Solar could do to continue moving toward that goal, including building up its cash reserves and management capacity and establishing its **worker-owner participatory processes**. Also, by simply initiating internal discussions about becoming a co-op, Cal Solar began cultivating interest and buy-in among its employees, which would be critical to a successful transition.

Five Plus Four

It took a full five years for Cal Solar to reach its next inflection point on its journey to becoming a **worker-owned co-op**. Having reached a more "comfortable" place financially, Lars sought advice on how to begin working to develop the requisite bylaws, operational procedures and decision-making protocols. He brought in the team from Project Equity to help.

California-based **Project Equity** is a non-profit organization that supports companies transitioning to **employee ownership**. It was co-founded in 2014 by Alison Lingane, whose career focused on mission-driven companies that create human impact at scale, and Hilary Abell, who had a background building **worker-owned co-ops**. Both women firmly believed in the social and financial benefits of employee-owned business models and sought to encourage employee ownership to become more mainstream by helping established organizations like Cal Solar transition to employee ownership.

Project Equity was eager to engage when Lars approached them in 2015, and after working with them for a period of time, Alison and Hilary's team realized that Cal Solar was in a big growth phase and was having trouble carving out the time to effectively manage its growth and to plan for the transition to **employee ownership**. As a solar company, Cal Solar's business was highly sensitive to economic volatility and environmental abnormalities. "We're very susceptible to micro-changes on global, state, and local issues, [including] any changes on the national scale, or if we have a bad-weather year, or if our local building department decides to change regulations," Lars explains. Cal Solar would have to grow beyond that "sensitivity threshold" before it could proceed with plans for a worker-owned transition.

By early 2019, with the help of an outsourced CFO recommended by Project Equity, Cal Solar was ready to re-engage Project Equity to move forward with plans to become a **co-op**. During those years, the company grew its employee headcount to 33 and achieved double digit year-over-year revenue growth. Lars attributes much of this growth to the thriving entrepreneurial culture and company dedication among Cal Solar's workforce, spurred by the ongoing worker-ownership discussions.

Project Equity mapped out an updated plan for a worker co-op transition, which Cal Solar returned to in 2019. First, they began training new staff on the transition process. Next, they launched a five-person transition committee to lead the transition planning, including landing the terms for the purchase and sale agreement, finalizing new bylaws and a decision matrix, and developing new operational and management approaches suited to the new structure. Within five months, Cal Solar set up a new worker **co-op** business entity with the requisite governance structures and executed the sales transaction that officially made Cal Solar a worker-owned company. The entirety of the Cal Solar team was able to participate in the company buy-in, making them all **worker-owners**.

Ownership and Resilience

What changed at Cal Solar once it became an established co-op? First, the company is now governed by a board of its **worker-owners**. Cal Solar appoints its board of directors through an election process with its **worker-owners** ("**representative democracy**"), and **worker-owners** occupy a majority of the board seats, in keeping with co-op guidelines.

Second, strategic decision making at the company also had to shift to become more participatory than when Lars was the principal business owner. But **co-ops** don't take a uniform approach to decision-making processes, and at Cal Solar, the only decision that requires unanimous **worker-owner** consensus is the addition of a new **worker-owner**. For this, Cal Solar's **worker-owners** established a process for evaluating a new candidate over the course of a year, in order to create a high enough bar for ensuring that the candidate is committed to Cal Solar's culture and growth. In early 2020, at the end of its first year as a **co-op**, Cal Solar underwent its first vote to approve new worker-owners.

Third, the company had to establish a management structure that would foster this more participatory culture within the organization. It has so far been able to do this even while maintaining a more traditional, top-down hierarchical structure (which most **co-ops** have).

Within its first year, the benefits of Cal Solar's new ownership model became clear. In particular, Lars says the company witnessed "instant payoff" in the company's flexibility and resilience amid a business climate deeply disrupted by the COVID-19 pandemic, economic instability, and mass social and political demonstrations in the U.S. He attributes this to better strategic decisions made by workers who think as business owners rather than employees. "We have to live in such an adaptable place and shift so frequently," he explains. "Having our employee base buy into the company's wider vision has made us a more adaptable company."

For instance, when California imposed state-wide lockdowns in response to the COVID-19 pandemic, Cal Solar faced certain financial hardship: It had a short cash **runway**, was waiting on a few large commercial orders to pay out and had no visibility into when deliveries or government services it needed would resume. The situation was far from unique to Cal Solar, and like many other companies, it temporarily furloughed all of its employees. But unlike many other companies, Cal Solar's employees—not just its senior managers—continued strategizing to figure out how to keep parts of the business running. The sales team figured out a way to partner with a battery manufacturer so Cal Solar could install energy storage units. By becoming an administrator of a storage rebate program, the company was able to generate a year's worth of battery sales in about three weeks. In turn, the company's 2020 financial projections fell by only 2%, in spite of a major and prolonged period of business disruption.

Cal Solar anticipates benefits of the **co-op** model to evolve and expand over time. Lars says one of the impacts Cal Solar expects to see is greater employee satisfaction. Also, it is possible the company will foster deeper customer loyalty, because customers may feel more secure knowing the person working on their home is directly invested in the success of the work and product they're delivering. And last but not least, co-op ownership enables Cal Solar to be authentically accountable to its mission of fostering a more responsible and sustainable society through clean energy.

"If you have a company that really cares for its employees and the employees care a lot about what they do," says Lars, "then **employee ownership** is a no brainer as a model to create longevity for that business."

Shared ownership is a model for everyone who cares about local businesses being retained across generations; as Alison from Project Equity says, "that's the real macro impact on an economic level."

Is Employee Ownership Right for You?

Founders

Employee ownership sends a powerful signal about a company's values and commitment to its workers and communities. And it can work for companies in any business sector, with only minor exceptions; for example, in U.S. law firms, only lawyers are allowed to own the firm.

You can pursue an **employee ownership** model at any time during your company's lifespan, whether from the outset of the business formation; amid a growth stage, as Cal Solar did; or when ownership naturally changes, like when a founder or owner decides to retire or sell the business. An **employee ownership** transition fundamentally entails:

1. *Business Entity:* The creation of an employee-owned entity (by transitioning the existing business, or setting up a new entity like a trust or a worker-owned co-op)

2. *Sales Transaction:* The current owner/owners sells/sell the existing business (or its shares or assets) to the employee-owned entity and executes a purchase and sale agreement. The sales transaction is typically financed by a group of lenders (see chart below). Specific to the worker co-op model, each worker-owner "buys in" to the co-op and receives a single voting equity share. In other models, employee ownership is treated as an employment benefit, i.e., is "free" to the employee.

3. *Roles and Culture Transition:* A transition of roles and the development of an ownership culture brings the many proven benefits of employee ownership to life. In a worker co-op, the worker-owners democratically elect a board of directors made up of a majority of worker-owners, on a one worker, one vote basis. Often, technical assistance from co-op developers specializing in this work helps smooth this transition.

4. *Profit sharing:* Though not built into all **employee ownership** models, profit-sharing is an important support for developing an ownership culture and is a highly recommended component. A **worker co-op** does have **profit sharing** (called "**patronage**") built into the model. All **worker-owners** earn profits based (essentially) on hours worked. For example, a three-quarter time **worker-owner** would earn three-quarters of the profit sharing that a full-time worker-owner earns.

Because the financial transaction that creates **employee ownership** can occur separately from the management transition, businesses can complete the financial sale first and then the management transition after. A phased approach can minimize risk by introducing less change to the business all at once.

Timing is an enormous consideration when it comes to transitioning to **employee ownership**, particularly in regard to the original owner and their relationship to the business. Project Equity notes that businesses need to consider in general: (1) Is it a good time for the owner to **exit**? (2) Is there a solid second-in-command ready to step in?

Project Equity generally sees two kinds of business owners considering conversions: those who are seeking to withdraw from the business to retire or focus on other pursuits, and those who are not exiting and have other management, economic, ethical or practical reasons for worker ownership.

Exiting owners must be focused on preparation. In an ideal world, retiring business owners would use a five-year **runway** for these planning considerations; as they must think through a wide host of legal, financial and human relations complexities like:

- How much money do I personally need to retire? What **valuation** does the business need in order to provide that? How close is the business to that point?
- Who will take over all the roles that I play (knowing that over a lifetime of running a business, the owner usually has a complicated variety of jobs)? Is that person/are those people present, or do I need to hire? In what ways will that person need to be groomed?
- Do I have outstanding personal loans that need to be transferred to the business? Other financial obligations?

For non-retiring business owners, the right time means there is bandwidth among at least a small team of employees to oversee the process and make decisions, and/or the business has the required resources on hand to go through the process.

Funders

Worker co-ops can raise external financing, but they cannot give up control (voting shares). Only **worker-owners** have voting shares (one voting share per owner), because of this, co-ops either raise debt or non-voting preferred equity shares.

Both public and private funders can look to finance **employee ownership** transitions as a way to build more resilient businesses and create lasting jobs. Receiving training from employee ownership support organizations like Project Equity and DAWN can enable small business services entities, law firms and financial institutions to better support existing businesses, assess the feasibility and requirements of transitioning to an **employee ownership structure**, and if necessary, to take on debt to finance this.

Support organizations like small business services, non-profits, law firms and finance institutions can be trained by **employee ownership** support organizations to work with existing businesses (small, medium and large) to assess feasibility for the enterprise to take on the debt for an **employee ownership** transition.

The capital gap for broad-based **employee ownership** exists mostly outside of the **ESOP** form (for worker **co-ops** especially)[1] partially because lenders rely on **personal guarantees**, which is hard to do for a business that truly has 20, 30 or 100 or more equal shareholders. This capital gap can be addressed by a dual-pronged approach. First, by increasing the pipeline of co-op transitions. Second, creating a more sustainable long-term horizon means there is a need to increase the capital under management available to finance these transactions both by growing funds that target employee ownership transitions, and by opening up lending from institutions that don't currently lend in this space.

In 2019, Project Equity partnered with Shared Capital Co-op to launch a joint initiative, *Accelerate Employee Ownership*. Shared Capital Co-operative is a national community development finance institution (CDFI), which specializes in financing employee ownership and **co-operatives**. The initiative was seeded by $5 million from the Quality Jobs Fund to support the sales transactions from small business owners to their employee base. Shared Capital Co-operative has the flexibility to provide both debt and equity investment depending on the needs of the business.

By bringing additional capital to the field, and engaging with and co-lending alongside other financiers, Project Equity and Shared Capital aim to drive alternative risk profiling to demonstrate to institutions how to lend without a **personal guarantee** (a distinctive element of the **co-op** transition's financial transaction) and how to approach **due diligence** for **employee ownership** business structures. This focus can have a ripple-out impact that fuels and scales the shared ownership movement: by first infusing employee ownership lending into dedicated CDFIs, then to mission aligned CDFIs, then to community banks. Ultimately the vision is that every major bank will lend for these transactions, once their volumes increase to a level where they become much more common and any regulatory hurdles are cleared across jurisdictions (Table 25.1).

---

[1]Another reason for ESOPs' widespread nature as an ownership instrument is that major banks traditionally have ESOP lending arms, creating a broader capital market to support financing the creation of these enterprises.

Table 25.1 Sources of capital for employee-owned companies

Source of capital	Considerations
DEBT	
Institutions (Banks, CDFIs)	Collateral and personal guarantee requirements can be barriers. Institutions that make cash flow small business loans, or those with experience in employee ownership are likely to be the best fit. Primary position on all assets except a secondary position on inventory; set repayment schedule
Vendors	Primary lien on business inventory
Selling owner	Subordinate, often unsecured, repayment contingent on primary debt repayment
Individuals (customers, community, friends, family, employees)	Subordinate, often unsecured, repayment contingent on primary debt repayment
EQUITY	
Worker-owner buy-in (in a worker co-operative)	Voting shares, usually small percentage of source of funding
Accredited investors (Private Placement)	In a worker co-op, equity investment is through preferred non-voting shares, with a targeted rate of return subject to co-op performance
Contributions or grants	No repayment required

26

Redesigning the Entire Funding Process

As we discussed at the beginning of this section, inequality in the global early-stage funding system is stark. I'm sure you have felt this on your own journeys. Unequal access to capital perpetuates global inequality. While all of the strategies and structures that we discuss in this book can play a role in making capital more inclusive, this section is perhaps the most powerful when thinking about how to address systemic inequality. Each chapter in this section addressed a different stage of the early stage funding process and each chapter suggested ways that funders and founders can redesign their funding processes to encourage diversity, inclusivity and a focus on community ownership of decisions, assets and profits (Table 26.1).

Founders

As a founder who is keen to redesign your own funding process, you have many choices to break out from the traditional grind. As we've discussed here, some of the options include choosing to **crowdfund**, creating a profit-sharing structure with your employees or transitioning to **employee ownership**. As a founder, you must decide how you want to embed your mission in your funding process and in your long-term ownership plans for your company.

One philosophy that is gaining traction is the idea of Steward Ownership. In the introduction of this book, we met **Max** from the **Creative Action Network (CAN)**, whose anchor investor is a company called **Purpose**

© The Author(s), under exclusive license to Springer Nature
Switzerland AG 2021
A. Patton Power, *Adventure Finance*,
https://doi.org/10.1007/978-3-030-72428-3_26

Table 26.1 Chapter overview

Sourcing	Due Diligence	Exit
For **João, Domingos and Rui** (Chapter 23), the investment community in Portugal didn't understand **Code for All's** potential as a social business, so they turned to the larger Portuguese community to get the funding that they needed. In the end, **debt crowdfunding** provided them with the opportunity to raise capital, create brand awareness and build an investment track record	**Ross** (Chapter 24) took his inspiration for **Village Capital's** community-led decision-making process from the village banking model in India. He saw significant opportunity in addressing not just the WHAT (the kinds of structures used in investing), but the HOW (the way decisions are made around who can access capital)	For **Lars** (Chapter 25), transitioning **Cal Solar** into an **employee-owned organization** made sense from a business perspective and a sustainability perspective. For **Alison and Hilary** (Chapter 14), building out the transition to **employee ownership as an exit option** for owners and investors has been a key focus of **Project Equity**

Ventures. As a funder, Purpose supports companies that have **steward ownership**. **Steward Ownership** refers to a set of legal structures that instill two core principles into the legal DNA of a business: Self-governance and profits serve purpose. These structures ensure that control (voting rights) over the business is held by people inside the organization or very closely connected to its mission. Voting control in **steward ownership** forms is not a saleable commodity. Profits in steward-ownership companies are understood as a tool for pursuing the company's purpose.

After paying back capital providers and sharing economic upside with stakeholders, the majority of profits are reinvested in the business. Steward Ownership forms include an **asset-lock**, which prevents the proceeds of a sale from being privatized. This structure aligns decision-making power with active stakeholders close to the business, instead of remote investors or shareholders.[1] Equal Exchange's **"no exit" clause** in their preferred stock offering is a great example of **steward ownership** in action. We'll discuss this in a bit more depth in the next chapter.

---

[1] https://www.impactterms.org/.

Funders

While Village Capital has built its entire model on allowing founders to participate in the deal **due diligence** process, funders interested in integrating structures and decision-making processes that mitigate bias and make entrepreneurship more meritocratic have many options to do so.

One of the simplest is to just step outside of your comfort zone. Take the case of Antonia Opiah, who founded Un-ruly in 2013 after years working for New York City's top digital advertising agencies. She saw a huge gap in the black hair industry and was inspired by her own frustrations to create a company that truly catered to black women. Un-ruly was launched as a beauty blog dedicated to black hair and later, Yeluchi by Un-Ruly became a marketplace to facilitate at-home professional hair styling services for women of color.

Antonia had always wanted to run her own business, even writing that goal in her diary at a very young age. As the business took off, she was hesitant to raise capital for two reasons. The first was that she was disillusioned by the obsession with capital raising as a goal versus building a revenue generating company. Secondly, in the few conversations she had had with funders, she was astonished to discover their seeming inability to understand the issue she was addressing around black hair.

"Funders in general just need to step out of their comfort zones because opportunities lie everywhere," she said. "Black hair has been getting a little bit more attention than it has in the past, but to me, the potential of the black hair industry has always been there… Consumers in that space are spending nine times more than other types of consumers. And they're currently being underserved. To me, that just equals opportunity. But it's crazy, because it's taken so long for people to recognize that opportunity. I think it's just a result of people, investors or funders, just not being familiar and sticking with what they know, the archetype of successful founders as a white guy with a hoodie who looks like Mark Zuckerberg."

In the end, Antonia and her sister and co-founder, Abigail, ended up raising capital from Tyler Trinigas at Earnest Capital through a shared earnings agreement, a type of **redeemable equity**. Antonia and Abigail had reached out to Tyler based on his investment ethos of founder friendly capital that didn't prioritize growth at all costs. And during their initial meetings with him, they were impressed by how much research he had done into the black hair market. Although it was not a market that he was familiar with personally, he was able to look beyond his own experience to understand the opportunity and develop a funding structure that matched their needs for both risk and return.

In addition to stepping out of your comfort zone to find and understand funding opportunities, you can ensure that the decision-makers around you have a diverse set of world views and life experiences. This can be in your **investment team**, your **investment committee**, your **board** or your funding partners.

Other funders that we've met in this book, such as Project Equity (Chapter 25) and Candide Group (Chapter 6), have used their transactions to help companies make the transition toward more stakeholder focused structures. Many of these funders subscribe to the principles of **steward ownership** and use their investments to help companies create the legal framework to protect their mission and direct profits toward reinvestment and employee focused disbursements.

As founders and funders, we can reframe who participates in the **sourcing**, financing, **due diligence** and ownership. The problem is, if we don't address inequity in decision making and wealth accumulation, no matter how well we structure financing, we are likely to continue to perpetuate unequal systems.

27

Embedding Mission into Contracts

In our final chapter before we start putting everything together, I'd just like to build on a few of the points we discussed in the last chapter around mission and talk about ideas for embedding your social mission into your funding contracts.

For founders, as you go down your funding journey, you will likely engage with some funders who completely understand and support your mission. You may also encounter funders who are interested in your business but see your mission as secondary to, or even a hindrance to, your growth. Regardless, it can be important for you to evaluate how to include your mission statement into funding contracts as a way to reduce the risk that funders will pressure you to move away from your mission.

For funders, some of the financing structures that we've discussed throughout the book can expand the type of **founders** you can engage with beyond non-profit organizations, while still fulfilling your own social and environmental mission. This may mean that you start funding for-profit organizations for the first time. This can be a fraught situation for many funders used to the security of contractual mission alignment with non-profits. Being able to enshrine a mutually agreed upon mission into the funding contract can be a way to better align your contracts with your shared impact priorities.

The bottom line is that having a mission agreed upon in a funding contract can align the incentives of all parties involved. If you are all on the same page as to which financial, social and environmental goals you are looking to achieve, then your relationship with your founder/funder should be off to a

© The Author(s), under exclusive license to Springer Nature
Switzerland AG 2021
A. Patton Power, *Adventure Finance*,
https://doi.org/10.1007/978-3-030-72428-3_27

Table 27.1 Embedding mission options by category

Category	Relevant terms	Embedded mission options
Type of funding	*Security*	Type of funding structure
Use of funding	*Use of proceeds*	Ring-fenced use of proceeds
Ownership	*Vesting, employee ownership*	Steward ownership
Default provisions	*Covenants, events of default*	Mission drift default, put options, facilitated exits
Rights	*Information rights, voting rights*	Mission change voting, Impact reporting

good start. Let's go through a few different ways that you can think about embedding mission and impact into your funding (Table 27.1).

Type of Funding

One option that **founders** and **funders** have to embed their mission into their funding is by choosing funding structures that complement their mission. Take for example how Candide Group (Chapter 6), Adobe Capital (Chapter 9) and Village Capital (Chapter 24) have pioneered different types of **structured exits** to create funding options that are more inclusive and that are better suited to founders achieving their long-term impact goals.

As a **funder**, just the willingness to explore different types of funding options can have significant impact. As a founder, understanding your options enables candid conversations with prospective funders about the right kind of capital for you. These discussion can be extremely important for the future of your organization and your ability to achieve your social mission.

Use of Funding

Traditional **grant** contracts generally have quite specific requirements around what money can be used for. The types of contracts that we've been discussing in this book rarely have detailed requirements around **use of proceeds** as they can be quite restrictive for founders and not well suited to organizations that need flexibility and freedom around how they use their capital. For most founders, having grant capital be unrestricted is the best possible option. Nonetheless, if you are bringing in **mission aligned** capital for a specific purpose, there are times you might want to consider putting that purpose into the contract and **ring-fencing** how that capital can be used.

An example of this would be a foundation giving a **convertible grant** to a social enterprise, like UBS-OF did to Trackosaurus (in Chapter 17), for the development of a specific product. UBS-OF was granting Trackosaurus this funding to develop an evaluation tool for early childhood development (ECD). In the contract, the use of the funds is restricted to the project description and goals written by Luke for the funding. If Luke decided one day that he actually wanted to build a gaming platform to increase high school scores in science instead of an evaluation tool for ECD with that capital, he would have to submit a modification request to UBS-OF, which could be denied.

A similar clause could be put into a loan agreement's **use of proceeds**, where the funder was interested in a company developing, for instance a "Spanish language version of the product and development of mobile features to make the product more accessible to low- income people".[1]

Ownership

In this section, we discussed different forms of **distributed ownership** as well as the idea of **steward ownership**, where stewards must pass voting rights onto successors upon leaving their role and must be committed to protecting the company's purpose and mission over time.[2]

In the U.S., the most widely utilized broad-based employee ownership model is **Employee Stock Ownership Plans (ESOPs)**. It's common for companies to design partial **employee ownership**, and it's possible for that ownership arrangement to stay partial in perpetuity; though in many cases, an initial partial ownership through an **ESOP** can establish the basis for an eventual transition to become 100% employee owned. Companies outside of the U.S. can create partial **employee ownership** options in the form of an **employee option pool**. This is standard among early-stage equity investors.

You can take this a step further by creating an **employee ownership trust (EOT)** or an **employee benefit trust (EBT)**.[3] These are trusts established to hold assets to provide benefits for the employees of a company or group of companies and sometimes also former employees and employees' dependents.

---

[1]Impact Terms Project.

[2]Impact Terms Project & Purpose Capital https://purpose-economy.org/content/uploads/purposebo oklet_en.pdf.

[3]Also sometimes called a perpetual employee trust.

EOTs and EBTs preserve the business over the long term for the benefit of the employees. Employees don't pay for their ownership benefits, and they receive a share of the company's annual profits. **EOTs** have lower set-up costs as compared to **ESOPs**.[4] This form of **employee ownership** is more common in Europe, and most in the UK are familiar with The John Lewis Partnership which is structured as an **EOT**.

Other legal options that embed mission into ownership structures include: **Golden Shares**, which divides voting and economic rights between classes of stakeholders. In this structure, 1% of voting rights are classified as the "Golden Share", which includes the right to veto an attempted sale of the company or changes to structure. Another such structure is a **Single Foundation**, where the business is majority owned by a self-governing non-profit institution, often with two boards: Corporate and Charitable. A third option is a **Trust Foundation**, which separates voting rights and dividend rights by placing them into separate legal entities: a charitable foundation and a foundation managed by stewards (this decouples profits from charitable contributions).[5]

Default Provisions

As an impact focused funder, you might be concerned about the future direction of the company that you are funding and want to have some protections around **mission drift**. This is particularly true if the funding you are providing is below market rate. In that case, it might be important for you to include an opportunity to recoup your funding if the company is no longer creating the impact that you had originally mutually agreed upon.

If you are interested in being able to incorporate a social or environmental mission into events of **default**, you need it clearly stated in the contract. One option is to specify the **mission statement** of the company, the social or environmental purpose of the investment, or the **use of proceeds** of the investment somewhere within the agreement.[6] Once the wording of the missions is explicitly stated and agreed upon in the contract, it can be used as **covenants** or **events of default**. An example of this would be a social purpose covenant that "The social purpose of the purchase of the Note (the "Investment") is to improve access to, and delivery of, quality, affordable healthcare

---

[4]https://project-equity.org/learn-about-employee-ownership-options/.

[5]Impact Terms Project & Purpose Capital—https://purpose-economy.org/content/uploads/purposebooklet_en.pdf.

[6]For examples of wording for these clauses, please see the online companion to this book.

for low income and other underserved people and communities across the United States, by accelerating the development and implementation of online programs for disease prevention and management for patients primarily serviced by federally qualified health centers (FQHCs) and other safety net organizations that provide medical services to underserved people".[7]

Another option is to include wording within the **default** provisions that clearly delineates mission-related actions that could cause a default. In their investments, the Global Innovation Fund (GIF) regularly includes specific social mission related provisions in the events of default. Examples include "the company's business ceasing to primarily benefit people earning less than USD 5 per day" or "the business is no longer involved in providing clean drinking water to poor, underserved populations" in a specific geography. They have also expanded this to include **Environmental, Social and Governance (ESG)** violations and other compliance related violations that might affect GIF's reputation as a charity with government funding.

Next, you'll need to lay out what happens if an event of **default** is triggered. If the funding is a loan, or a **structured exit** debt agreement, the **funder** might require the **founder** to repay the **total amount outstanding**. If it is a **grant**, the **funder** might require the relevant **grant** funds to be repaid. If the funding is **equity**, the most common approach is to have a **put option**, which allows the funder to request that the company or a third party purchase the funder's ownership within a specified period. The **valuation** of that ownership might be **fair market value** as agreed between the parties or determined by an independent third-party expert or, in the case of a **redeemable equity** agreement, the amount due would be the **total redemption price**.

When Ginny Reyes Llamzon, the associate general counsel for GIF, reflects on the use of **mission defaults**, she sees them as "a very big stick" that encourages founders to return to the table. They give the GIF the ability to push for a re-negotiation or changes to ensure the company keeps to its intended impact or social mission.

Rights

Protecting the mission of a company shouldn't just be the concern of a funder. Founders should also consider how their funding journey will affect their ability to create social and environmental impact. In addition to choosing

---

[7] https://www.impactterms.org/.

funders that share your social mission or a funding structure that is designed to protect your mission, you can choose to include rights in an investment contract that give you, as the **funder**, the ability to resist changes to the company that go against its social or environmental mission. One option is to include language that restricts changes to mission without a vote of a specific percentage of founder shares.[8]

Another area to embed mission is **information rights**. Funders can put in specific requests around how **impact metrics** are reported and if there is a required independent **impact audit**. Similar to a financial audit, an **impact audit** uses a third party to verify a company's reported performance against its agreed-upon **impact metrics**.

It is important for funders to balance the desire for additional data with an understanding of the cost and complexity of founders collecting additional information. Ideally, all **impact data** that is reported should directly align with the **impact data** the company needs to run their organization effectively.

Conclusion

As a founder or funder, you have a variety of options to embed your mission into how you structure your funding contracts. Whether you include any or none of these provisions, it is worth considering how your funding agreements reflect who you are as a company and the goals that you are trying to achieve.

---

[8]https://www.impactterms.org/.

Part VI

What If: You Want to Plan Your Journey?

Ok, we've come to the final part of the book. This is where we are going to try to pull everything together to help you evaluate all of the different options that we've discussed throughout our time together. This last part of the book is written entirely from a founder's perspective and builds on the questions that we asked way back in Part I.

In Chapter 28, we'll dive into the first three parts of the checklist: *who you are as an organization, how mission driven you are* and *what your funding needs are*. In Chapter 29, we'll focus on the questions you need to ask to understand what kind of funder you want to work with. And finally, in Chapter 30, we'll look at the whole spectrum of funding options.

Just one note, this part is not designed to be a fulsome guide to getting **investment ready**. There are many resources available around preparing yourself for investment and you'll find a whole set of recommended ones on the online companion to this book. Rather these chapters focus on what information you need and what questions to ask in order to choose the financing instruments that will work for you.

28

Who Are You and What Do You Need?

Ok, so let's kick this off by focusing on who you are as an organization and what your goals are. Your goals and what you are wanting to build should be the foundation for deciding what type of funding you pursue. You should use this chapter as a chance to really reflect on who you are as a founder and as a company and how that links to your own funding decisions (Table 28.1).

Table 28.1 Founder's self-evaluation with relevant terms

	Questions	Relevant terms
Who are we?	How is our company registered?	For-profit, non-profit, social enterprise, co-operative, hybrid
	How do we make money? Who are our customers?	Revenue model, internal finance, seasonality, cyclicality
	What stage company are we?	Concept, Early-stage, Growth Stage, Scaling, Established, Intellectual property, proof of concept, minimum viable product
	What are our growth projections?	Revenue model projections, Free cash flow projections, exponential growth (J curve), high growth venture, niche venture, dynamic enterprise, category pioneer, livelihood enterprise

(continued)

Table 28.1 (continued)

	Questions	Relevant terms
How mission driven are we?	How embedded is our mission in our company?	Mission, Purpose, Theory of Change
	Do we have an impact track record?	Impact Measurement
What are our funding needs?	How much funding do we need?	Burn rate, capital expenditure, operating expenditure
	What do we need to spend it on? How long do we need it for?	Proof of Concept, Working capital, Growth Capital, Assets, research and development, assets, Time Frame, Term
	Do we have assets available for collateral?	Collateral
	How do we want to pay it back?	Internally (Revenue), externally (borrow or future funding) or through an exit (trade sale, secondary sale, IPO)
	What are our ownership expectations in the short/medium term? Long term?	Dilution, distributed ownership, employee ownership
	What kind of funding are we going to need in the future?	Sell shares to equity funders, borrow money, internal cash flow generation
	How involved do we want our funders to be?	Mentorship, board seats, board observer rights, information rights, voting rights

Who Are We?

What Is Our Business Registered as?

When you start a company, one of the most important decisions that you make is selecting what type of legal structure your organization will take. This decision is intimately linked to the future of your company and its impact will be felt in your organization's daily decision making and communication flows, administration, and financial realities.

The best time to select the appropriate legal structure for your organization is after you have developed your **business model** or your **business plan**. Traditionally, a business plan will articulate your company's name and location, its mission and vision, market analyses, descriptions of the products and services, and your financial plan. Once you have developed this plan, you'll need to ask yourself (and hopefully a trusted advisor) the questions in this chapter to help you determine the appropriate legal structure.

In the table below, I have expanded upon the initial categories of the legal structures in the beginning of the book and added in characteristics of ownership and profit distribution, as well as the limitations around funding eligibility.

Because each jurisdiction is different, I would suggest you engage with materials produced in your own country or region around the specific type of legal entity that would be the most suitable for your organization (Table 28.2).

Table 28.2 Comparison of types of legal structures

Type	Examples	Ownership	Profit distribution	Funding eligibility
Mainstream[a] Market Company	MyTurn, GetVantage	Combination of internal and external shareholders	To shareholders	Eligible for all kinds of equity and debt investment. Not a likely candidate for grant funding, except in very specific circumstances.
Company Allocating Percentage to Charity	Warby Parker	Combination of internal and external shareholders	To shareholders and a set percentage to charities	Eligible for all kinds of equity and debt investment. Funders must be aligned with commitment to distribute percentage or profit or products. Not a likely candidate for grant funding.
Co-operative/Distributed Ownership	Cal Solar, Equal Exchange	Significant ownership by employees or customers	To shareholders	Eligible for all kinds of debt. Equity only relevant if it has structured exit, as any investment that requires a sale of the company is not suitable.

(continued)

Table 28.2   (continued)

Type	Examples	Ownership	Profit distribution	Funding eligibility
Profit Distributing Social Enterprise	*Maya Mountain Cacao, Clinicas del Azurcar, Viwala, SOKO, Powered by People, Provive, Code for All*	Combination of internal and external shareholders	To shareholders	Eligible for all kinds of equity and debt investment. Funders should be mission aligned or contract should have protection against mission drift. Able to access grants on a limited basis.
Hybrid Organization	*Trackosaurus/Early Bird*	Non-profit: not owned by shareholders	Non-profit: none	Eligible for all kinds of debt and grants. No ability to access equity funding.
		For profit: Combination of internal and external shareholders	For-profit entity: To shareholders	All types of debt and equity. Grants on a limited basis.
Profitable Surplus Reinvested Social Enterprise	Many Steward-Ownership companies	Combination of internal and external shareholders	No surplus profit distribution	Eligible for debt. Not suitable for equity, although depending on the specific legal structure, redeemable equity might be an option.
Combination of trading revenue and grants non-profit	*Riders for Health, Studio Museum in Harlem, Upaya*	Not owned by shareholders	None	Eligible for all kinds of debt and grants. Not eligible for equity.
Grants only non-profit	*IkamvaYouth*	Not owned by shareholders	None	Eligible for all types of grants and debt. Not eligible for equity.

[a]Financing for Social Impact: The Key Role of Tailored Financing and Hybrid Finance. (2017). Available at: https://evpa.eu/knowledge-centre/publications/financing-for-social-impact

How Do We Make Money and Who Are Our Customers?

If your company has a **revenue model** that is **seasonal**, raising funding like **secured debt** from a bank that requires you to commit to a fixed repayment model may not be possible. You'll want to have flexibility around your repayments so they are in line with your **cash flow**.

If you are a **social enterprise** whose customers are **underserved**, you may want to evaluate how to **link impact to your financing** to be able to get your products out to more **underserved customers** that may not be able to support high margins.

If your customers are highly incentivized to buy your product, you can consider how to use them in your funding plans, including through **crowdfunding** or supply **chain financing**.

For non-profits, you'll want to link **external financing** to your most secure form of revenue. This may be a **fundraising stream** that has a historical track record and consistency such as a specific set of donors or an event. Or it could be earned revenue from assets or **income streams** with a history. Or it could be a contract for funding in the future.

What Stage Company Are We?

There are lots of terms that are used to describe the stages of company growth. Let's revisit the typology that we first discussed in the first section.

Concept stage: You generally have an idea, but not necessarily a minimum viable product (MVP) or a **proof of concept**.

Early stage: You may have an **MVP** or **proof of concept** here and you may even have started protecting your IP legally, but you still only have a small number of paying customers, if any at all.

At both the **concept stage** and **early-stage**, you are a high-risk company, so funding that you consider must have a high willingness to accept risk. For **social enterprises** and non-profits, **grant** funding is often used for **research and development (R&D)** and initial product or service development. While a traditional **grant** with no repayment obligations may be your preferred option, you'll want to weigh up how restrictive that funding is and what the restrictions will mean for your ability to change or pivot your strategy. In conversations with **grant** funders, you'll want to keep options around **embedding your mission** and **linking impact into the financing** close at hand to be able to negotiate a contract that works for the short and long term of your company. For instance, you might find that a funder would be willing to allow you more freedom around your use of the funding if there are financial milestones that turn the grant funding into a loan once you are financially successful.

Equity funding is designed as **risk capital**. As we've discussed throughout this book, you need to be conscious around the implications of taking on **equity** funding in the early stages of your company as you will need to promise and pursue **exponential growth**. Although **revenue-based financing** (RBF) will not be available to you at the **concept stage**, you might find funders that would be willing to negotiate a contract that includes **redeemable equity,** which would give you the opportunity to regain your ownership of the company in the medium term.

Growth stage: You have defined your product or service offering and have a base of paying customers. You are building your internal infrastructure to grow.

At the **growth stage**, there are a larger number of funding options available to you based on your risk profile and track record. Depending on the kind of **collateral** that you have and your **credit history**, you'll likely be able to choose from a few different types of **debt**. The evaluation of these options will be dependent on the questions below around the use of the capital. For most **structured exit funders**, this is their sweet spot. If you have raised **equity** capital previously, you'll be able to access **Venture Debt**.

As a non-profit, you should have a diversified **revenue model** and will want to balance accepting **grants** and other types of **subsidized financing** with building a **credit history** and/or **collateral** to access cheaper **commercial capital** that may be suited to your needs.

Scaling: You have a large and growing customer base, have built your internal infrastructure and are in the process of scaling up your operations and potentially adding new products or services.

At the **scaling stage**, you should have a wide variety of options for funding and the evaluation of these options will depend on your funding needs and the price. **Redeemable equity** will likely not be applicable at this stage, but **RBF** and **Convertible RBF** style contracts could provide options for capital.

Established: You have a steady base of paying customers and a successful business track record. As an **established business**, you should also have a wide variety of **debt**-based options that you can access. Your ability to access **structured exit** financing will depend on your growth rate.

As a **social enterprise**, you'll find that the availability of **grant** capital will decrease as you grow unless you are able to demonstrate a strong rationale for market failures that require continued **subsidization**. If this is the case, you'll want to develop a plan for **impact-linked financing** options that can integrate your **social, environmental and financial milestones** in a way that works for your business.

What Are Our Business Growth Projections?

To better be able to combine all of the above variables, let's use the growth profiles that we first introduced in Chapter 5.

High Growth Venture—you have a **disruptive business model**, large addressable markets, high growth projections, ability to scale quickly and are quite risky. You may have **J curve projections** and **exponential growth**, but you may not.

High growth projections often require significant amounts of capital. You can consider options with **high risk/high return** calculations such as **equity** and **structured exits**. Depending on the type of collateral you have available and the stage of your business, you may also qualify for specific types of debt like **venture debt, mezzanine financing** and **invoice or purchase order financing**.

As a **social enterprise**, you will want to be purposeful in the type of structure you select and the contracting terms around your **mission** and impact as you may attract funders that do not see your **social or environmental mission** as center to your strategy. This can create **mission drift** as well as conflict between founders and funders.

Category pioneer—you have **disruptive products and services**, new markets that are likely large, variable growth and the potential to scale.

With variable growth and the potential to scale, you are a prime candidate for **structured exits**. While your markets may not be well defined, the potential to repay investors a **risk-adjusted rate** may also create opportunities for you to access **mezzanine debt** and **venture debt**.

As a **social enterprise**, if your customers are **underserved** and/or markets are very underdeveloped, you'll want to consider how you can use **forgivable loans, recoverable grants** or **impact-linked finance** to reduce your risk in early stages when there is a lack of market data available.

Niche venture—you have an innovative product or service, niche markets and customer segments and are projecting steady to high growth.

With niche customer segments, you can consider how to make your customers part of your funding strategy through **debt-** or **rewards-based crowdfunding, invoice factoring** and **supply chain financing**. If you are projecting high growth, you may also consider **structured exits**, which would allow you to access **risk capital** without needing to project **exponential growth**.

If you are a **social enterprise**, you may want to evaluate how **forgivable loans** could be useful to you to build up a **credit history** or assets to transition to more **commercial debt**.

Dynamic enterprise—you are in an established industry and sector, you have existing products that are tried and tested, a proven business model and are projecting steady growth.

As you do not have high risk/high return options, you will need to be purposeful around matching the type of funding that you need to the right **collateral** or **revenue streams**. If you have not yet built-up **a credit history** and **collateral** to access **secured bank financing**, looking at specialist offerings such as **invoice factoring, supply chain financing** or **unsecured mezzanine debt** may be appropriate. You may also look for **guarantees** to increase your access to appropriate **debt** capital and/or reduce your cost.

If you are a **social enterprise** or non-profit, you might find that **forgivable loans** or **recoverable grants** can provide flexible financing at a low cost of capital that allows you to serve your target market effectively.

Livelihood enterprise—you are a family run, high localized business that is driven by local opportunity and are projecting limited future growth.

Without high growth projections, you will be precluded from the high risk/high return funding options, but if you have a significant track record, you should be able to access **debt** funding options. You might also consider how **employee ownership** would benefit your company from a tax and a revenue perspective.

As a **social enterprise** or non-profit, accessing local mission aligned capital that is focused on the geographic areas that you serve may allow you to decrease your **cost of capital**.

How Mission Driven Are We?

What Is Our Mission and How Embedded Is It in Our Company?

As discussed throughout this book, understanding your mission and/or your theory of change is incredibly important to understand what kinds of funders and funding structures would work best for your organization.

If you are a company with a high level of **mission embeddedness**, you will likely have your mission explicitly stated in your **articles of incorporation** as it forms a key part of why the business was founded, what kind of products and services you offer and to whom you offer them. You may also choose to

embed your mission into your funding contracts. You will likely identify as a **social enterprise** if you have a for-profit structure. By having a high level of **mission embeddedness**, you may qualify for funding from **impact focused funders**.

Alternatively, you may be a company that is **mission driven**, but does not identify as a **social enterprise**. Your mission will guide how you operate as a company and prevent you from behaving unethically. You may also be conscious of the social or environmental effect of your products or services. Although this may be considered a low level of **mission embeddedness** compared to a **social enterprise** or a non-profit, running a **socially conscious enterprise** is an excellent goal. You may be less likely to qualify for **impact focused capital**, but you also will be less likely to be perceived as inherently risky, which is something that **social enterprises** struggle with in our current funding market.

Do We Have an Impact Track Record?

If you are interested in accessing funding from **impact focused funders**, you'll need to be able to provide evidence that your end users are **underserved**. This might be in the form of socioeconomic status such as the percentage of customers that are in the **base of the pyramid (BOP)** or the **emerging middle class** or it might refer to gender or other classifications that use data to show how underserved they are in the market.

You'll also need to have evidence that the product or service you are providing has significant impact. This should be data in line with your **theory of change**. If you are creating positive environmental impact, you'll need to have scientific evidence. If you are creating positive social impact, you'll need **verifiable data** from your end users and other stakeholders of the efficacy of your product or service.

If you do not yet have a track record of **verifiable impact**, either because you are a start-up or because you have not been collecting impact data, you will need to create a realistic plan to collect the relevant data. You should be able to draw upon **proxies** or **research**, or both, to demonstrate the scale, depth and significance of your company's impact potential. For more on impact measurement, please see relevant materials on the online companion to this book.

What Are Our Funding Needs?

How Much Funding Do We Need?

As we discussed in Chapter 5, you'll need to calculate your current **burn rate** and your projected burn rate.

Burn rate= *Monthly cash in (cash flow) — monthly cash out (expenses)*

You'll need to make sure that you are including all of the costs that you will need to incur to reach your growth targets. Often, founders underestimate how much it will actually cost to create the growth that they are projecting.

If you are revenue positive, then you will want to look at how much additional cash you will need over and above any **retained earnings** to be able to finance your growth plans. You should always consider your **internal cash flow generation** as your first source of funding and only look for **external funding**, when actually necessary.

If your need is related to **working capital** you'll need to budget this on a monthly, weekly or even daily basis to identify any **liquidity** shortfalls based on timing of receipts and payments, taking into consideration any existing facilities such as **overdrafts** and **credit lines**. Many businesses fail due to timing of cash inflows and outflows not being aligned.

What Do We Want to Spend Our Funding on?

What you are planning to spend your money on is important when deciding what type of funding you need. Here are the main categories for spending:

Proof of Concept—this is cash spent to test your **proof of concept** or build your initial **MVP**. This might be for your first product or can be for expansion into a new market or product. **Proof of concept** funding is inherently risky and funders need to be very risk tolerant. If you are a **concept stage** business, this will likely need to be **equity** or **equity**-like funding (such as **redeemable equity**) or **grant** capital. If you are an **early-stage** or **growth-stage** business that is developing additional products or services for new markets, then you can either use **internal funding** or look for additional risk tolerant funding. This will need to be medium-term to long-term capital as the ability to repay quickly will likely be low.

Growth capital—this is cash spent on hiring people, investing into new product development, putting systems into place, marketing anything that helps you build toward the future. **Growth capital** is generally medium- to long-term capital as you are investing in the growth of the business and it takes time for that capital to produce a **return on investment**. If growth capital is a shorter-term need, then the repayment should be linked to revenue or cash flow to ensure its affordability.

Working Capital—this is cash spent to buy inputs, stock or materials required for your product or service. **Working capital** funding is generally more short term as you can often manage your inventory on a shorter-term basis. If possible, you should make sure to fund **your working capital** with short-term financing such as **debt** or **revenue-based financing** or **invoice factoring** or **supply chain financing**. Selling ownership in your company in order to finance your **working capital** needs means that you are selling a permanent stake in your company for a very short-term funding need. If you are evaluating a **structured exit contract** for working capital, you'll need to compare the cost of that funding with other short-term options.

Assets—this is money that is invested into **physical or intangible assets** such as buildings, equipment and brands. Capital used to purchase assets will depend on the type of assets purchased and the size, if they are smaller **assets** and immediately income producing, they may have a shorter repayment term compared to larger assets **or assets** that take a longer time to create income. If these assets can act as **security**, then there is the possibility of accessing **secured debt** to fund them.

Do We Have Any Assets to Use for Collateral?

You'll need to take stock of the assets that you currently have to see if any of them could work for **collateral** and if you would feel comfortable putting them up as **surety** to secure funding. Having some sort of **collateral** can decrease the **cost of your capital**, but it is important to remember that if you default on your obligation, those assets will potentially be seized. If you have valuable assets such as buildings, machinery or other physical assets owned by the company and have **a credit history**, then you may be eligible for **secured lending** from a bank or other type of financial institution. These lenders will be interested in being **senior** to any other creditors or investors in your **capitalization table** but will be able to offer you relatively inexpensive rates compared to other options discussed in this book.

You can also use **guarantees** as surety. These can be a **personal guarantee** or from a third party and can be **funded** or **unfunded**. While **personal guarantees** may be required for some types of **structured exits**, a **funded guarantee** like Riders for Health had or an **unfunded guarantee** from a large, respected entity can help you to qualify for secured debt from a financial institution.

If you have **purchase orders** or **invoices**, you can use these to access **purchase order financing** or **invoice factoring** as we discussed in the **SOKO** and **Powered by People** case.

Finally, you can use recurring revenue streams and the reputation of your current funders as a type of surety to qualify for **RBF**.

The value of these assets is important whether it is a building or the reputation of a **guarantor**. Funders will evaluate how your **surety** affects your risk profile depending on how valuable the **surety** is perceived to be.

How Do We Want to Pay It Back?

There are three distinct strategies around how you anticipate repaying funders that affect your funding options. The first strategy is repayment through a **third-party exit**. The second strategy is to repay from **internal cash flows**. The third strategy is to repay using **future funding**. Technically, you have a fourth option, which is not to pay it back, but unless it is a grant that doesn't have any repayment requirements, that means that you will **default**, so that's not a great plan.

A **third-party exit** is a **future sale of the company, a merger, a public listing** or a **secondary sale**. If this is your expectation, this means that you are on either an **exponential growth** curve or have a realistic path to a sale of the company (or a **merger** with another company). A **secondary sale** means that a future investor will be willing to buy-out current funders. Funders will need to be convinced that this is a viable strategy to accept this as their return strategy. Founders that believe this is the appropriate return strategy for their potential funders can consider equity options such as **convertible notes, SAFEs** or **priced equity rounds**.

Internal cash flows mean that you will use revenue, cash flow or some other calculation to pay back the funding. Examples of this include **RBF** and most types of **debt**. If your revenue is **seasonal** or **cyclical**, you'll need to make sure that your funding options allow for repayment that is aligned with the fluctuations in your revenue.

Repaying using **future funding** means you are planning to access new types of funding to repay your previous funders. When you are a **concept** or **early-stage company** with no **collateral** or **credit history**, your options for funding are generally quite expensive, but over time, you will hopefully build up a track record and even potentially assets to borrow against. This means your plan may be to qualify for longer-term, cheaper financing or to **roll-over your debt**. In this case, you can plan over time to replace expensive capital with cheaper forms of capital. An example of this might be repurchasing redeemable equity with **debt**, which you can pay off over time using your internal cash flows. Most companies continue to keep some sort of debt on their books throughout their operations. Long-term secured debt can be an inexpensive way to fund growth, expansion and working capital fluctuations. If this is your plan, you'll need to be building toward the ability to raise enough debt funding and will need to prove to funders that this will be possible.

What Are Our Ownership Expectations?

From an ownership perspective, you need to evaluate your current status as well as your plans for the future. If you are a for-profit, do you want to continue as the founder to own the company in the future? Do you want to transition to more distributed ownership among your employees? The kind of money you take on may help or hinder you in achieving your ownership expectations down the road.

Debt and **grant**-based funding options do not require you to give up ownership in the company, but equity funding will, although funding options like **redeemable equity** can give you the opportunity to repurchase equity and maintain control of the company. Allowing external funders to own shares in your company means that you give up control as well as ownership in your business, so you need to evaluate how willing you are to give up ownership in the short, medium and long term.

What Kind of Funding Are We Going to Need in the Future?

Equity: Do you think you will want to sell shares in the business in the future? If this is the case, then you'll need to be cognizant of this when you raise funding now. For instance, many **equity** funders do not understand **structured exit agreements** and may not wish to have a share of revenues or cash flows being paid out to a previous funder. Thus, if you are considering a **structured exit agreement**, you'll need to make sure that you have a clear understanding of the timing and implications of the contract. If you are planning to raise **equity** in the future, you will also be **diluted** in future rounds. So you may wish to source as much non-dilutive capital as possible in the early-stages of your business. **Non-dilutive** capital is any capital that doesn't require you to sell or ownership (and can include **redeemable equity** where you can buy your ownership back), so any type of **grant** or **debt capital** is applicable here.

Debt: Are you hoping to build up your **credit history** to be able to access **debt** capital?

If you are wanting to build up a **credit history** to secure **debt** capital, then you should focus on developing a history repaying obligations, earning revenue and building **collateral**. Using **crowdfunding, RBF, invoice factoring, forgivable loans** or **recoverable grants** are all ways to create a credit history using flexible **debt** capital. A **guarantee** can be useful to lower the **cost of capital** while you are building a **credit history** or can serve as a stand-in for **collateral**. Whether you are a for-profit or a non-profit showing potential creditors that you can pay back debt in a timely manner will increase your access to **debt** funding and decrease the cost of that funding.

Internal Cash Flow Generation: Are you hoping to generate enough cash flow internally that you don't need to access external funding in the future? If your goal is to be internally funded in the future, then you'll need to make sure that you are accessing types of funding that don't require you to access external funding to generate a return. This means that **equity** funding is not a good option for you to consider.

How Involved Do We Want Our Funders to Be?

One of the main reasons that founders look for **equity** financing is that **equity** funders generally come to the table with much more than just funding. As they are aligned to the growth of the founder, **equity** funders are prepared to bring their expertise and their networks alongside their cash to help founders build fast growing businesses.[1] **Structured exit funders**, particularly **Convertible RBF** and **Redeemable Equity** funders are similarly aligned to growth.

If you are looking for a funder to be involved in shaping your business, you'll need to be willing to provide the correct incentives for them to do so. Generally, this means some kind of **upside** if the business does well, so this will need to play into your evaluation of different funding options.

You'll want to understand the priorities and capabilities of potential funders to figure out what kinds of incentives and terms make the most sense for them as a funder. You'll need to do active due diligence to understand what kind of funder can provide the involvement and value-add that you need as a company. You can use the next chapter to help you evaluate potential funders (Table 28.3).

---

[1] As we have discussed, this may cause issues if the founder and funder are not aligned around the type of growth that the company is seeking. Founders and funders should be very clear around the type of company they are trying to build and how they will receive their return.

Table 28.3 Funder approach by type of capital

Category	Grant Capital	Debt Capital	Equity Capital
Focused on:	Social upside and social downside focused	Financial downside focused	Financial upside focused
Level of Involvement:	Lower involvement	Lower involvement	High ongoing involvement
Risk mitigation strategies:	Impact reporting	Financial reporting around covenants	Board seats, Voter Rights

29

What Type of Funder Is Right for You?

Ok, so now you know a bit more about your own company's needs, let's take some time to talk about the type of funder that you'd like to work with. In order to determine if a funder is right for you, you'll need to do your own **due diligence** on them. Here are some of the questions that you'll need to ask whether you are determining what funders to approach for funding or evaluating a partnership with a specific funder (Table 29.1).

Table 29.1 Fund evaluation

Questions	Relevant terms
Do you fit their investment thesis?	Investment thesis, market fit
Are you mission aligned?	Mission, theory of change, mission alignment
Who else have they funded and what do those founders have to say?	Referrals/references
What type of resources can they provide?	Creditworthy collateral, debt, distribution channels, equity, fundraising support, financial management, geographic knowledge/presence, grants, governance support, human capital support, impact strategy, outcomes/industry knowledge/experience in issue areas, purchasing power, social capital, strategic support, technology experience, visibility

(continued)

A. Patton Power, *Adventure Finance*, https://doi.org/10.1007/978-3-030-72428-3_29

Table 29.1 (continued)

Questions	Relevant terms
What level of risk are they comfortable with?	Low to high financial risk, low to high impact risk, Angel, Early-stage, Growth
What return do they require? When do they require that return?	IRR, CoC, Money multiple, Principal, risk-adjusted return, Time frame, fund life
Who are their stakeholders? How does funding get approved?	LP/GP structure, limited life funds, donor advised Funds, foundations, Family office, government, Investment Committee, Non-profit board

Do You Fit Their Funding Thesis?

A funder's **investment thesis** lays out the types of companies that they invest in. Their thesis should identify the sectors they fund, the geographies, the stage of companies, the types of instrument(s) and the size of funding. Thus, you'll need to carefully evaluate a potential funder's funding thesis to understand if you are a fit for them from a sector, geography, stage and size of investment.

If a funder doesn't currently use the type of funding instrument that you believe would be best for your company, but you fit the rest of the criteria, it will likely still be worth a conversation. If you are wanting to use an innovative type of funding from this book, they might not even know about the type of funding that you are looking for.

Are You Mission Aligned?

Regardless of whether you are a mainstream market company, a co-op, profit distributing social enterprise or a non-profit, you need to have an understanding of your underlying **mission** and what kind of company you are building. Thus, before you decide to engage with a funder, you should interrogate their **mission**. What are their priorities? How do those align with your own **mission**?

In addition to the organization, you also need to evaluate the individuals that you'll be working with. Do they understand your business? Are you excited about working with them for months or years to come?

If you are a **social enterprise** or non-profit with a firmly embedded **impact thesis**, then you'll want to understand the funders' **theory of change** and how that aligns with your own. If you are a mainstream market company, you'll want to evaluate what priorities the funder has, beyond financial return. You can evaluate this through interrogating their **mission statement**, but the best way to gauge your **mission alignment** is to speak to others that have received funding from them or funded alongside them. Their historical actions will speak volumes about who they are as a funder.

Now this doesn't mean that you can only deal with mission aligned funders, but remember, the more control and involvement a funder has, the more opportunities to compromise your mission, regardless of the contractual terms that might be designed to protect it. Additionally, in tough times when you might be required to come back to the negotiating table, a non-mission aligned funder will be less likely to consider additional factors outside of their own short-term financial return.

In my research for this book, I spoke to over 150 founders and funders from across the innovative finance spectrum. The one concept that came up in nearly every interview was *trust*. Founders and funders need to be able to trust each other, otherwise no matter how elaborate or innovative the contract, it is bound to fail. Mission alignment is necessary in order to build trust.

Who Else Have They Funded and What Do Those Founders Have to Say?

You need to look at who else they have funded historically. Are their other portfolio companies similar to your company? What do the other founders have to say about their experience working with this funder? Just as if you were hiring a new employee, doing a reference check on a funder is a key step to make sure that you are making the right decision.

What Type of Resources Can They Provide?

In your self evaluation, you should determine what kinds of support your business needs right now. So you need to make sure that your funders have the capability to provide the resources that you need. Here is the list of resources from Chapter 5 paired with the types of funding we have spoken about during the book (Table 29.2).

Many of these resources will be portfolio support that they can provide. Some of these resources will be at a firm level, others may be at a personal level meaning that you should evaluate who at the organization you are going

Table 29.2 Types of resources with funding options

Type	Description	Can be used for
Creditworthy collateral	Assets that have significant value, as determined by public and private markets	Guarantees
Debt capital	Capital that can be lent out	Secured debt, revenue-based financing, convertible RBF, venture debt, mezzanine debt
Distribution Channels	Ability to distribute products or services through proprietary or shared channels	Invoice factoring, supply chain financing, revenue generation
Equity capital	Capital that can be used to purchase ownership	Priced rounds, convertible notes, SAFE/KISS, redeemable equity
Fundraising Support	Support, advice and connections for future funding	All types of fundraising
Financial Management[a]	Help develop financial management capabilities, financial and accounting systems	Non-financial support
Geographic Knowledge/Presence	Knowledge of or presence in the geography targeted	Non-financial support
Grant capital	Capital that does not expect a financial return	Forgivable loans, recoverable grants, convertible grants, guarantees
Governance Support[b]	Support to develop board of directors, strengthen governance systems	Non-financial support
Human capital support[c]	Connecting you to talent for hiring, helping to strengthen existing management	Non-financial support
Impact strategy	Support developing theory of change and impact measurement and management strategies	Non-financial support

(continued)

Table 29.2   (continued)

Type	Description	Can be used for
Outcomes/Industry Knowledge/Experience in Issue Areas	Experience working in the identified outcome areas	Non-financial support
Purchasing Power	Ability to commit to purchasing products/services	Invoice factoring, supply chain financing, revenue generation
Social Capital	Influence and/or trust as an entity or individual with relevant people/communities.	Non-financial support, crowdfunding
Strategic support	Business model development, business planning	Non-financial support
Technology Experience	Ability to use and build relevant technology	Non-financial support
Visibility	Ability to disseminate information to large numbers of relevant people	Crowdfunding support, Non-financial support

[a]EVPA NFS report—https://evpa.eu.com/knowledge-centre/publications/adding-value-through-non-financial-support-a-practical-guide
[b]EVPA NFS report—https://evpa.eu.com/knowledge-centre/publications/adding-value-through-non-financial-support-a-practical-guide
[c]EVPA NFS report—https://evpa.eu.com/knowledge-centre/publications/adding-value-through-non-financial-support-a-practical-guide

to be dealing with. This is particularly true if they are going to sit on your board.

What Level of Risk Are They Comfortable with?

You'll need to understand what level of risk funders are comfortable with. A fulsome discussion of early-stage funding risks could, and has, filled entire books,[1] so we'll just go over some key issues here to help you begin to assess a funders' risk tolerance.

---

[1]You'll find suggestions for additional resources on the online companion to this book.

Enterprise Risk: If your company scores high on the risk spectrum in the previous chapter, you have a high risk of failure. Some funders are comfortable with the potential for failure. These funders have a high enterprise risk tolerance. They might mitigate their risk by adopting a VC approach to building a portfolio that only requires one or two companies to do exceptionally well to make up for the failure of the rest. Or they may look for risk tolerant capital themselves (like Prime Impact Fund from Chapter 15) to allow them to take significant risk. They may also engage in a "**back the jockey not the horse mentality**," where they find entrepreneurs that they believe in and invest in them, even if the business model still needs a lot of work. These high enterprise risk tolerant funders believe that good entrepreneurs can pivot to build successful businesses.

Funders that have a medium or low enterprise risk tolerance may require **collateral, guarantees** or **surety** in order to fund high risk companies, while others will not be willing to engage with high risk companies regardless of the protections offered.[2]

Market Risk: There is always the risk that regardless of how astute the enterprise it will fail due to larger market risks. These can be a myriad of possibilities from a global pandemic to political upheaval to currency devaluations to the emergence of a giant competitor to climate change. Funders that have a low market risk tolerance may choose to mitigate their risk by investing in companies in established markets and countries with low levels of political risk or through diversification of their investments, but there is no way to completely mitigate market risk.[3]

Scalability Risk: Scalability risk is the risk that a company will not reach the necessary scale to achieve the projected financial or impact return. In investment terms, scale is the ability for an enterprise to operate with greater profit margins as it grows. For impact focused funders, this concept is extended to incorporate social impact: Scalable social enterprises should be able to achieve greater impact per unit of input as they grow in size. Funders can mitigate this risk through the amount they invest as well as the structure.

Liquidity Risk: **Liquidity** risk is the risk that a funder will not be able to extract capital when it is necessary for them to do so. If a funder has a

---

[2]This section has been adapted from a set of cases compiled by Cynthia Schweer Rayner and the author for the Bertha Centre for Social Innovation and Entrepreneurship in 2017. Those cases were originally based on the Impact Assets Issue Brief #2, Risk Return and Impact: Understanding Diversification and Performance Within an Impact Investing Portfolio by Jed Emerson.

[3]An interesting theory about impact investing is that it provides an additional level of diversification by focusing on businesses that serve underserved populations that are less likely to make buying decisions based on market movements. This means that these businesses are less correlated to market fluctuations. There is not yet enough data to prove out this hypothesis.

high tolerance for **liquidity** risk, they will be willing to wait a longer period of time to start making **returns on their investment**. Capital that is locked up in an investment for a long period of time is generally more expensive than capital that can be withdrawn at any point or that has a short payback period, this is called a **liquidity premium**. Private equity and venture capital investors generally assume that their capital is going to be locked up for long periods of time, this is one of the reasons that equity capital is so expensive (i.e., requires such high returns).

Exit Risk: Whereas liquidity risk relates more to withdrawing your invested capital, **exit** risk is the possibility that you won't be able to achieve a successful **exit** from an investment to make your return. Funders with a high exit risk tolerance will be more likely to use traditional **equity** instruments, whereas funders with a medium exit risk tolerance may use instruments like **structured exits** to mitigate their risk. Funders with a low exit risk tolerance will be inclined to use **debt** instruments with a clear path to repayment.

Transaction Cost Risk: If you are attempting to use a new type of funding structure, there is the risk that the costs to structure the deal will be considerable. If the funder is committed to increasing their own toolkit of funding options, they may have a high tolerance for transaction cost risk. Otherwise, they might not be willing to consider structures that do not align with their current templates.

Tax Risk: If there is not settled case law or clear tax regulation in a country regarding the use of a specific type of investment structure, there is a tax risk associated with funding via that structure. If a funder has a high tax risk tolerance, they may be willing to take that risk to establish a precedent. Otherwise, they may deem trying something new to be too risky from a tax perspective.

Impact Risk: Impact risk is the risk that an investment will not achieve the social or environmental impact that is projected. Impact risk includes the risk that a successful project or intervention may create negative impacts in other areas, resulting in reduced or no net benefit to society or the environment. Funders that have a high impact risk tolerance will be willing to invest in companies that have the potential for high impact, even if it carries a high possibility of failure. Funders that have a low impact risk tolerance will need a strong impact track record and verifiable impact data to mitigate their impact risk.

During 2020, the awareness of the risks of climate change, racial injustice, and social and gender inequity came to the forefront of the global economic and political conversation. Some of this was prompted by the global pandemic, but much of it had been lingering below the surface for years. In a post-2020 funding landscape, all of these issues are beginning to factor into how funders view risk. Diversity, equity and inclusion are now, more than ever, sought after by **impact investors** as they evaluate an entrepreneurial team and environmental impact is coming to the forefront of even the most mainstream funders' risk analysis.

What Return Do They Require? When Do They Require that Return?

Many funders will be looking for a **risk-adjusted financial return**. This means that they will design the potential financial return based on their evaluation of the risk that they are taking in the investment and will look for a return that compensates them for the risk they are taking. When funders say they are looking for **a market-rate return**, they mean they are looking for returns similar to other investments with a comparable risk profile.

Funders can calculate their expected financial return using the different terms we have discussed throughout the book including **Internal rate of return (IRR)**, **Cash on Cash (CoC)**, **Money Multiple** and **Interest Rate**. All of the risk factors that we discussed above will be taken into account when determining the type of return they require.

As we discussed in Sect. 4 of the book, some mission aligned funders might be willing to trade-off financial return for defined social or environmental outcomes. Other mission aligned funders might be focused on the impact of an organization and any financial return will be secondary to their calculation.

In any of the structures that we have discussed in this book, understanding the financial and/or impact return expectations of the funder is paramount.

You also need to understand the timing for that return. If a funder has a **limited life fund**, they need their returns within their 10 or 12 year investing cycle. If they've invested in you in the third year of that fund, then they will need to see their return prior to the end of the **fund life**, which means within the next 7–9 years. If they have an **evergreen fund** or do not have **external funders**, then you'll need to understand their own internal timing expectations.

Who Are Their Stakeholders?

In order to understand funders' opportunities and limitations around disbursing funding, you need to look at what type of stakeholders they have and how their funding gets approved.

Many funders will have external stakeholders such as **limited partners (LPs)** or **external donors**. If this is the case, then you'll need to understand that the funder has a criteria for success that they have pre-agreed with those funders. If they are **LPs**, then they will have specific types of companies they can invest in, return requirements, levels of risk they can take and a timeline to make their returns. For instance, a VC fund might raise capital from **LPs** by saying that they are going to invest equity in early-stage healthtech start-ups in Asia, target returns of 20%+ and their fund will be a 12-year fund, which means that they promise to return **LPs** capital (plus returns) in 12 years. Since the **LPs** invested their capital into this fund based on that description, it would be hard for the fund to change the type of company, the return they were seeking, the level or risk or the timeline for returning capital to investors.

Funders that are responsible to external stakeholders (like VC or debt funds to **LPs**) are likely to be less flexible in their structuring and less able to be flexible in the type of resources they can provide. This doesn't mean that they cannot be innovative, but you need to recognize that their future fundraising is dependent on them meeting the criteria for success of their **external stakeholders**.

Funders that have a specific impact focus that they have promised **external donors** must be cognizant of the **mission embeddedness** and **impact track record** of companies. In Chapter 15, Upaya raised **recoverable grants** to create jobs in India through working with local entrepreneurs. While these **recoverable grants** gave Upaya flexibility in how they were spent (could be through **loans**, **equity investments**, **RBF** or other types of support), Upaya must use the capital to create the impact they promised donors, in this case jobs for people at the base of the pyramid in India.

Funders like family offices and endowed foundations may not have external funders themselves, but they will still have internal stakeholders to whom they are responsible. This means that any funding they allocate must meet their internal criteria for success. Funders that are not responsible to external stakeholders are able to be more flexible in how they structure deals and around the types of resources that they can provide.

Another thing you need to evaluate is how their funding gets approved (or resources get allocated). Funders might have an **investment committee** or a **board** or a **senior management committee** that determines which deals get approved, this might be a short or a long process and depending on the type of deal might require significant **due diligence** documentation.

Finally, **fund life** is important. If you remember back to Chapter 2, GBF was unable to adapt their funding for SOKO because they were at the end of their **fund cycle**. Understanding where a funder is in their fund cycle can be important.

30

What Type of Funding Is Right for You?

So now you know a bit more about where you are as a company and the kind of capital and type of funder that best suits you, the next thing to consider is what type of funding is best for you. As you've seen in the previous 29 chapters, organizations need different types of funding based on who they are and what their funding needs are. What type of funding you might be able to attract depends on things like your risk profile, collateral, cash generation potential, attitudes toward ownership/dilution and exit prospects. These needs are varied and can be quite unique, so while I can give you suggestions about the characteristics of companies that these structures seem to work best for, I cannot tell you which type of contract is best for you.

> I think if nothing else, entrepreneurs need to understand that there's no one kind of capital that's good or bad, you may need it all over the lifetime of your growth. And so, understanding how it fits in with your cash flow and your vision for the business and the scale that you want to grow to are the important pieces to remember.
> —Janice St. Onge, Flexible Capital Fund, L3C.

© The Author(s), under exclusive license to Springer Nature
Switzerland AG 2021
A. Patton Power, *Adventure Finance*,
https://doi.org/10.1007/978-3-030-72428-3_30

It is important to remember that you as a founder will change over time and your company will as well. So, you'll want to continue to re-evaluate in different stages of life and company growth. With all of those caveats, let's look at the content that we've covered in this book summarized in table form below.

What Are My Options?

For a comprehensive summary of your options, please 30.1, 30.2 and 30.3. On the online companion to this book, you'll find interactive versions of these tables.

Table 30.1 Summary of options by criteria

Do I...?	If yes, then consider:
Mission / Impact	
Have mission embedded in our governing documents	Grant, Recoverable Grant, Forgivable Loan, Convertible Grant, Impact-Linked Finance
Have a verifiable social/environmental track record	
Collateral	
Have Physical Assets and a credit history	Secured Debt
Have a Guarantee	
Have Invoices / Purchase orders / History of Fulfilling Orders	Invoice factoring, Purchase order financing, Supply Chain financing
Have Recurring Revenue	Revenue-based financing (RBF)
Have Venture Capital Funding	Venture Debt
Planned investor return via	
Plan to sell our company, merge with another company or complete a public listing	Equity (Convertible Note, SAFE, Priced Equity Round)
Plan to repay (or redeem) from internal cash flows or external borrowing	Mezzanine Debt, Structured Exits (Convertible RBF, Redeemable Equity)

Table 30.2 Comprehensive summary table of funding options

	Equity (Priced Equity, SAFE, Convertible Debt)	Secured Debt	Mezzanine Debt	Venture Debt	Factoring (Invoice Factoring, Shipping Financing, Purchase Order Financing)	Supply Chain Financing	Revenue-based Financing (RBF)	Convertible RBF	Redeemable Equity	Guarantees	Traditional Grant	Recoverable Grant	Forgivable Loan	Convertible Grant
Description	Purchase of ownership or the future right to ownership in a company*	Loan that is secured by collateral.	A loan that is paid back with a fixed interest and has upside through kickers such as warrants or profit share	Loan made to fast growing venture-backed companies	Short-term funding option that allows you to borrow against your invoices/shipping bills/purchase orders	Uses pre-payments from your customers to help finance working capital	Loan that is repaid as a percentage of future revenue or cash flows	Loan that is repaid as a percentage of future revenues or cash flows with an option to convert to equity	Purchase of shares that can be bought back at a pre-agreed multiple or mutually agreed price.	Security provided by a third party.	Capital that has no expectation of financial repayment	Grant that converts into debt	Debt that converts into a grant	Grant that converts into equity
Your profile:														
Business registration	For-Profit, Social Enterprise	Non-profit, For-profit, Co-op, Social Enterprise	For-profit, Social Enterprise	For-profit, Social Enterprise	Non-profit, For-profit, Co-op, Social Enterprise		Non-profit, for-profit, co-op, Social Enterprise	For-profit, co-op, Social Enterprise	For-profit, co-op, Social Enterprise	For-profit, non-profit, co-op, Social Enterprise	Non-profit[1]	Non-profit[1]	For-profit, non-profit, co-op, Social Enterprise	Social Enterprise
Revenue Model	May not be determined yet	Consistent or mildly seasonal	May have some seasonality		Likely seasonal or highly variable		Can be seasonal and variable, must have revenues and high margins	Can have some seasonality or variability, must have existing revenue and high margins	Pre- or post-revenue	Any				May not yet be established

(continued)

Table 30.2 (continued)

	Equity	Secured Debt	Mezzanine Debt	Venture Debt	Factoring	Supply Chain Financing	RBF	Convertible RBF	Redeemable Equity	Guarantees	Traditional Grant	Recoverable Grant	Forgivable Loan	Convertible Grant
Company Stage	Concept, Early-stage, Growth	Growth, Scaling or Established	Early-stage, growth or scaling	Early-stage, growth or	Early-stage, scaling or established	Early-stage, growth,	Early-stage, growth, scaling or established	Early-stage, growth or scaling	Concept or early-stage	Any				Concept stage
Business Growth Projections	Unicorn aspirations or High Growth Venture. Some Category Pioneers.	High growth venture, Category pioneer, Niche venture, Dynamic enterprise, Livelihood enterprise	High growth venture, category pioneer, niche venture	High growth venture, category pioneer	High growth venture, Category pioneer, Niche venture, Dynamic enterprise, Livelihood enterprise	High growth venture, Category pioneer, Niche venture, Dynamic enterprise, Livelihood enterprise	Category pioneer, niche enterprise, dynamic enterprise, livelihood enterprise	Category pioneer, niche enterprise, dynamic enterprise	High growth venture, category pioneer, niche enterprise	Any				High growth venture or category pioneer
Your mission:														
Embedded-ness	If you have high mission embeddedness, you will want to seek out impact funders for your equity partners.	Not exceptionally relevant	If you have high mission embeddedness, you may want to seek out funders that are mission driven.		Not especially relevant	If you and your buyer/customer have high mission embeddedness, you may find your financing goals are aligned as well	Not especially relevant	If medium to high embeddedness, you should look for a mission aligned funder		For a guarantee from a mission-driven funder, high mission embeddedness will be necessary	High mission embeddedness required			
Track Record	You may not yet have an impact track record, but you can build a comprehensive IMM plan.	Unless you have social or environmental milestones in your debt agreement, this will not be relevant.	Impact investors may look for an impact track record for later stage companies.		Not especially relevant			Mission aligned funders will likely require an impact track record		Significant impact track record may be required for a concessional guarantee from a mission-driven funder	Impact track record likely to be required		Impact track record will be important if impact milestones are used for forgiveness or interest rate rebates	No track record required, but commitment to measure impact is necessary.

	Equity	Secured Debt	Mezzanine Debt	Venture Debt	Factoring	Supply Chain Financing	RBF	Convertible RBF	Redeemable Equity	Guarantees	Traditional Grant	Recoverable Grant	Forgivable Loan	Convertible Grant
Your funding needs:														
Spend funding on	POC or Growth for long term	Working capital, assets, growth capital over medium term	Growth capital, Working capital over the medium term		Working capital over the short term		Working capital or growth capital over the short term	Working capital or growth capital over the medium term	Proof of concept or growth capital over the medium to long term	Assets, Working Capital	Proof of Concept, Growth Capital, Working Capital, Assets			Proof of Concept
Assets for Collateral	None required	Physical assets and credit history	Some mix of physical assets and alternative types of collateral. Some funders may be willing to be completely unsecured.	Venture capital funding and potentially some level of collateral	Invoices, shipping bills or purchase orders	Customer goods	Historic revenues and may require personal surety	May require personal surety	None	Guarantee acts as collateral for another transaction	None required		Dependent on funder, but generally low	None
Planned Payback Source	Third-party exit through sale, IPC, merger or secondary	Internal cash flows or external borrowing	Internal cash flows for interest rate and cash kicker, if warrants are included then also a third-party exit		Customer payment	NA	Internal cash flow generation	Internal cash flow or future funding		If payment required, internal cash flows	None	None or internal cash flow	None, internal cash flow, or future funding	None or third-party exit through sale, IPO, merger or secondary
Ownership	Willingness to dilute control of business over time	No impact on ownership	If payback is interest + cash kicker, it is not necessary to be willing to dilute ownership. Warrants will require willingness to dilute ownership.	Willingness to dilute control of business over time due to VC funding	No impact on ownership		No impact on ownership	No effect on ownership unless convertibility is triggered	Willingness to dilute ownership in short term, but potential for long-term ownership or transition to employee ownership	No effect on ownership				Willingness to dilute ownership of company in the future

(continued)

Table 30.2 (continued)

	Equity	Secured Debt	Mezzanine Debt	Venture Debt	Factoring	Supply Chain Financing	RBF	Convertible RBF	Redeemable Equity	Guarantees	Traditional Grant	Recoverable Grant	Forgivable Loan	Convertible Grant
Funding in Future	Mix of equity and debt.	Can be used alongside any type of future funding	Can work with both equity and debt funding in future		Can create credit history for future debt funding	No impact on future funding	Equity can be raised in future, but generally designed for companies planning to use debt and internal cash flow generation for future funding	Equity can be raised in future, but generally designed for companies planning to use debt and internal cash flow generation for future funding	Equity can be raised in future, but generally designed for companies planning to use debt and internal cash flow generation for future funding	Can help create credit history for future debt funding	No significant impact on future funding	Can help create credit history for future debt funding	Can help create credit history for future debt funding	Supports equity funding in the future
Funder Involvement	Financial upside focused. High ongoing involvement including board seats, significant voting rights and information rights	Financial downside focused. Low ongoing involvement based on covenants in the debt agreement.	Both upside and downside focused. Will have ongoing involvement. Covenants will act as downside protection, and voting rights and information rights may be used as upside involvement.		Focused only on specific transaction(s) that are financed	Must initiate the transaction	Generally financial downside focused, although may be interested in growth, which could result in quicker repayment. Low ongoing involvement based on covenants in the debt agreement.	Both upside and downside focused. Will have ongoing involvement. Covenants will act as downside protection and voting rights and information rights may be used as upside involvement.	High involvement while shares outstanding including board seats, voting rights and information rights.	If mission driven, funder will be both impact and downside focused with covenants relating to both. Otherwise, just downside focused.	Will be focused on impact and financial spend reporting	Likely to be impact focused with covenants used to embed mission in contract (such as convertibility or cost of capital linked to impact achievement)		Impact and upside focused. Likely to be focused on ongoing involvement with potential for board seats, voting rights and information rights, if converted.

	Equity	Secured Debt	Mezzanine Debt	Venture Debt	Factoring	Supply Chain Financing	RBF	Convertible RBF	Redeemable Equity	Guarantees	Traditional Grant	Recoverable Grant	Forgivable Loan	Convertible Grant
Most likely funders	VC fund, Private Equity Fund, Angel Investor, Incubator Accelerator, Development Finance Institution, Family Office	Bank, Development Finance Institution, Debt fund, Non-Bank Financial institution	Debt Fund, Mezzanine Fund, Bank, Non-bank Financial institution		Mezzanine Fund, Non-Bank Financial Institution	Customer	Non-Bank Financial Institution, Specialized Fund, Debt Fund, Mezzanine Fund	Mezzanine Fund, Debt Fund, VC Fund, Specialized Fund, Non-Bank Financial Institution, Family Office	Angel Investor, Incubator, Accelerator, Family Office, Specialized Fund, VC Fund	Development Finance Institution, Foundation, Family Office, Non-Profit Funder	University, Foundation, Government		Foundation, Family Office, Development Finance Institution, Government, Non-Profit Funder	University, Foundation

Table 30.3 Linking impact and embedding mission summary

		Relevant terms	Impact linking options	Funder motivations	Founder motivations
Linking impact to	Cost of capital	*Interest, dividend/profit share, repayment, redemption*	Interest rate rebate, margin step down, outcomes-based payments	Can encourage companies to achieve social and environmental milestones	Can link financial incentives with social and environmental milestones
	Distribution	*Disbursement schedule*	Impact milestone tranched disbursements	Can reduce impact risk by tying impact achievement to the distribution of capital tranches	Can offer the ability to prove impact track record to access larger amounts of capital
	Convertibility	*Vesting, employee ownership*	Impact-linked vesting, equity earn back	Can link the type of security to impact milestones	Can set clear goals or requirements for the conversion of a security
	Ownership	*Convertibility*	Impact milestone linked convertibility	Can incentivize founders with additional ownership through impact milestones	Opportunity to earn back or accelerate the vesting schedule, based on impact achievement
Embedding mission alignment through	Type of funding	*Security*	Type of funding structure	Create funding options that are more inclusive and that are better suited to founders achieving their long-term impact goals	Understanding what your options are so that you are able to have a candid conversation with prospective funders about the right kind of capital for you, can be extremely important for the future of your organization and your ability to achieve your social mission

(continued)

Table 30.3 (continued)

	Relevant terms	Impact linking options	Funder motivations	Founder motivations
Use of funding	*Use of proceeds*	Ring-fenced use of proceeds	Can be used to ensure that capital is used for the specified purpose or to support the social or environmental mission	Can create clear expectations around capital use
Ownership	*Vesting, employee ownership, stakeholder ownership*	Steward ownership, ESOP, EOT, worker co-operative, golden share, single foundation, trust foundation	Protect the mission of a company over time and incentivize additional impact	Protect the mission of a company over time
Default provisions	*Covenants, events of default*	Mission drift default, put options, facilitated exits	Can allow the funder the opportunity to renegotiate the agreement and/or require the company to arrange an exit for the funder if there are significant changes to the company's mission	Can be used to legally protect the company's mission when non-mission aligned funders are part of funding, but founders must be careful that the restrictions are not overly onerous from a strategic perspective
Rights	*Information rights, voting rights*	Mission change voting, impact reporting	Can establish the type of information that the company must provide around their mission	Can include the ability to resist changes to the company's mission without the founders' vote

Conclusion

Thank you so much for joining me on this journey through the colorful world of innovative finance for purpose-driven companies. I hope you have been able to gain the knowledge and the insights that you need to take your own funding journey forward. Being a founder is not an easy job; it requires creativity, ingenuity, grit, and a lot of perseverance. I admire everything that you are building and the work that it will take to continue building your company. Similarly, being a funder that is dedicated to creating the right type of funding options is no walk in the park. I know that if you are committed to walking this journey and finding ways to make your funding better suited to the needs of the founders that you work with, you will see profound and meaningful impact.

I absolutely love being able to be interact you as you strive to change the world and I look forward to engaging with you going forward. Here is hoping that we meet very soon.

31

Glossary

Accelerator	Time-limited programs that work with cohorts or "classes" of ventures to provide mentorship and training, with a special emphasis on connecting early stage ventures with investment.[1]
Alternative financing	Financing gained from outside traditional bank loans or venture capitalists.
Angel investor	Individuals or networks with resources who invest in very early start-ups (typically in exchange for equity) and provide additional support (often in the form of expertise).
Articles of incorporation	A set of formal documents filed with a government body to legally establish the existence of a corporation and generally contain pertinent information, such as the firm's name, address, number of shares and outline for corporate governance among others.
Asset class	A grouping of financial instruments that behave similarly in the market.

---

[1] https://www.galidata.org/accelerators/.

© The Author(s), under exclusive license to Springer Nature
Switzerland AG 2021
A. Patton Power, *Adventure Finance*,
https://doi.org/10.1007/978-3-030-72428-3_31

287

Asset Owners	Individuals or institutions that own assets. These generally refer to insurance companies, pension funds, banks, foundations, endowments, family offices, as well as individual investors.
Asset-lite	A business that owns relatively fewer capital assets compared to the value of its operations.
Asset-lock	A clause that prevents the sale of a company (or part of a company) to certain buyers.
Assets	Physical or intangible resources such as buildings, equipment, and brands that are expected to generate value.
"Back the Jockey"	Early stage investing often relies on the "back the jockey not the horse mentality." Savvy investors find entrepreneurs that they believe in and invest in them, even if the business model still needs a lot of work. Good entrepreneurs can pivot to build successful businesses.
Bank Loan	Cash loan provided by formal banks to borrowers based on their perceived creditworthiness.
Bankruptcy	A legal proceeding that allows individuals or businesses freedom to continue trading without servicing their debts, thus offering creditors an opportunity for repayment.
Base of the Pyramid (BOP)	Base of the pyramid refers to individuals at the bottom of the economic pyramid of earning, i.e., those making less than $2–5 per day (depending on the context).
Benefit Corporation Certification (B Corp)	Certification that measures a company's entire social and environmental performance. The B Impact Assessment evaluates a company's operations and business model impact your workers, community, environment and customers.
Blended finance	Transactions where public or philanthropic funders collaborate with private investors in order to catalyze (additional) impact.

Board of Directors	An elected group of individuals that represent shareholders that typically meets at regular intervals to set policies for corporate management and oversight.
Bootstrapping	The process in which an entrepreneur takes on the financial responsibility of setting up a company with personal savings and operating revenues with minimal or no external funding.
Break-even	The point at which the revenue generated by the business equals its costs.
Bridging Capital	Temporary funding that helps a business cover its initial costs.
Broker-dealer	A financial entity that trades securities or execute orders on behalf of its clients.
Burn Rate	The net amount cash that you are spending to grow your company. Generally calculated on a monthly basis. Burn rate = *Monthly cash in (cash flow) – monthly cash out (expenses)*
Business loan	Cash loan specifically intended for business purposes and which require some form of collateral.
Business model/business plan	Articulates your company's name and location, its mission and vision, market analyses, descriptions of the products and services, and your financial plan.
Business to Business (B2B)	Businesses that sell their product to businesses.
Business to Consumer (B2C)	Business that sell their products or services directly to customers.
Capitalization Table	A table that lays out the ownership of a company and the amount that equity investors have invested.
Capital Structure	A company's capital structure, otherwise known as **capital stack or waterfall**, is made up of various types of financing used for the business operations. This includes external funding, which is raised from debt

and equity funders, and internal equity funding, which is earned in the form of net profits or retained earnings.

Cash on Cash return (CoC)   A rate of return ratio that calculates the total cash earned on the total cash invested.

Catalytic Capital   Investment capital that is risk-tolerant which aims to unlock impact and additional investment that would not otherwise occur.

Category pioneer   Disruptive products and services, new markets that are likely large, have variable growth and the potential to scale.

Change of Control/Sale of company   The change in ownership of more than fifty percent (50%) of the voting capital of a company in one or more related transactions; the sale of all or substantially all the assets of a company; any merger; the consolidation or acquisition of a company with, by or into another corporation, entity or person.

Community Interest Companies (CICs)   Is a special form of non-charitable limited company in the UK, which exists primarily to benefit a community or with a view to pursuing a social purpose, rather than to make a profit for shareholders.[2]

Collateral   Lenders often require companies (or individuals) to pledge something valuable to act as **security** for a loan. If a business defaults on the loan, i.e., stops paying, the lender can seize this, collateral to sell it to recover some of their principal.

Commercial bank   Financial institution that accepts deposits, offers checking account services, makes business, personal, and mortgage loans to individuals and small businesses.

Contracting infrastructure   The legal agreements necessary to create and execute contracts.

---

[2]https://www.informdirect.co.uk/company-formation/community-interest-company-cic-advantages-disadvantanges/#:~:text=A%20community%20interest%20company%20(or,make%20a%20profit%20for%20shareholders.

Convertible clause   Agreements that convert from one type of
                                          security to another. For types of funding
                                          that have a convertibility clause, you can
                                          choose to have that conversion be triggered
                                          by financial or impact milestones.

Below are all of the different types of convertible agreements that we have
discussed throughout the book (Table 31.1).

Table 31.1 Convertible instruments

Called:	Converts:	Made to:	By:	Funder motivation	Founder motivation
Convertible debt	From debt to equity	For-profits	Venture capitalists, impact investors, individuals	Put capital into a very early-stage business without having to put a value on the business	Access risk capital without having to commit to a valuation
Convertible RBF	From debt to equity	For-profits	Fintechs, specialist funds, impact investors	Create liquidity through a structured exit and create a more inclusive portfolio	Access risk capital without having to commit to a valuation or to exponential growth
Redeemable equity	From equity to debt	For-profits	Specialist funds, impact investors	Create liquidity through a structured exit and create a more inclusive portfolio	Access risk capital, but still have a clear path toward continued ownership of the company

(continued)

Table 31.1 (continued)

Called:	Converts:	Made to:	By:	Funder motivation	Founder motivation
Recoverable grants	From grant to debt	For-profits or non-profits	Non-profit entities: foundations, donor-advised funds	Recover capital to recycle to other grantees	Access timely bridging capital, low risk proof-of-concept funding, flexible capital to on-lend or build a credit history
Forgivable loans	From debt to grant	Non-profits or for-profits	Non-profit or for-profit entities: foundations, impact investors, individuals, governments	Use social milestones to reward an organization or use financial milestones to recycle capital	Access debt funding that aligns incentives around achievement of social milestones or flexibility in case of underperformance financially
Equity earn back	From equity to grant	For-profits	Impact investors, foundations, DAFs, individuals	Incentivize funders to create additional social and/or environmental impact	The opportunity to earn back ownership based on achievement of social and/or environmental goals
Convertible grants	From grant to equity	For-profits	Non-profit or for-profit entities: foundations, impact investors, individuals, universities	Fund very early-stage, potentially high impact organization with potential for significant upside	Access funding that may not otherwise be available

Convertible Grant   Capital allocated to allow companies to develop a product or service before raising investment capital. If a company raises equity financing in the future, the grant converts to equity ownership.

Convertible Note/Convertible Debt Agreement	A debt agreement that converts into equity at a later date, normally when the investee raises a round of equity funding. In a convertible debt agreement, an investor agrees to loan a certain amount of money to an organization. This loan generally accrues interest, but that interest isn't paid in cash. Instead, it is added to the amount of the loan over time. When the organization raises a round of equity capital, the amount of the loan outstanding is used to buy shares of the company. The cost of these shares is calculated by taking the price the equity investors are paying and applying a discount.
Convertible Revenue-Based Financing (Convertible RBF)	Loan that is repaid as a percentage of future revenues or cash flows with an option to convert to equity.
Co-operative (Co-op)	Partially or completely employee-owned companies. Also called **Worker Co-ops**.
Cost of capital	The return that funders expect for providing capital to the company.
Covenant	An agreement to do something or refrain from doing something. In early stage funding agreements, these are clauses in contracts that specify specific actions that the company can or cannot take. If these clauses are "breached" or broken, they can lead to the consequences spelled out in the document, often defaulting on the agreement.
Credit line	A type of standing loan that allows organizations to borrow cash when they need it, repay what they have borrowed, and continue borrowing without applying for a new loan.
Creditworthiness	In addition to collateral, lenders generally require proof that a business has a **credit history**. This credit history can be in the form of audited financial statements, history

	of other borrowing or outstanding orders for goods.
Creditworthy collateral	Assets that have significant value.
Crowdfunding	A fundraising method of collecting small amounts of capital from your community of supporters, end-users and everyday individuals in order to finance a new business venture or the evolution of your existing business.
Currency Risk	Also called exchange rate risk. It is the risk that exists when financial transactions are dominated in a different currency to the base currency of the organization.
Customer Orders	A commercial document issued by the customer of goods to the seller.
Cyclicality (of revenue)	Variations in revenue caused by business cycles, again caused by external factors.
Debt and mezzanine funds	Pools of capital that invest in businesses through mezzanine and debt instruments.
Debt capital	Capital that can be lent out or borrowed.
Debt crowdfunding	Individuals lending money to a company over a set period of time. Also called **Peer to peer (P2P)** or **loan-based crowdfunding**.
Default	Occurs when a borrower is unable to pay back a loan or breaches other covenants in a loan agreement.
Demand Dividend	A type of convertible RBF agreement that uses profit sharing to repay investors initial risk capital investment.
Deposit Account Control Agreement (DACA)	The agreement in which a debtor, a lender and the bank maintaining the deposit account have agreed that the bank will comply with instructions from the lender directing the use of the funds in the deposit account without further consent by the debtor.
Development finance institution	Specialized development banks or subsidiaries that are set up to support

	private sector development in developing countries.
Development Impact Bond (DIB)	A results-based contract in which private investors provide pre-financing for social programs and public sector agencies pay back investors their principal plus a return if, and only if, these programs succeed in delivering social outcomes.[3]
Dilution	The decrease in existing shareholders' ownership percentage that results from issuing new shares; such shareholders own a smaller, or diluted, percentage of the company after the new shares have been issued. Dilution may also result when holders, such as company employees, exercise their share options. Capital that does not dilute founders' ownership is called **non-dilutive capital**.
Direct Public Offering (DPO)	A type of offering in which a company offers or sells its securities (without the help of an underwriter) directly to the public in order to raise capital.
Discount Rate	A discount that is applied to a calculation. In this book, we are referring to a discount applied to a future transaction, i.e., how much less the SAFE investors would pay per share than the Series A investors. If the discount rate is 40%, then the SAFE investors would pay 60% of the Series A investors' price per share.
Disruptive innovation	An innovation that creates a new market and value network and eventually disrupts an existing market and value network. A company that has a **disruptive business model** is harnessing disruptive innovation. This concept was pioneered by Professor Clayton Christiansen.

---

[3]https://www.cgdev.org/topics/development-impact-bonds.

Distributed ownership	Refers to democratic ownership of a company in the form of management or community buy-out, worker co-operative conversion and other ownership types.
Distribution Channels	How companies distribute products or services through proprietary or shared channels.
Dividend	Payments made to shareholders from the profits of a company.
Donation-based crowdfunding	Individuals donating money toward a social or environmental project.
Donor-Advised Fund (DAF)	A tax-preferred philanthropic vehicle similar to a private foundation. A donor can establish a DAF with an initial tax-deductible contribution, and then recommend the DAF donate funds to other non-profits at a later time. This allows donors to separate the timing of the tax decision from the giving decision, and to give money out over time while claiming a tax benefit in the year (or years) most beneficial to her.
Down round	When a company raises an equity round at a valuation that is lower than its last round.
Downside protection	A risk-management strategy that attempts to reduce the amount of capital that is lost in an investment.
Dry powder	Capital that can be invested by an investment fund.
Dynamic discounting	Similar to early payment, it allows small suppliers to secure early payment from buyers by offering a discount on their orders.
Dynamic enterprise	Company in an established industry and sector that has existing products that are tried and tested, a proven business model, and is projecting steady growth.
Early payment	Allows small suppliers to secure early payment from buyers by offering a discount on their orders. A type of **Supply Chain Financing**.

Earnings before tax, amortization and depreciation (EBITDA)	A measure of a company's overall financial performance and current operating profitability.

$$EBITDA = \text{Net Income} + \text{Interest} + \text{Taxes}$$
$$+ \text{Depreciation} + \text{Amortization}$$

Elective payments	Optional payments in structured exits that can be made in addition to scheduled payments to reduce the number of shares outstanding or the total obligation. The decision to make these payments lies solely with the investee.
Electronic invoicing	A form of electronic billing.
Emerging middle class	This term refers to the growing middle-class population in emerging markets.
Employee ownership	An arrangement in which an employee owns shares of a company's stock which they work in. This is also referred to as a **Shared Ownership** model.
Employee Ownership Trust (EOT)	Also known as Perpetual Employee Trust or **Employee Benefit Trust** (EBT). EOTs are designed to preserve the business over the long term for employees' benefit. Employees don't pay for their ownership benefits, and they receive a share of the company's annual profits.
Employee Stock Ownership Plan (ESOP)	ESOPs are the most common broad-based employee ownership model in the U.S. They effectively function like a **401(k) employee benefit plan** in the U.S. that allows a company to transfer full or partial ownership to its employees. With an ESOP, there is no requirement for profit sharing or democratic governance, wherein employees have strategic decision-making rights.
Endowment	Donation of money or property to a non-profit organization, which uses the resulting investment income for a specific purpose.

Enterprise risk	Enterprise risk is the overarching set of risks that affect the entire organization. Enterprise risk comprises several subtypes such as liquidity risk and financial risk.
Environment, Social and Governance (ESG)	Refers to the three central factors in measuring the sustainability and societal impact of an investment in a company or business.
Equity capital	Capital that can be used to purchase ownership.
Equity crowdfunding	Individuals investing into a company in return for ownership in the company.
Equity earn back	Clause that allows founders to earn back ownership from funders through the achievement of impact milestones.
Evergreen fund	A fund that does not have a limited life, rather it exists in perpetuity. Funders in evergreen funds will need to have clauses in their funding contracts that specify how they will get their capital out of the fund. This will generally be through a combination of liquidity events such as dividends and selling their shares in the fund to other funders.
Exit risk	The possibility that you won't be able to achieve a successful exit from an investment to make your return.
Exit	Getting out of an investment. For equity investors an exit event is generally, a listing on a public stock exchange called an **Initial Public Offering (IPO)**, a purchase of the company by a larger competitor or a purchase by a financial investor (**trade sale**). Very rarely, early equity investors will be bought out by later stage VC funders (**secondary sale**). For lenders, an exit event is repayment of the loan.
Expenditure responsibility	A U.S. accounting and tax requirement that grant funding that is given to a for-profit

	entity must track the use of the capital to ensure that it is used for social purposes.
Exponential growth	"growth whose rate becomes ever more rapid in proportion to the growing total number or size" (Oxford Dictionary). For start-ups, we often call this a **J curve** or a "**hockey stick**" projection as the graph of future revenues looks like a J or a hockey stick—flat and then suddenly straight up.
External stakeholders	When referencing funders' external stakeholders, we mean their Limited Partners (LPs) or other types of funders that provide capital to a fund or foundation. These stakeholders will have specific criteria around how they want their capital to be allocated.
Factoring	A loan that uses invoices or purchase orders as collateral.
Fair Trade	An arrangement designed to help producers in developing countries achieve sustainable and equitable trade relationships. Members of the Fair Trade movement add the payment of higher prices to exporters, as well as improved social and environmental standards (Fairtrade.net).
Fair Market Value	The value of an asset or a company as determined by the external or internal evaluators.
Family office	Private wealth management advisory firms that serve ultra-high-net-worth investors.
Flexible Capital	Capital is very flexible and, unless specified, it can be used for anything the entrepreneur wishes to use it for.
Follow-on Investment	When funders follow their initial investment with an additional investment in the next round of fundraising. For instance, an investor that invested $50 k in a seed round might decide to invest $200 k in the series A round. The $200 k would be a follow-on investment.
Forgivable Loan	Loan that converts to a grant and is used to support non-profits and social enterprises.

For-profit	An organization that is run with the primary aim of capturing value in the form of money (profit) for its owners.
Foundation	Independent legal entity set up solely for charitable purposes, often drawing on the resources of a single individual, family or corporation.
Founder	An individual who comes up with an idea and transforms it into an organization. In this book, it can also mean anyone that works for an organization raising capital.
Free Cash Flow	A way of looking at a business's cash flow to see the available cash that can be distributed to its securities holders without causing issues in its operations.
Friends, Family and 'Fools' (the 3 Fs)	Generally, the first people that a founder looks to invest in a start-up company.
Fund Life Cycle	Refers to the timing of a closed-in fund. Generally closed-end investment funds have a 10- to 12-year fund life cycle. This means once they have raised their capital, they invest it into companies for the first 2–3 years, manage those companies for 4–5 years and then begin to look for exits from those companies in the last 3 years of the fund, so they can return the capital to their LPs.
Funder	An individual or an institution that provides an organization with capital or other resources to support its operations, growth or other business matters.
Fundraising stream	A historical track record and consistency such as a specific set of donors or an event.
Fundraising Support	Support, advice and connections for future funding.
Governance Support	Supporting the development of a board of directors, and strengthening governance systems.

Government agency

Government institutions established for the specific purpose of promoting economic growth and development through a variety of direct or indirect support mechanisms.

Grace Period

A period which allows a borrower to delay payment for a short period of time.

Grant capital

Capital that does not expect a financial return.

Gross margin

The difference between revenue and cost of goods sold, i.e., direct costs.

Gross Margin = (Total Revenue

− Cost of Goods Sold)/Total Revenue.

Growth Capital

This is cash spent on hiring people, investing in new product development, putting systems into place, marketing anything that helps you build toward the future.

Guarantee

Is very similar to, say, relying on a friend or relative to co-sign an apartment rental agreement. If you're a young person without a history of paying rent, a landlord might not be willing to rent to you because they don't know whether you'll be able to pay. But when someone with a longer credit history steps forward and promises that you'll pay your rent, that reduces the land-lord's sense of risk. Getting a guarantor for your debt basically has the same effect on lenders and can help you to access debt capital and/or borrow at a much lower interest rate. The catch is that you need to have a guarantor that has a strong enough reputation or a dedicated amount of cash to set aside on your behalf.

There are two ways guarantees can be set up: "funded," which means the guarantor places some or all of the amount into an account that can be accessed by the lender, (as Skoll did on Riders for Health's behalf);

	and "unfunded," which is really more of a pledge that the loan is guaranteed.
Guarantor	An individual who promises to pay a borrower's debt in the event that the borrower defaults on his or her loan obligation. Guarantors pledge their own assets as collateral against the loans.
Hackathon	An event where a large group of people meet to engage in collaborative computer programming or brainstorming to build or develop start-up company ideas.
High growth venture	Companies with a disruptive business model, large addressable markets, high growth projections, and the ability to scale quickly. These companies are quite risky and are often referred to in the start-up world as **Gazelles**.
Hollywood accounting	The practice of being very creative with your financial reporting. Can be used to reduce your payments to convertible RBF funders that rely on dividends from free cash flow.
Hybrid organization	A company that has two different types of legal structures, being both a for-profit and a non-profit.
Impact audit	Similar to a financial audit, an impact audit uses a third party to verify a company's reported performance against its agreed-upon impact metrics.
Impact bond fund	Multiple outcomes-based contracts joined together into a fund structure.
Impact bond investors	A funder that provides the upfront capital for the service provider to achieve the social or environmental outcomes. The investors' return is based on how effectively the service provider creates the social or environmental impact.
Impact investing	Investments made with the intention to generate positive, measurable social and environmental impact alongside a financial

return.[4] See also **impact focused funders, mission-aligned funders**.

Impact measurement and management (IMM)	The process of identifying the positive and negative effects of a business' activities on people and the planet, and managing these effects toward the business and/or the investor's social or environmental objectives.
Impact metrics	A standard of measurement that is used to assess the impact or progress of a company.
Impact risk	The risk that an investment will not achieve the social or environmental impact that is projected.
Impact strategy	A plan that articulates how the impact of an investment in the future, typically through a theory of change and supporting impact measurement and management methodologies.
Impact thesis	A succinct and evidence-based proposition that indicates how an investment strategy will achieve its intended social or environmental impact.
Impact track record	The historical performance of a business toward its stated impact objectives.
Impact-linked debt	A type of impact-linked financing where the debt agreement has contractual clauses that link the cost or distribution of funding to impact milestones.
Impact-linked finance	Refers to linking financial rewards for market-based organizations to the achievements of positive social or environmental outcomes.
Income streams	The different ways in which a company creates revenue. This can refer to different products or services, different parts of the business model or different segments of customers.

---

[4]https://thegiin.org/impact-investing/.

Incubator	Institution that helps ventures define and build their initial products, identify promising customer segments, and secure resources.
Information rights	A clause in a funding agreement that requires a company to provide investors with company information and financial statements.
Initial Public Offering (IPO)	When a company lists on a public stock exchange. It can also be called "taking a company public." An IPO involves selling shares of the company to the general public, by way of investment banks.
Intellectual Property (IP)	Intangible assets which can extend beyond things like software, or an actual design, process or methodology and can include the trade secrets of the business (customer and client lists) as well as the know-how of the employees.
Interest-free loan	A zero-interest loan where only the principal balance must be repaid.
Interest Rate Rebate	Reducing the cost of a loan based on achievement of impact milestones.
Interest	Nearly all forms of debt accrue interest and require the borrower to make interest payments of some kind. Generally, these interest payments are required at regular intervals (i.e., monthly) and are calculated as a percentage of the **principal** (the original amount borrowed) and can also be linked to national interest rates.
Intermediary	An organization that helps to set-up transactions.
Internal Rate of Return (IRR)	A metric used in financial analysis to estimate the profitability of potential investments. IRR is more or less the **return on investment** if the investment had been a traditional loan, paid annually.

Internal stakeholders	When referencing funders' internal stakeholders, we mean their management, board or investment committee.
Investment Advisor	A financial professional that makes investment recommendations in securities such as stocks, bonds, exchange-traded funds or conducts security analysis for its clients in exchange for a fee.
Investment Committee	The primary authority on developing the corporation's investment objectives and corporate policies on investing. An investment committee approves or declines investments that are presented to them by fund employees.
Investment pitch deck	A slide presentation of a business to showcase to investors or any other capital providers which typically include key financials, competitors analysis, market research and value proposition.
Investment Process	For an **equity** or **mezzanine** investment, this is generally called "the investment process," while a process for **debt** may be called a "loan process" or a "credit process."

See Table 31.2.

Table 31.2 Investment process description

Founder	Step	Funder
As a founder, you need to find funders who are interested in investing money into your business. Once you connect with them, your initial conversations will involve descriptions of your business and what you are looking to build	Sourcing	As a funder, you need to get creative to source the best deals by engaging your network, attending conferences and pitch days and scouring social media to find new and interesting businesses. You may also want to have an application form that founders can fill out to initiate a conversation

(continued)

Table 31.2 (continued)

Founder	Step	Funder
When a funder decides that they are interested in your business, they'll begin the process of doing diligence on you and your company. This will involve collecting data on your current business, the market and potential customers. It will also involve probing any legal or intellectual property (IP) issues.	**Due Diligence**	Due diligence is your chance to understand the opportunities and risks of investing in a company. Many funders have a pre-due diligence period where they do an initial check before they spend time and resources on a full due diligence process
In order to make an investment official, you'll need to sign legal agreements. For debt and equity investments, this will start with a term sheet, which lays out the terms of the funding. This term sheet will then be used to create the legal documentation necessary to finalize the deal. In Chapter 10, we'll go through the different terms on a term sheet one by one	**Contracting**	To negotiate the terms of the investment, you'll need to either have templates ready or work with lawyers to build the necessary legal agreements. If the investment involves a business valuation, you'll need to build that out here as well

Funding term

The amount of involvement funders have during the investment term will depend on the type of investment. Debt funders are typically less involved in day-to-day operations than equity funders

Exit

For an equity funder, the exit marks the end of their investment in a business, either through a sale of the company, a merger, or a listing on a public exchange (called an IPO). For debt funders, their "exit" is when the loan is repaid (although the term "exit" is usually only used in equity investments)

Note that some activities in the above steps can be in a slightly different order and that the boundaries between the steps are not always clear. For example, investors will usually start exploring terms early in the process, so before the actual due diligence starts.

How long does an investment process take? That is hard to answer as it depends on a number of different factors: the type of investment, the type of investor, the geography, and the entrepreneur. Some angel investors are able to close equity deals in just a few days while others take months to get through the due diligence and contracting process. As you saw in Chapter 7, tech-enabled funding platforms VIWALA and GetVantage are both able to close debt investments in less than a week, whereas a bank might take several months. So with that giant caveat, here are some basic guidelines for raising equity and debt funding:

If you are a founder raising equity funding, expect to spend several weeks to months having initial conversations with investors. They will want to get to know you and your business before beginning due diligence, as going through the due diligence process takes time and resources, which are scarce. For commercial VC investors doing an equity deal involving a valuation, you can expect the due diligence process to take at least a month, likely more. You'll also need to negotiate a term sheet, which may be done in the midst of the due diligence process. Depending on how many terms you want to change, this process can require a lot of back and forth. Then you have the legal documentation, which is the lawyer's remit and often requires filing paperwork with regulatory bodies, so expect this process to take a few weeks as well.

If you are raising debt funding, the biggest factor is the type of institution you are borrowing from. If you are borrowing money from a large financial institution, the process will be very regimented and often quite manual. You may have long waiting times between submitting required information and hearing back about the decision. If you are working with smaller lenders or tech-enabled lenders, the process could be more transparent and streamlined, and they should be able to give you an idea of how long it will take from the outset.

Investment readiness framework	A framework designed for early stage impact ventures to assess their readiness for investment.
Investment risk	The uncertainty or probability of losses rather than expected return from an investment.
Investment thesis	Lays out the types of companies that a funder invests in. The thesis should identify the sectors they fund, the geographies, the stage of companies, the types of instrument(s), and the size of funding.
Investor Demo Days/pitch events	An event where a founder pitches his/her idea to potential investors.
Investor group/network	A group of individuals that meet with the purpose of pooling money to invest or sharing investment ideas or due diligence.

Investor repayment

If you secure funding from external funders to cover your business's spending and growth needs, there are three ways to repay your funders. The first is repayment through a third-party exit. Basically, this means that you expect to repay your funders sometime in the future, either by selling your company or listing it on a stock exchange. The second strategy is repayment from internal cash flows. In this case, you plan to repay funding based on cash that your business generates while your funding agreement is in place. The third strategy is to use future funding to repay your financial backers. For this strategy, you may use funding in the early stages of your business, or in the short-term, to build a credit history and track record that allows you to access better, less expensive funding with which to repay your initial financial supporters.

Invoice

Document that records a transaction between buyers and sellers.

Invoice Factoring

Is a short-term funding option that allows you to borrow against your invoices to finance your working capital.

Junior (aka subordinated) debt

Junior debt is unsecured and has a lower probability of being paid back should an organization default, since higher-ranking debt is given priority.

Keep it Simple Security (KISS)

An agreement that is a cross between a convertible note and a SAFE. It accrues interest at a stated rate and establishes a maturity date after which the investor may convert the underlying investment, plus accrued interest, into newly created preferred stock of the company.

Kicker

An additional payment. **Mezzanine financing** generally has some kind of kicker, in addition to a fixed interest rate,

	that provides **upside** to investors. These can be in the form of **cash kickers** (revenue or profit shares) or **warrants.**
Lead the round	When an investor is the lead investor on a deal. This usually means they are the one to take charge of due diligence and drafting the term sheet and legal documents. They also may put in the largest amount of capital in the deal, compared to other investors.
Licensing income	Income earned from licensing the right to products, services or brands.
Limited life fund	A fund with a specific date by which the fund managers need to return their capital to their LPs.
Limited Partners (LPs)	An investor into a fund or business that does not have a day-to-day role. Most Venture Capital and Private Equity funds are structured so that their investors are LPs. The Venture Capital and Private Equity funds are then the **General Partners (GPs)** that manage the assets on behalf of the LPs.
Limited Liability Companies (L3Cs)	An L3C is a variation of a limited liability company (LLC), which is a private organization where the owners actively participate in management and don't face personal liability for the organization's debts and obligations. An L3C, though, is a hybrid of an LLC and non-profit business model, which is where an organization operates to benefit the general public without shareholders and without a profit motive.[5]
Liquidation preference	A contractual clause that sets out the order in which investors, debtholders and creditors are paid if a company is liquidated. Investors and holders of preferred shares (stock) usually have a higher priority than holders of ordinary shares (common stock) or debt.

---

[5] https://nonprofithub.org/starting-a-nonprofit/jargon-free-guide-l3c/.

Liquidity	When an investment is liquid, it means that it can be easily converted to cash. Thus, liquidity means being able to convert your investment into cash.
Liquidity event	An acquisition, merger, IPO or other event that allows founders and investors to cash out their shares in a company. A bankruptcy is also considered a liquidity event for contractual purposes, although it is generally not what is meant when talking about exits.
Liquidity premium	Capital that is locked up in an investment for a long period of time is generally more expensive than capital that can be withdrawn at any point or that has a short payback period, this is called a liquidity premium.
Liquidity risk	Liquidity risk is the risk that a funder will not be able to extract capital when it is necessary for them to do so.
Livelihood enterprise	Family run, highly localized business that is driven by local opportunity and is projecting limited future growth.
Management buy-out	A transaction where a company's management team purchases the assets and operations of the business they manage.
Market risk	There is always the risk that regardless of how astute the enterprise it will fail due to larger market risks. These can be a myriad of possibilities from a global pandemic to political upheaval to currency devaluations to the emergence of a giant competitor to climate change.
Market traction	Evidence that a product or service has established consumer demand in the market.
Market-rate return	Returns similar to other investments with a comparable risk profile.
Maturity Date	This is the date that the total amount owed is expected to be paid back and/or shares redeemed.

Mentorship	Equity investors expect to be very involved in their investee businesses, providing mentorship and valuable connections. In an equity investment, both the investor and the investee are incentivized to grow the business.
Mezzanine Debt	Loan that is paid back with a fixed interest and has upside through kickers such as warrants or profit share (cash).
Mezzanine financing	Combines elements of debt and equity to create funding that has more flexibility than pure debt and equity. Mezz funders are willing to consider different forms of risk assessment, such as the presence of a Venture Capital funder (**venture debt**). They are also willing to lend money that is completely unsecured. As they are taking additional risk by funding earlier stage businesses or sitting **subordinated** to other funders, they look for higher returns than secured debt funders. These returns come from a fixed interest rate and some kind of upside opportunity in the form of a kicker.
Microfinance institution	Formal institutions whose major business is the provision of financial services and insurance products to low-income individuals and micro- and small businesses.
Microfinance loan	Cash loan provided by small organizations to borrowers who lack access to traditional banking.
Milestone	A milestone is a goal or target that is predefined. It can be financial (X $ of sales) or social (number of women employed) or environmental (X megawatts of solar power installed).
Minimum Viable Product (MVP)	A version of the product with just enough features to make it usable for initial users with the primary aim of getting feedback.
Mini-Bond	Form of debt that allows investors to invest in a company and receive a fixed return over

	a set period of time, with the initial investment returned at the end of the prescribed duration. Mini-bonds allow you to lend money directly to businesses.[6]
Missing middle	In terms of business, this refers to a company that is too small for big investors and too big for small investors.
Mission drift	Moving away from your social and/or environmental mission.
Mission embeddedness	How deeply your social and/or environmental mission is embedded in your company. If you are a company with a high level of mission embeddedness, you will likely have your mission explicitly stated in your articles of incorporation as it forms a key part of why the business was founded, what kind of products and services you offer and to whom you offer them.
Mission lock	Contractually protecting your mission in your founding documents or funding agreements.
Mission-related investment (MRI)	MRI is not a legal term but describes an investment that integrates mission alignment into the investment decision-making process. Impact Investment is often used interchangeably with MRI. MRIs are a component of the foundation's overall endowment and investment strategy and must comply with the state and federal prudence requirements applicable to a foundation's investing activities generally.
Mission statement	A formal summary of the aims and values of a company, organization, or individual. (Oxford Dictionary)
Money Multiple	A multiple that describes how much an investor made compared to their initial investment. Money Multiple = Amount of

---

[6]https://www.syndicateroom.com/alternative-investments/mini-bonds#:~:text=Mini%2Dbonds%20are%20a%20form,lend%20money%20directly%20to%20businesses.

money returned to an investor/amount of money put into investment. An investment that returned $100 k on a $20 k investment would have a money multiple of 5x ($100/20 = 5).

Niche Enterprise
A company that has an innovative product or service is in niche markets, and customer segments and is projecting steady to high growth.

"no exit" clause
A type of mission lock clause that is meant to dissuade an outside acquisition. Simply put, there would be no upside for investors if some deep-pocketed competitor dangled a large acquisition check. For Equal Exchange, it means that if Starbucks or Nestle, for example, wanted to acquire them, the company's bylaws require Equal Exchange to repay investors only what they invested, and to give all net proceeds from the sale to another Fair Trade organization.

Non-bank financial institution
Institutions that provide certain types of banking services but do not have a full banking licenses (e.g., credit unions, CDFIs, fintech, etc.).

Non-convertible loan
Debt that cannot be converted into equity.

Non-dilutive capital
Capital that doesn't require you to sell ownership (and can include redeemable equity where you can buy your ownership back), such as grant or debt capital.

Non-profit
A type of company that is value-based and depends in whole or in part, on charitable donations and voluntary service with a focus on value created (impact) for society in the achievement of mission, and subsists on fundraising and earned income from goods and services provided by the organization.

One-way option
An option that can be triggered to one party, usually a funder. For instance, an option for a funder to convert debt into

equity if the founder of the company raises an equity round.

Original issue discount (OID)
The difference between the face value of the bond and the price at which it was originally sold to an investor.

Outcomes
The goals and objectives a company aims to achieve which come as a direct result of outputs.

Outcome-based financing
A financing contract where the funder only pays once the pre-agreed social and/or environmental outcomes have been achieved by the service provider.

Outcomes payor or Outcomes Funder
A funder that is willing to pay for social and environmental outcomes.

Outputs
The measurable quantity and quality of products and services that illustrate/highlight the activities of a company.

Overdraft facility
An overdraft is a short-term credit facility provided by a bank through which an account holder can borrow up to a certain sum once their account balance is at or below zero. The lender levies an overdraft fee on the borrowed amount, and the money is to be returned within stipulated time frame(s).

Ownership
In general, early stage equity investors do not buy more than 50% ownership in a company during an investment round. This is because early stage investors need to invest into many companies and they do not have the time or expertise to manage all of these companies. Nevertheless, after multiple investment rounds, an entrepreneur might find themselves owning less than 50% of the business, meaning they no longer control the company.

Participation rights
Participation rights or the right of first refusal outline how funders can participate in future equity rounds.

Participatory budget	Is a pool of public grant capital that citizens decide how to allocate.
Patient capital	Patient capital is another name for long-term capital. With patient capital, the investor is willing to make a financial investment in a business with no expectation of turning a quick profit.
Patronage	This is when company profits are shared among worker-owners based on their status as full- or part-time workers.
Pay as you go (PAYG)	Business models that are based on PAYG allow customers to pay for goods and services as they receive them. The most common example is home solar systems like M-KOPA where customers pay for their solar electricity each month instead of paying upfront for the solar home system.
Payment guarantee	An assurance that a buyer will pay a specified purchase price on a set date.
Peer-based decision making	Allowing decisions to be made by a group of participants. The **Village Banking model** is an example of this, as is Village Capital's **peer-driven investment approach**.
Perceived Risk	Risks that are based on a lack of data.
Permitted indebtedness clause	A precautionary lender protection that gives funders the option to stipulate that written permission or approval is needed for the company to take on additional debt obligations.
Personal guarantee	A written agreement made by an individual to repay credit issued to their business using their own personal assets in the case of default.
Pipeline	Access to high-quality deals, projects or entrepreneurs. Generally used by investors to describe their potential deals, i.e., we have built a pipeline of incredible entrepreneurs from our work with University science departments.

Portfolio-level return

For an investor, each individual investment will have a financial return. When they look across their entire portfolio, these will sum up into a portfolio-level return.

Portfolio Return Expectations (VC)

Early stage equity investing is very risky. Most small companies fail. This is true in every country in the world. Thus, equity investors need to bet on a lot of companies (by building up a portfolio) and bet on companies that are projecting exponential growth to make the kind of return that merits this risky investment. The math would typically look like this:

If an early stage investor invests in 10 companies, they need 1–2 of them to blow the lights out (i.e., return over 10 times the money invested or 10× as this is often called). This is because they expect 4 or so to just middle along and not provide much return and then 3–4 to fail completely. So that 1 superstar (or 2 if they are lucky) will provide most of the return for the whole fund and cover the losses of the failed businesses.

Post-revenue

Company that has current sales or revenue, also called revenue positive.

Prepayment penalty/discount

In most debt contracts there is a prepayment penalty, if you pay down the debt early. This is because lenders create their own financing models based on the assumption that outstanding borrowers will continue to pay interest until the maturity date. If the borrowers prepay the loan, then the lenders forgo that interest. For structured exits, there are examples (such as Adobe) of a prepayment discount, where the borrower repays the total obligation early and thus negotiates a discount to the total obligation.

Pre-revenue	Company that does not yet have sales or revenue.
Priced Equity Round	Buying a specific amount of shares in a company for a specific price per share.
Private equity fund	Medium- to long-term finance provided to an investee company in return for an equity stake in potentially high growth companies.
Private placements	Stock sales directly to investors instead of on an exchange.
Pro rata	Allocated in proportion.
Profit share	An agreement to share in profits of a company.
Program-related investments	The legal catch-all term for any type of non-grant financial commitment made to advance a foundation's mission. They are not a grant and they are not an investment. They are a legally distinct third option that only appears in the U.S. tax code.
Proof of Concept	A process to validate the feasibility and viability of an idea, product, or service in principle.
Proxies and econometric research (in relation to impact measurement)	Proxies are strongly correlated substitutes that are used to indirectly measure a desired outcome when direct measures of that outcome are unobservable and/or unavailable.
Public Benefit Corporation	A specific type of company that allows for public benefit to be a charter purpose in addition to the traditional corporate goal of maximizing profit for shareholders.

1. Have an expanded purpose beyond maximizing share value to explicitly include general and specific public benefit.
2. Are required to consider/balance the impact of their decisions not only on shareholders but also on their stakeholders.
3. Are required to make available to the public, except in Delaware, an annual benefit report that assesses their overall social and environmental performance against a third party standard. Such a report does not need to be certified or audited by a third party but uses the standard as an assessment tool.

Purchase order financing	A way for businesses to use orders from customers as a form of collateral to secure a loan.
Purchasing Power	Ability to commit to purchasing products/services.
Put option	A contractual clause that gives the owner the right to sell. In early stage funding, this means that a funder can force the founder to repurchase their shares or repay the outstanding debt.
Quasi-Equity	Funding that is a combination of equity and debt.
Real Risk	Real risks, such as currency risk, political risk and early stage risk are risks that we can build into our financial models and can use to price capital accordingly.
Recoverable Grants	Recoverable grants are grants that are repaid to the funder if the grantee achieves certain pre-agreed financial outcomes.
Redeemable Equity	Shares that can be repurchased by founders at a pre-agreed multiple or mutually agreed price.
Redemption price	The price at which an investment company will buy back its shares from the owner. Generally calculated as a **redemption multiple**.
Repayment risk	The risk of a borrower not being able to repay back a loan in accordance with the loan terms.
Research and development (R&D)	Costs incurred to create new products and services.
Residual stake	Shares that cannot be redeemed except through a **change of control** (sale of the company) or a **liquidation event** (i.e., IPO or bankruptcy).
Results-based finance	Is an umbrella term referring to any program or intervention that provides rewards to individuals or institutions after

	agreed-upon results are achieved and verified.[7]
Retained earnings	These are the profits that a company decides to keep instead of distributing them as dividends to shareholders. These are located in the shareholder's equity section of the balance sheet.
Return on capital hurdle	A funder will have a minimum amount of financial return that they are looking to achieve. They will often call this their return on capital hurdle rate. Another term for this is a **Return Target**.
Return on Investment	Measures the gain or loss generated by an investment in relation to its initial cost.
Return Variable	Can be a single, well-defined financial metric, such as gross revenue, retained earnings, or net income, or a custom formula, such as the "Founder Earnings."
Revenue-based financing (RBF)	Loan that is repaid as a percentage of future revenues or cash flows. Also called: revenue share agreement.
Revenue model	Internal financing model describing targeted resources harnessed, resources offered, to whom, at what price.
Rewards-based crowdfunding	Individuals donating to a project or business with the expectation of receiving a non-financial reward in return, such as goods or services, at a later time.
Ring Fence	To separate assets or funding. Funders or founders can ring-fence capital for specific uses.
Risk/Return	Calculation which suggests that greater risk leads to greater return.
Risk Capital	Funds allocated for high-risk, high-reward investments.
Risk-adjusted financial return	The expected return on the evaluation of the investment risk and upside expectations.

---

[7] https://www.worldbank.org/en/programs/reach.

Roll-over debt funding   Extending a loan's due date.

Runway   The duration for which a business can sustain itself before it runs out of money. This is dependent on how much cash they have on hand and how large their burn rate is.

Scalability risk   Scalability risk is the risk that a company will not reach the necessary scale to achieve the projected financial or impact return.

Scheduled or mandatory payments   Payments that are scheduled over a defined period of time or at the request of the investor. In structured exits, this could mean quarterly payments equaling 3% of revenues.

Seasonality (of revenue)   Variations in revenue that occur over a similar period in a year often caused by external factors.

Secondary Sale   When the investor sells their shares in the company to another financial buyer such as a venture capital firm. A secondary sale is generally part of a larger raise that the company has completed where the new investors would prefer to buy the old investors out to make the ownership of the company simpler.

Secured Debt   Secured Debt that is secured by **assets** or other forms of collateral. A longer-term loan that is used for purchasing equipment, buildings and other income-producing assets is called a **Term Loan**. A shorter-term loan that is used for day-to-day expenses is called a **working capital loan**.

Self-Liquidation   Debt is considered a self-liquidating instrument. This means that it does not require an exit event for the lender. The agreement states that the borrower will repay interest over time and by some date the principal borrowed. This means that the borrower has a plan for when they will be fully repaid.

Senior Debt	Senior or secured debt is debt that is secured by assets or other forms of collateral and as a result it takes priority over unsecured or junior debt.
Senior Management Committee	A committee made up of senior management within an organization.
Service Provider	An organization that attempts to create the social or environmental outcomes specified in the outcomes contract.
Shares	To purchase equity in a business, investors have to buy shares. Generally, these are preferred shares as they come with a set of terms that give them preferential treatment over common shares held by the founders.
Shipment financing	A short-term funding option that allows you to borrow against your shipping bills to finance your working capital.
Side letter	An arrangement that is not part of the primary agreement.
Simple Agreement for Future Equity (SAFE)	An agreement between a founder and a funder that stipulates that the funder will invest into the founder's business, but allows the major terms of that investment to be set by the next round of equity funders.
Small business	A type of company that does not have revenue of more than X million, a balance sheet total of more than X million and does not have more than X employees. Depending on the country, the numbers differ.
Social Capital	Influence and/or trust as an entity or individual with relevant people/communities.
Social enterprise	A relatively new category of business, originating from a confluence of traditional business (marketplace) and philanthropy (mission). Social enterprises use the methods and disciplines of business and strive toward "common good"—a social, environmental or human justice mission by generating revenue.

Social entrepreneur	A founder that runs a social enterprise.
Social Impact Bond	A type of outcomes-based contract that operates like an equity agreement but instead of linking investors' returns to a company or organization's financial performance, returns are linked to impact achievements.
Social Impact Incentive (SIINC)	A type of impact-linked finance, where an investor, a service provider and an outcomes payor come together to create impact through a financing agreement that incentivizes the service provider to achieve specifical social outcomes.
Social impact	An effect on people, communities or the planet that happens as a result of an action or inaction, an activity, project, program or policy.
Social metrics	The use of data to gauge or measure the performance of social media campaigns on a company's revenue.
Social milestones	Milestones or outcomes that represent impact progress.
Social mission	A statement of a cause that benefits the society.
Start-up	A type of company that is an entrepreneurial venture in its early stages of operation.
Steward Ownership	A set of legal structures that instill two core principles into the legal DNA of a business: self-governance and profits serve purpose. These structures ensure that control (voting rights) over the business is held by people inside the organization or very closely connected to its mission. Voting control in steward ownership forms is not a saleable commodity. Profits in steward-ownership companies are understood as a tool for pursuing the company's purpose.
Strategic support	Business model development, and business planning.

Structured Exits	A risk capital agreement where founders and funders contractually agree on a plan for the funder to fully (or partially) exit the investment. Unlike equity funders, who have an open-ended agreement that relies on exponential growth and an unknown future buyer or listing on a stock exchange, structured exit funders have a specific, achievable plan for how they are going to receive their return through dividends, profit sharing, redemptions or a combination of payment types.
Subsidies	An amount of money provided to an organization to help reduce the cost of production, usually in the form of government payments or tax cuts. Can also be in the form of cross-subsidization where a company sells a good or service for a higher price to one set of customers to be able to sell it to a lower price to another set of customers (generally based on need).
Supply Chain Financing	Also known as reverse factoring. Uses prepayments from your customers to help finance your working capital needs. Can be in the form of **early payment**, where suppliers pay companies early voluntarily, or **dynamic discounting**, where suppliers are offered a discount based on how early they pay. Some suppliers have established supply chain financing programs that you can participate in. If you have good relationships with larger, regular customers, you can initiate conversations with them outside of formal programs as well.
Sustainable Development Goals (SDGs)	A collection of 17 interlinked global goals designed to be a blueprint to achieve a better and more sustainable future for all. The SDGs were set in 2015 by the United Nations General Assembly and are intended to be achieved by the year 2030. [ref] Each

	SDG consists of a list of targets and indicators.
Tax risk	If there is not settled case law or clear tax regulation in a country regarding the use of a specific type of investment structure, there is a tax risk associated with funding via that structure.
Technical assistance	Pots of money that are reserved for skills building, capacity development and for the specific consulting needs of a company.
Technology Experience	Ability to use and build relevant technology.
Term Sheet	A nonbinding agreement/document that sets out the basic terms and conditions under which an investment will be made. It serves as a template to develop more detailed legally binding documents.
Theory of Change	A schematic depicting the rationale and plan for achieving social and environmental outcomes. It makes explicit the connections and logic between activities (what you will do), outputs (the short-term, direct results), and outcomes and impacts (the longer-term shifts that occur, either directly or indirectly, from your activities).
Third-party assessor	An organization that assesses whether the outcomes have been achieved by the service provider.
Total Obligation	The total amount that needs to be repaid to the funder.
Total Amount Outstanding	The outstanding loan amount that needs to be repaid to the funder.
Trade Finance	Options that allow organizations (borrowers) to use customer orders or invoices as collateral to access working capital.
Trade Sale	When the entire company (otherwise known as the "target") is sold to another buyer. This buyer could be a corporate that is in the same industry as the target and is interested in acquiring them to grow their

market share. It could also be a financial buyer such as a private equity firm that is interested in investing in the company to resell it again down the road.

Tranching — Releasing specific amounts of capital.

Transaction cost risk — If you are attempting to use a new type of funding structure, there is the risk that the costs to structure the deal will be considerable.

Underserved population — A group which has limited access to goods and services or faces other material forms of social exclusion based on their attributable characteristics.

Unicorn — A term used in the venture capital industry to describe a privately held start-up company with a value of over $1 billion.

Unsecured Debt — Loans that are backed by no collateral and as a result present a greater degree of risk.

Upside — The potential increase in value, measured in monetary or percentage terms, of an investment.

Use of Proceeds — What you plan to spend capital on.

Valuation Cap — The maximum valuation at which the SAFE will convert in the next round. This "Val Cap" limits the dilution for SAFE investors by putting a cap on the price per share they will pay when they convert.

Valuation — It can be exceptionally hard to value a small business or start-up given the number of variables, uncertainty and the lack of information. The process of collecting the data to value a company is part of the **Due Diligence** process, and it can be expensive and time-consuming. Therefore, many investors take shortcuts in early stage valuations by either making very high-level assumptions or putting off the valuation all together by using convertible notes. There are two different ways to talk about the valuation of a company: **Pre-Money** or **Post Money**. If you are investing $200,000 in a company and you think it is worth $800,000 before you put your money into it. Then it had a $800,000 pre-money valuation and a $1,000,000 post-money valuation.

Variable payments

Payments that vary in amount and are made based on a company's performance.

Variable payment obligation

Loan that is repaid as a percentage of future revenues or cash flows with an option to convert to equity.

Variable rate loans

A loan where the interest changes relative to changes in market interest rates.

Variable-interest rate

An interest rate on a given loan that is not fixed but is determined/influenced by an underlying benchmark that is constantly changing.

Venture-backed company

Company that has received venture capital equity investment.

Venture capital fund

A subset of private equity that specifically invests in start-up companies and provides advice and other non-finance resources.

Venture Debt

Loans made to fast growing, venture-backed companies.

Venture Finance

Funding small businesses and start-ups.

Verifiable data

Data that can be independently verified. An example would be check-ins to a clinic that can be verified with cell phone GPS data.

Vesting

Releasing ownership of shares.

Village Banking model

A peer-driven investment approach with its roots in ancient cultures, whereby financial services are administered locally rather than centralized in a formal bank.

Visibility

Ability to disseminate information to large numbers of relevant people.

Warrants

Contracts that allow a funder to purchase shares in the future. These are generally attached to mezzanine debt agreements to allow debt funders to participate in the

	future growth of the company, i.e., to have upside.
Worker co-op transition	Worker co-operative transition is similar to a management buy-out, but instead of just a few key managers purchasing the business, most or all employees are offered an equal ownership stake and have the opportunity to participate in profit sharing. These owners are then called **worker-owners**.
Worker co-ops	Company that is owned and managed by its employees. Also referred to as an **Employee owned enterprise**.
Worker-owner participatory processes	Also called **Representative democracy**. Where worker-owners collaboratively make decisions.
Working Capital	This is cash spent to buy inputs, stock or materials required for your product or service.
Written off	When an asset or an investment is considered to be worthless, the value of that asset or investment is reduced (or taken all the way down to zero) on the balance sheet.
Zebra	Businesses that combine profit and purpose and come in many different stripes, representing the diversity of their founders and the problems they are trying to solve. They are collaborative but feisty, ambitious but not motivated by a quick exit, and are building companies with impactful solutions while also taking care of their workforces, communities and environments.

Index

A

accelerator x, 5, 17, 45, 64, 73–76, 78, 105, 117, 167

Adobe Capital 68, 91, 93, 97, 101, 244

affordability 78, 79, 88, 98, 102, 109, 118, 119, 124, 127, 261

alternative financing 93, 226

Angel Investors 4, 45, 52

articles of incorporation 258

asset class 140

asset-lite xi, 124

asset-lock 240

asset owners 82, 127

assets 43, 52, 105, 114, 141, 145, 150, 163, 173, 231, 261

B

back the jockey not the horse mentality 11, 272

balance sheet 7, 28, 33, 149, 150, 175, 176

bank loan ix–xi, 18, 217

bankruptcy 5, 109

Base of the Pyramid (BOP) 211, 259

benefit corporations 37

blended finance 197

board of directors 36, 231

bootstrapping xi

borrow 15

break even 43

bridging capital 155

broad-based employee 230

broker-dealers 219, 221

burn rate 42, 260

business growth projections 39, 257

business loans 18

business model 4, 11, 18, 20, 37, 38, 40, 67, 87, 192, 194, 232, 252, 258

business plan 73, 106, 109, 110, 145, 252

C

Cal Solar 229–234, 240

Candide Group 67–69, 93, 107, 123, 242, 244

capitalization table 7, 25, 261

© The Editor(s) (if applicable) and The Author(s), under exclusive license to Springer Nature Switzerland AG 2021
A. Patton Power, *Adventure Finance*,
https://doi.org/10.1007/978-3-030-72428-3

capital stack 22, 23, 54
capital structure 22, 25, 100, 156
cash flow 22, 28, 29, 32–34, 39, 70,
    96, 97, 105, 107, 109, 110,
    114, 124, 255
cash flow based financing 108
cash kickers. *See* cash flow
Cash on Cash (CoC) 66, 274
catalytic capital 157
category pioneer 40, 129, 257
change of control 79, 80
Code for All 215–220, 240
collateral 15, 18–20, 22–25, 27, 29,
    32, 34, 47, 51, 52, 54, 69,
    109, 114, 116, 119, 130, 143,
    174, 252, 256–258, 261, 262,
    264, 267, 270, 272, 277
commercial bank 46, 85
commercial capital 256
commercial debt 258
common shares/common
    shareholders 5, 12, 220
Community Interest Companies
    (CICs) 37, 290
concept stage 255, 256, 260
Contingent-payment debt instru-
    ments. *See* Revenue-Based
    Finance (RBF)
contracting infrastructure 205
convert 95, 100
convertible clause 95
convertible debt 6, 8, 168
convertible grant 152, 165, 168–171,
    174, 211, 245, 270
convertible note 7, 8, 12–14, 54, 66,
    81, 125, 169, 220, 262, 270.
    See also convertible debt
Convertible Revenue-Based
    Financing (Convertible RBF)
    81, 91, 94, 95, 97–101, 103,
    105, 108–111, 113, 119,
    123–125, 128–131, 256, 264,
    270

co-operative ownership. *See*
    co-operatives (co-ops)
co-operatives (co-ops) 28, 32, 37,
    52, 54, 83–86, 126, 231–234,
    237
cost of capital 127, 143, 149, 150,
    185, 188, 208, 258, 264
covenants 102, 110, 128, 246
Creative Action Network (CAN) x,
    xii, 239
credit history 15, 18, 44, 52, 54, 55,
    70, 109, 125, 148, 149, 155,
    174, 256, 258, 261, 262, 264
credit line 260
creditworthy. *See* credit history
crowdfund/crowdfunding 215,
    217–221, 240, 255, 264, 271
    debt crowdfunding 217, 221
    donation-based crowdfunding
        217
    equity crowdfunding 215, 217,
        219, 221
    loan-based crowdfunding 217
    rewards-based crowdfunding 217,
        257
currency risk 148–150
customer orders 27, 143
cyclical cash flow 19, 22

D

debt x, 7, 11, 13, 15, 18, 19, 22–25,
    27, 32, 34, 46, 47, 51, 52,
    54, 55, 64, 67, 70, 74, 85,
    87, 95–98, 100, 101, 105,
    107, 108, 110, 111, 113,
    115, 119–121, 125, 128, 131,
    137, 145, 148–150, 153–155,
    163–165, 170, 174, 177, 184,
    185, 187, 188, 196, 236–238,
    240, 253–258, 261–265, 267,
    270, 273, 275
    debt capital 47, 125, 148, 258,
        264, 270

debt financing 15, 21, 22, 70, 97, 109, 113, 119, 143, 145

debt-based crowdfunding. *See* peer-to-peer lending (P2P)

default xvii, 15, 18, 99, 109, 120, 131, 149, 150, 174, 177, 261, 262

demand dividend. *See* Convertible Revenue-Based Financing (Convertible RBF)

Deposit Account Control Agreement (DACA) 20

Development Finance Institutions 46, 149

dilute. *See* dilution

dilution 6, 8, 70, 78, 120, 125, 277

Direct Public Offering (DPO) 215, 219

discount/discount rate 7–9, 100, 169

disruptive business model 40, 257, 295

disruptive products and services. *See* disruptive business model

distributed ownership 245, 263. *See also* shared ownership

dividends 5, 23, 36, 37, 69, 79, 80, 83, 85, 87, 88, 99, 111, 124, 141

Donor Advised Fund (DAF) 157, 174, 176, 177

down round 14

downside protection 13, 131

DPO. *See* Direct Public Offering

dry powder 21

due diligence 20, 44, 50, 113, 116–118, 149, 150, 223, 225, 227, 237, 240–242, 264, 267, 276

dynamic discounting 28

dynamic enterprise 40, 258

E

early payment 28, 32

early purchasing. *See* early payment

Earnings before tax, amortization and depreciation (EBITDA) 94, 96, 98, 102, 105, 128

elective payments 79, 80

electronic invoicing 118

emerging middle class 259

Employee Benefit Trust (EBT) 245

employee option pool. *See* Employee Stock Ownership Plan (ESOP)

employee-owned. *See* employee ownership

employee ownership 130, 229, 230, 232, 234–240, 252

employee-owned enterprises 230

employee ownership structure 236

Employee Ownership Trust (EOT) 231, 245, 246

Employee Stock Ownership Plan (ESOP) 230, 231, 237, 245, 246

endowment 47, 137, 140

enterprise risk 272

Environmental, Social and Governance (ESG) 247

Equal Exchange 28, 32, 54, 83–89, 123, 240

equity x–xii, 3, 4, 6, 7, 9–14, 17, 19, 21–25, 39, 45, 46, 51, 52, 63–70, 74, 77, 85, 87, 91, 92, 94, 95, 97, 99–101, 105, 107–111, 113–115, 120, 124–126, 131, 137, 139, 140, 151, 153, 156, 157, 165, 167–171, 174, 177, 184, 195, 196, 200, 207, 235–238, 252–254, 256, 257, 260, 262–264, 267, 270, 273–275, 325

equity capital 47, 54, 265, 270, 273

equity financing 3, 15, 17, 19, 52, 64, 67, 86, 93, 98, 105, 106, 110, 184, 195, 264

equity investments 11, 14, 17, 51, 107, 139, 153, 168, 210
equity earnback 211
events of default 246, 247
exit/exit event 11, 51, 54, 64, 65, 68, 69, 71, 74, 75, 82, 93, 94, 98, 99, 105, 106, 110, 123–126, 130, 154, 168, 218, 226, 235, 240, 252, 253, 256, 261–264, 273, 277
expenditure responsibility 175, 176
exponential growth xi, 3, 11, 12, 39, 51, 52, 54, 69, 75, 91, 251, 256, 257, 262
exponential rates. *See* exponential growth
external donors 275
external financing 37, 236, 255
external funders. *See* external financing
external funding. *See* external financing
external stakeholders 36, 49, 50, 275

F

factoring 29–34, 70. *See also* purchase order financing
fair market value 76, 247
Fair Trade 84, 86, 87, 103
family offices 47, 50, 67, 118, 188, 268, 275
financial milestones 155, 210, 256, 257
fintechs 118, 119
fixed interest rate 24, 25
Fledge 74–77, 123
flexible capital 69, 152, 154, 155
flexible VC. *See* redeemable equity
follow-on investment 151
Ford Foundation 136–138, 174
foreign exchange losses 147, 149

forgivable loan 139, 155, 159, 163–165, 170, 171, 174–176, 183, 211, 257, 258, 264
foundations 42, 46, 49, 50, 67, 135, 137–142, 144, 149, 151, 153, 157, 160, 163, 168, 175, 188, 201, 203–205, 227, 228, 268, 275
401(k) employee benefit plan 230, 297
free cash 42
free cash flow. *See* free cash
frequency 98, 109
friends, family and 'fools' 4
funded guarantee 148, 261
fund life cycle 21, 274, 276
fundraising stream 255
future financing plans 78, 79, 99, 110, 120, 124
future funding. *See* future financing plans
future sale of the company 262

G

GetVantage 115, 116, 119–121, 124, 253, 307
golden share 246
grace period 20, 70, 95, 96, 98, 101, 105, 107, 109, 127
grant committees 89
grant makers 173
grant(s) ix, x, 16, 17, 37, 44, 48, 49, 96, 126, 136–141, 143–145, 152–157, 161–163, 165, 167–171, 173–177, 183, 186, 187, 203, 216, 238, 253–258, 260, 262–265, 267, 270, 275
grant capital 143, 165, 168, 173, 193
Grassroots Business Fund (GBF) 19, 54
gross margins 99

growth capital 43, 83, 85, 105, 108, 124, 152, 192, 193, 220, 260
growth funding. *See* growth capital
growth stage 70, 97, 100, 108, 119, 219, 234, 256, 260
growth targets 43, 260
guarantee/guaranteed/guarantees 32, 54, 85, 87, 105, 137–139, 143, 145–148, 149, 150, 174, 196, 258, 261, 264, 270, 272, 301. *See also* funded guarantee

H

hackathon 73, 74
Helium Health 3, 4, 10, 39
high growth venture 40, 129, 257
High Net-Worth Individuals (HNWI) 4
hollywood accounting 108
hybrid organizations 37

I

IkamvaYouth 159–164, 174, 183
impact audit 248
impact bond 203, 206, 209
  impact bond fund 206
  impact bond model 206
impact data 147, 197, 248, 259, 273
impact goals 50, 183, 195, 208, 244
impact investing xi, 63, 93, 117, 139, 149, 153, 156, 157, 168, 188, 194, 197, 201, 272
  impact focused capital 259
  impact focused funders 42, 259, 272
impact investment. *See* impact investing
impact investor. *See* impact investing
impact-linked finance(ing) 183, 191, 196, 198, 256, 257
  impact-linked debt 185, 187, 188, 191

impact-linked payments 193, 195
impact measurement 48, 170, 188, 189, 205, 259. *See also* Impact Measurement and Management (IMM)
Impact Measurement and Management (IMM) 140
impact metrics 188, 248
impact milestones. *See* impact metrics
impact risk 268, 273
impact thesis 163, 170, 197, 268
impact track record xx, 197, 273, 275
income statement 98
income streams x, 255
incubators 4
information rights 110, 248
Initial Public Offering (IPO) 11, 22, 52, 65, 68, 80, 93, 106, 125, 126, 219, 252, 298
Intellectual Property (IP) 4, 38, 51, 131, 171
interest 6, 7, 12, 15, 19, 22, 23, 25, 34, 54, 79, 87, 88, 98, 102, 116, 128, 130, 141, 188, 203
interest-free loan 162, 163
interest payment. *See* interest
interest rate. *See* interest
interest rate rebate 183, 186, 188, 208, 209
intermediary 183, 200, 204
internal cash flow generation 260, 264
internal cash flows. *See* internal cash flow generation
internal funding. *See* internal cash flow generation
Internal Rate of Return (IRR) 77, 82, 101, 127, 274
inventory 17, 21, 28, 43, 85, 261
investment advisors 221
investment committee 20, 50, 82, 127, 227, 228, 242, 275, 305

investment pitch deck xi
investment readiness 227
investment readiness framework. *See*
    investment readiness
investment ready. *See* investment
    readiness
investment risk 49, 221
investment team 242
investment thesis 268
investor xi, xii, 6–13, 19, 22, 25,
    36, 42, 49, 63–70, 73, 74, 78,
    81, 83, 85–88, 93–95, 97–99,
    105, 108, 110, 118, 123, 127,
    139, 153, 169, 195, 200, 203,
    205, 209, 217, 220, 221, 240,
    273
investor demo days 64
investor groups and networks 64
invoice factoring 30, 33, 34, 55,
    257, 258, 261, 262, 264
invoices 27, 29–31, 33, 55, 143, 262

J

J curve projections 257

K

Keep it Simple Security (KISS) 12
kicker 19, 24, 54, 128

L

lead the round 67
licensing income 171
Limited Liability Companies (L3Cs)
    37, 309
Limited Partners (LPs) 50, 275
liquidation preferences 5
liquidity 23, 70, 71, 81, 82, 98, 101,
    124–126, 260, 273
liquidity event. *See* liquidity
liquidity premium 273
liquidity risk 272

livelihood enterprise 40, 258
loan xvii, 6, 7, 18, 29, 32, 36, 54,
    77, 94, 95, 97, 99, 101, 105,
    111, 115, 128, 145–147, 149,
    164, 177, 183, 186, 211, 218,
    220, 275. *See also* debt
loan-based crowdfunding. *See*
    peer-to-peer lending (P2P)
low interest loans 139

M

management buy-out 230
mandatory payments 80, 98, 99
Mapula Trust 162, 174, 183
market rate 140–142, 149, 154, 156,
    167, 246
market risk 272
market traction 156
maturity date 95
Maya Mountain Cacao (MMC) 68,
    104, 124
merger 68, 94, 125, 221, 262
mezzanine 19, 21, 23–25, 27, 46,
    51, 54, 93–95, 101, 113, 161,
    257, 258, 270
mezzanine debt. *See* mezzanine
mezzanine financiers. *See* mezzanine
mezzanine financing. *See* mezzanine
mezzanine fund 46
mezzanine structure. *See* mezzanine
Michael and Susan Dell Foundation
    (MSDF) 183
microfinance 18, 185, 221, 223
microfinance institution 46
microfinance lenders. *See*
    microfinance
microfinance loans. *See* microfinance
micro-loans. *See* microfinance
milestones 43, 89, 163, 164, 175,
    193–195, 207, 209–211, 227
mini-bonds 220
Minimum Viable Product (MVP)
    38, 43, 255, 260

missing middle 95, 221

mission aligned 49, 87, 88, 99, 129, 164, 173, 177, 188, 197, 206, 237, 244, 254, 258, 267–269, 274

mission default 247

mission drift 42, 64, 246, 257

mission driven 259

mission embeddedness 258, 259, 275

mission lock 89

Mission Related Investments (MRIs) 157

mission statement 42, 243, 246, 269

money multiple 274

multiple of cash invested. *See* money multiple

myTurn 73–77, 80, 123

N

net profits 22, 95

networks. *See* investor groups and networks

niche enterprise 40, 129

niche venture 257

no exit clause 85, 86, 88, 89, 123, 240

non-bank financial institution 46

non-convertible loan 185

non-dilutive 115, 120, 124, 263

non-profit x, xvii, 36, 37, 52, 75, 139, 140, 145, 150, 152, 155, 156, 160, 162, 164, 174–177, 188, 200, 207, 217, 236, 256, 258, 259, 264

non-profit organization. *See* non-profit

O

one-way option 100

ordinary income 111, 176

Original Issue Discount (OID) 111

outcome funder 205

outcomes 152, 183–185, 188, 189, 193, 195, 196, 201, 202

outcomes-based contract 200, 205. *See also* results-based finance

outcomes fund 205, 206, 208

outcomes payor. *See* outcome funder

outputs 189, 208

ownership xi, xii, 5–7, 10, 11, 13, 19, 24, 36, 39, 52, 69, 70, 75, 85, 86, 100, 105, 110, 124, 145, 168, 171, 211, 217, 219, 229, 230, 232, 233, 246, 247

P

participation rights 110

participatory budget 216

patient capital 152, 252

patronage 231, 235

pay as you go (PAYGO) 34

peer-based decision making. *See* peer selection

peer-driven investment approach. *See* peer selection

peer selection 224–227

peer selection process. *See* peer selection

peer-to-peer lending (P2P) 217

perceived risk 150, 174

performance aligned redeemable convertible preferred stock. *See* redeemable equity

permitted indebtedness 100

perpetual employee trust. *See* Employee Ownership Trust (EOT)

personal guarantee 33, 54, 101, 105, 118, 127, 237, 238, 261

physical assets 15, 23, 27, 114, 261

pipeline 9, 152, 237

pitch events 64

political risk 150, 272

portfolio-level return 153

Post-Money SAFE 12
post-money valuation 5, 7, 12, 78
post-money valuation cap 8
post-revenue 97, 100, 108, 115, 119,
    120
Powered by People 29–31, 33, 34,
    55, 262
preferred equity 66, 86, 87, 236
preferred shareholders 5
preferred shares. *See* preferred equity
preferred stock. *See* preferred equity
preferred stock agreement 87
preferred stock offering. *See* preferred
    stock agreement
pre-money valuation 5, 12, 78
pre-paying 85
prepayment discount 97
pre-revenue 75, 81, 97, 120
pre-seed 4, 9, 52
priced equity 12, 13, 81, 125, 262
priced equity rounds. *See* priced
    equity
principal 20, 22, 34, 136, 141, 154,
    156, 185–187, 211
private equity fund 45
private placements 87
profit sharing 54, 230, 235
Program Related Investments (PRIs)
    135–141, 145, 150, 157, 174,
    175
Project Equity 232, 234–237, 240,
    242
Proof of Concept (POC) 38, 43,
    123, 255, 260
proxies 259
public listing 262
purchase order financing 29, 30, 32,
    55, 257, 262
purchase orders 20, 29–31, 33, 262
Purpose Ventures xi, xii, 240
put option 247

Q
quasi-equity 19, 51, 54

R
real risk 150
receivables factoring 30, 220. *See
    also* invoice factoring; purchase
    order financing
receivables financing 70
recoverable grants 126, 151–157,
    159, 171, 174–177, 211, 257,
    258, 264, 275
redeemable equity 68, 70, 73–75,
    78–83, 88, 98, 100, 123–126,
    128–131, 218, 220, 241, 247,
    254, 256, 260, 263, 264
redemption multiple 78
redemption price. *See* redemption
    multiple
reimbursable grants. *See* recoverable
    grants
repayment risk 153
repurchase price 88
require personal guarantees 120
Research and Development (R&D)
    165, 174, 255
residual stakes 79, 81
results-based finance 197
retained earnings 22, 260
return on capital hurdle 140
return on investment 11, 77, 101,
    127, 157, 260, 304
return variable 94, 98, 105, 109, 110
revenue-based debt agreements. *See*
    Revenue-Based Finance (RBF)
Revenue-Based Finance (RBF) 70,
    74, 94, 97, 113, 115–120,
    124, 125, 128–131, 220, 256,
    261, 262, 264, 270, 275
revenue-based investing. *See* Convert-
    ible Revenue-Based Financing
    (Convertible RBF)

revenue-based loans. *See* Revenue-Based Finance (RBF)

revenue-based mezzanine debt. *See* revenue-based finance (RBF)

revenue-based structure. *See* Revenue-Based Finance (RBF)

revenue model 37, 150, 255, 256

revenue share agreement. *See* Revenue-Based Finance (RBF)

reverse factoring 29

revolving credit line 20

Riders for Health 143–149, 174, 261

ring-fencing 245

risk-adjusted financial return 49, 274

risk-adjusted rate 257

risk capital xi, xii, 13, 51, 63, 64, 69, 71, 78, 79, 81, 97, 100, 113, 123–125, 156, 256, 257

risk profile 49, 52, 150, 256, 262, 274

risk/return 25

royalty financing 128

runway 21, 43, 233, 236

S

scalability risk 272

scaling 17, 256

scaling stage. *See* scaling

scheduled or elective payments 80

scheduled payments. *See* scheduled or elective payments

scheduled repayment. *See* scheduled or elective payments

seasonal 22, 255, 262

secondary sale 11, 52, 65, 94, 252, 262

secured bank financing. *See* secured debt

secured debt 18, 19, 23, 24, 29, 52, 97, 263

secured lending. *See* secured debt

securities-based crowdfunding 220

securitized loan. *See* secured debt

security 10, 22, 27, 52, 261

Seed round 6, 7

self-liquidating 22

self-liquidating instruments. *See* self-liquidating

senior debt 25

senior management committee 50, 275

senior secured debt. *See* senior management committee

senior(ty). *See* senior management committee

Series A 7, 8, 10, 52, 107

service provider 200, 204, 205

Shared Earning Agreement 128, 241

shared ownership 229, 230, 234

shares xii, 5, 6, 8, 11

shipment financing 30, 32, 55

side letter 12, 155–157, 175

Simple Agreement for Future Equity (SAFE) 8–10, 12–14, 52, 81, 125, 168, 270

Single Foundation 246

Skoll Foundation 144, 145, 148, 174

small business ix, 18, 27

social enterprise xi, 37, 45, 73, 75, 106, 139, 144, 154–156, 159, 167, 170, 171, 173, 174, 191–193, 200, 207, 223, 251, 255–259, 268

social entrepreneur. *See* social enterprise

social impact xi, 17, 85, 92, 164, 186

Social Impact Bond (SIB) 199, 200, 203

Social Impact Incentives (SIINC) 191–196, 209

social metrics 164

social milestone. *See* social metrics

social mission xi, 87, 89, 103, 123, 124, 163, 169, 192, 194, 219, 247, 248
SOKO 16–21, 23, 24, 28, 52, 262
sourcing 103, 104, 153, 240, 242
start-up ix, x, 4, 5, 8, 9, 12, 14
Steward Ownership 240, 242, 245
steward Ownership xi
stock offering 83, 85, 87, 240
structured exit agreements. *See* structured exits
structured exits 68–71, 80, 82, 98–101, 108, 123–127, 131, 223, 257, 261, 263, 273
Studio Museum 135–138, 174
Subordinated variable payment debt. *See* Convertible Revenue-Based Financing (Convertible RBF)
subsidies 137, 156, 197
supply chain 28, 29, 32, 33, 54, 55, 255, 258, 261, 270, 271
supply chain financing. *See* dynamic discounting; early payment; supply chain
surety 130, 261, 262, 272
sustainable business 41, 70, 174

T

tax risk 273
Technical Assistance (TA) 17, 177, 231
10x returns 65
term loan debt. *See* term loans
term loans 18, 24, 25, 34
Term Sheet 11
the 3Fs 4
theory of change 48, 258, 259, 267, 268, 270
the village banking model 224, 240
third-party exit 22, 43, 262
total amount outstanding 99, 100, 110, 120, 247

total obligation 94, 98–100, 108, 109, 119
total payments made 100
total redemption price 247
trade finance 27, 33, 51
trade financing. *See* trade finance
trade sale 11, 65, 94, 252, 298
tranche 210, 211
transaction cost risk 273
Trust Foundation 246

U

UBS-OF 166–170, 174, 245
underserved customers 255
unfunded guarantee 149, 150, 261
unicorn 5, 11, 13, 39, 40, 52, 63, 64, 70, 81, 125
unsecured 21, 23, 24, 54, 113, 130, 238, 258
upside 19, 24, 25, 44, 49, 54, 81, 125, 127, 170, 171, 240, 264, 309
use of proceeds 244–246

V

valuation 5–8, 12–14, 39, 78, 79, 114, 169, 204, 236
valuation cap 8, 9
variable-interest rate 185
variable payment 91
variable payment obligation 107
variable-rate loans. *See* variable-interest rate
variable VC. *See* redeemable equity
VC investor. *See* venture capital
venture-backed companies 19
venture capital ix
venture capital equity funding. *See* venture capital
venture capital firms. *See* Venture Capitalists (VCs)

Venture Capitalists (VCs) 64–66, 89, 131, 272, 275
venture debt 19, 20, 24, 54, 101, 106, 256, 257, 270
venture finance xvii, 199
verifiable data 259
verifiable impact 259
vesting 210
Village Capital 68, 223, 225–227, 240, 241

W

warrants 20, 24, 25, 54, 128, 130
waterfall. *See* capital structure 289

worker co-op. *See* shared ownership
worker co-op transition 230, 232
worker-owner 86, 231, 233, 235, 236
worker-owner participatory processes 231
working capital 18–21, 27–30, 32, 33, 43, 52, 54, 55, 113–116, 119, 124, 125, 155, 200, 220, 260, 261, 263
written off 177, 211

Z

Zebra 39, 40, 63, 68, 69